A WORLD OF
BAKING

A WORLD OF
BAKING

DOLORES CASELLA
ILLUSTRATED BY LORETTA TREZZO

DAVID WHITE • NEW YORK

Acknowledgement is made to *The National Observer* for permission to use material on pies which was first published in that newspaper.

DAVID WHITE, INC.
60 EAST 55TH STREET, NEW YORK, N. Y. 10022

MANUFACTURED IN THE UNITED STATES OF AMERICA

*This book is lovingly dedicated
to my children*
LOURICE. LEONARD, WAYNE, *and* TERESA ANN
*who faithfully encouraged,
tasted, and enjoyed.*

Contents

Foreword

Most women like to bake. It provides us with a satisfying sense of accomplishment, and fills the house with those delicious odors that linger in the memory, and are part and parcel, it seems to me, of a happy home. And since few of us can react indifferently to the warmth of a home filled with the fragrance of home-baked breads, pies, and cakes, it seems to provide an impetus towards the harmony that we all desire.

I learned to bake *after* I was married, and in those early years many a culinary catastrophe churned its way down the garbage disposal. One of the more memorable disasters occurred when I was first learning to make bread. I had come across an old recipe for homemade yeast, and with the optimism that only a teen-ager can have, I decided to try the recipe. The recipe cautioned against filling the bottles too full, or putting the lids on too tightly, but neglected to explain *why*! Being short of bottles I filled each brim-full, but fortunately did not cap them tightly or the resulting chaos I'm certain would have been much worse. The hours that I spent cleaning the foaming, bubbling mass of home-made yeast off the kitchen floor indirectly led to my habit of extensive notes with almost every recipe that I've made since.

I was making all of the breads, rolls and coffeecakes we could eat, before we were married a year. But, as foolish as it now seems, I didn't attempt biscuits for another 5 or 6 years. Reared on the jokes and comments about new bride's biscuits, to my mind there could be no greater test of culinary ability. Imagine my chagrin when I discovered how really simple it is to make a flaky, tender biscuit!

It was about that time that I made up my mind to eventually write my own books on baking. The average woman's magazine goes into such lengthy detail with even the simplest recipe, that they make a frightening project out of what should be creative pleasure. And, unfortunately, many cook books go to the opposite extreme of being overly vague, so that only an experienced cook can find them of value. And of course, there is always the somewhat selfish pleasure, and value, of having all of *my own* favorite recipes at hand.

My hope is that you, the reader, will find this book informative, pleasurable, and useful, and that someday someone will say to you, as a dear friend once said to me, "I love to walk into your house. It *smells* so happy!"

AUGUST 1968

DOLORES CASELLA

A WORLD OF
BAKING

1. *Cakes*

To make a "great cake" in Colonial times was a task to awe the most energetic housewife. Everything had to be done by hand, often with directions that were slightly less than vague. One recipe, in Marion Tyree's 1879 edition of *Housekeeping in Old Virginia,* calls for "the whites of 20 eggs, 1 pound of flour, 1 pound of butter, 1 pound of almonds," and the only directions given are to "use a little more flour, if the almonds are omitted." The housewife *was* warned not to use bad eggs, and some old books strongly advised against using pulverized sugar because it might contain plaster of Paris!

The directions for making fine icings were no less awe-inspiring. In *The Art of Cookery Made Plain and Easy,* published in 1805 by Mrs. Glasse, a recipe is given as follows: "Take the whites of twenty-four eggs and a pound of double refined sugar . . . and with a whisk,

3

whisk it well for two or three hours, till it looks white and thick." But in spite of all this, the housewife whipped and beat and pounded, and used the finest ingredients (available mainly because they were home-grown), and turned out cakes that the modern housewife with her labor-saving equipment would be proud of.

Many of the early-day cakes were based on a basic Pound Cake, and varied by the addition of spices, liquors, nuts, grated fresh coconut, and candied fruits. The use of a scale was taken for granted, and it was common to see a recipe direct the baker to use "14 eggs, the weight of 10 in sugar and the weight of 6 in flour."

Today the housewife has mixers, blenders, controlled oven heat, and standard ingredients of a consistent quality. For these reasons, among others, cake-making should be a pleasure and we should not let our-selves be beguiled into relying on commercial mixes. They are overly sweet and have a distinct floury taste, and we know that artificial flavorings and dried eggs will never give a quality of flavor that we wish. I have never found the commercial mixes to be less expensive than the homemade cake, either—unless we fool ourselves into com-paring a mix that uses 2 eggs with a made-from-scratch cake that calls for ½ pound butter and 5 or 6 eggs.

If time is the problem—and there is no denying that a tall, glamorous cake does take time to make—perhaps we should bake less often and make the dessert cake for a special occasion. Or we could make other, less time-consuming desserts. If occasionally we do have a spare after-noon, the freezer can be put to good use by making several cakes at a time and freezing the layers, which are then easily assembled and frosted when desired. Many of the fruited cakes and spice cakes, such as CARROT-PINEAPPLE CAKE (page 31), DATE CAKE (page 26), and PRUNE SPICE CAKE (page 70), are very easily made and store well.

As with any collection of cake recipes, the biggest problem comes in deciding what to include and what to leave out. I settled on recipes that would be most representative of our American style of baking, although some, because of the melting-pot character of our culture, are definitely at home in other countries. There were many that had to be omitted, but I hope that you will enjoy this cross-section of the old and the modern.

"Comfort me with apples." SOLOMON

GENERAL INFORMATION

1. Always read the recipe through first, checking to see if you have all the ingredients called for.

2. Assemble all ingredients, including bowls and pans.

3. Prepare the pans first. Unless otherwise directed, butter the bottom and sides of the pans, then sprinkle with a tablespoon of flour and tap and shake the pans lightly to coat the butter with the flour. Shake out any excess flour. If desired, you may omit the flour and place a small circle of waxed paper over the bottom of the buttered pan. Butter the waxed paper also. This method is my favorite, as it practically eliminates the frustrating experience of having part of the cake adhere stubbornly to the pan. The waxed paper does not have to fit the pan perfectly, as long as it is over the center part.

4. Use standard measuring utensils. No longer do we measure by "teacupfuls."

5. When measuring the dry ingredients, heap the cup or spoon, and then level with a spatula. Be careful not to shake the measuring cup, as you might pack in the flour and add an unnecessary tablespoon or two of flour. If by chance you do not have cake flour, you *can* substitute all-purpose flour. Use ⅞ cup (1 cup minus 2 tablespoons) all-purpose flour for each cup of pastry or cake flour that is called for.

6. Unless otherwise specified, all ingredients should be at room temperature.

7. The flour should be sifted before measuring, preferably several times.

8. The egg size should be carefully noted. Large eggs weigh about 2 ounces each. If you use small eggs where large are called for, the batter will not be of the proper consistency.

9. I use butter in all cakes, as we greatly prefer the flavor. You can use margarine if you wish. Vegetable shortenings do not give a cake good flavor. The least expensive margarine is preferable to the canned vegetable shortenings.

10. The tenderest cakes are made with water, but milk makes a richer cake.

11. Where brown sugar is called for, it must be firmly packed. Superfine granulated sugar (*not* powdered or confectioners') is the best for cakes calling for granulated sugar.

12. Where baking powder is called for, use double-acting baking powder.

13. The single most important facet of cake making is the proper creaming of the butter before and after the addition of the sugar. The butter should always be beaten until it is light, soft, and airy. *Then* gradually, a few spoonfuls at a time, add the sugar and continue beating until the mixture is very light and fluffy and there are no grains of sugar to be seen or to be felt with the fingertips. This takes time but is well worth it. When whole eggs are used, they are added one at a time and beaten in thoroughly before the next egg is added.

14. When the eggs are separated (some of the finest cakes call for separating the eggs), the whites must be beaten until very stiff before folding into the batter. Preferably the whites should be folded in by hand, but a whisk or even a large spoon will do. The whites should be folded in just until there are no remaining patches of white.

15. After the batter is turned into the pans, the pans should be lightly tapped on the counter top to release any bubbles of air that would make unsightly holes in the finished cake. *Do not do this if there is stiffly beaten egg white in the batter.*

16. The oven must always be preheated to the correct temperature.

17. Place cake pans on a rack in the *center* of the oven, and bake the directed time.

18. The cake is done if the edges have pulled away slightly from the sides of the pan and if the top springs back when lightly touched with the finger. A cake tester inserted in the center of the cake will come out clean.

19. Cool cakes on racks to allow air to circulate around them. Cool completely before frosting unless otherwise directed.

TO FREEZE CAKES

Most cakes freeze well. I prefer freezing all cakes unfrosted. Wrap cake layers in aluminum foil or freezer wrap, and seal them securely. Freeze for no more than 3 or 4 months. Defrost before unwrapping and then fill and frost the cakes.

PAN SUBSTITUTIONS

IF RECIPE CALLS FOR:	YOU CAN USE:
2 8-inch round layer pans	1 8-inch square pan or tins to make 18 cupcakes
3 8-inch round layer pans	2 8-or 9-inch square pans
2 9-inch round layer pans	2 8-inch square pans, or tins to make 30 cupcakes
3 9-inch round layer pans	10-inch tube pan or Bundt pan
1 13 by 9 by 2-inch oblong pan	2 9-inch round layer pans
1 9 by 5 by 3-inch loaf pan	1 9-inch square pan or tins to make 24 cupcakes

VANILLA WAFER CAKE

This admittedly expensive cake, a cross between a pudding and a cake, uses no flour. You might dust it with sifted powdered sugar, but don't frost it. And remember that with this and the following GRAHAM CRACKER CAKE the pans used, even Teflon pans, *must* be buttered and dusted with flour. These cakes show a remarkable propensity for sticking to anything.

½ pound butter or margarine
2 cups sugar
6 medium or large eggs
3 cups vanilla wafer crumbs (a 12-ounce box)
2 teaspoons baking powder

¼ cup milk
1 or 2 teaspoons grated lemon rind (optional)
1 cup flaked coconut
1 cup finely chopped nuts, or slivered, blanched almonds

Cream the butter or margarine and sugar until light and fluffy. Beat in the eggs 1 or 2 at a time, beating until smooth and fluffy. Combine wafer crumbs and baking powder and stir to blend. Stir into the creamed mixture alternately with the milk and lemon rind (if used), beginning and ending with dry ingredients. Fold in the coconut and chopped nuts. Turn into a buttered and floured 10-inch tube pan, Bundt pan, or 2 9-inch round layer pans. Bake in a 325° F. oven for 1 hour and 15 to 30 minutes for the tube or Bundt pan, 30 to 40 minutes for the layers. Cool in the pan on a rack for 10 to 15 minutes before turning out. If you have made the layers, put them together with whipped cream and top with more whipped cream.

GRAHAM CRACKER CAKE

½ pound butter or margarine
2 cups sugar
4 large eggs
1 pound graham cracker crumbs
1 teaspoon baking powder

1 teaspoon baking soda
1 cup milk
1 teaspoon vanilla extract
1 cup chopped nuts
1 cup flaked coconut

Cream the butter or margarine and sugar until light and fluffy. Beat in the eggs 1 or 2 at a time, beating until smooth and fluffy. Combine cracker crumbs with the baking powder and soda. Stir to blend. Add to the creamed mixture alternately with the milk and vanilla, beginning and ending with dry ingredients. Then stir in the nuts and coconut. Turn into a buttered and floured 10-inch tube pan, Bundt pan, or 2

9-inch round layer pans. Pans must be buttered and floured even if Teflon-lined, as this cake has remarkable sticking qualities! Bake in 350° F. oven for 1 hour to an hour and 15 minutes for the tube or Bundt pan, and for 25 to 35 minutes for the layers. Cool in the pans, on racks, for 10 to 15 minutes before turning out of pans. If you have made the layers, put them together with whipped cream and top with more whipped cream to serve.

CHRISTMAS CRACKER CAKE. Use ¼ cup brandy or Cognac in place of as much milk, and add 1 cup of candied fruits to the batter. If you use a Bundt pan, you can arrange nut halves on the bottom before spooning in the batter. It makes a very attractive cake with good keeping qualities.

PENNSYLVANIA DUTCH FUNNY CAKE

Nobody knows just where this got its name, except for the obvious explanation that, being baked in a pie shell, it's a funny kind of cake. The cake batter may be poured over a layer of any desired fruit butter, or drained, crushed pineapple, or canned blueberry or apple-pie filling which has been put in the pie shell. It can also be served with a choco-late sauce topping. The Pennsylvania Dutch serve it for breakfast. Have ingredients for the cake batter at room temperature.

9-inch unbaked pie shell with a high, fluted rim

CAKE BATTER

1¼ cups sifted pastry or cake flour	¾ cup sugar
1 teaspoon baking powder	½ cup milk
½ teaspoon salt	1 teaspoon vanilla extract
¼ cup butter or margarine, softened	1 large egg

Sift the flour with the baking powder and salt directly into the mixing bowl. Make a well in the center and into this put the softened butter or margarine, sugar, milk, and vanilla. With an electric mixer beat for 2 minutes, scraping down the sides regularly. Add the egg and beat for another minute. If you use any of the suggestions for fillings mentioned above spread the filling in a shallow layer over the unbaked pie crust and then pour the cake batter over the filling. Bake in a 350° F. oven for 50 to 55 minutes. If you wish to use the CHOCOLATE SAUCE TOP-PING (recipe below) pour it *over* the cake batter before baking. Bake as directed.

CHOCOLATE SAUCE TOPPING.   Put 1 square unsweetened choco-late in a small saucepan with ½ cup water. Cook over low heat until chocolate is melted. Then stir in ⅔ cup sugar and cook, stirring, until mixture just comes to a boil. Remove from heat and stir in ¼ cup butter or margarine and 1 teaspoon vanilla extract. Stir until butter is melted and cool before using.

NEW ORLEANS CARNIVAL KING'S CAKE

This very old recipe for "Twelfth-night Cake" is closely connected with the New Orleans Mardi Gras. Custom tells us that the cake was always served on the night they chose the king and queen, but the modern housewife serves it throughout the season from January 6th (Twelfth-night) to Mardi gras, the day before Lent.

8 cups of the very best flour, sifted	8 to 10 large eggs
1 cake yeast dissolved in ¼ cup lukewarm water	1 pound of the best quality butter or margarine
¾ cup rich milk, scalded and cooled	1½ cups sugar
	½ teaspoon salt

Take 6 cups of the flour and sift it again into a large bowl. Make a hole in the center of the flour and into the hole put the dissolved yeast. Now working the dough with one hand, add enough of the cooled milk to make a medium dough that is neither too soft nor too stiff. When the dough is smooth, brush it with melted butter, cover with a cloth, and set it aside to rise until doubled, about 5 hours. When the dough has doubled, punch it down and add the remaining 2 cups flour. Now beat 8 of the eggs with the butter or margarine, sugar, and salt until thor-oughly blended and then work this into the dough. Work it in thoroughly and if the dough is a little too stiff, add 1 or 2 eggs. Knead the dough lightly on a very lightly floured bread board, or knead right in the bowl. Brush it again with melted butter, cover with a clean cloth, and let it rise 45 minutes to an hour. When it has risen, punch it down again and work it lightly so that there will be no large air holes. Place the dough in a large, buttered, 5-quart ring mold or, lacking a mold that size, shape the dough by hand into a large ring and place it on a buttered cookie sheet. Cover with a clean cloth and let the bread-cake rise again for an hour. Then bake in a 325° F. oven for 1 hour and 25 to 35 minutes. Glaze and decorate as desired when the cake is completely cooled.

RUM LAYER CAKE

This is a rich-flavored rum cake. We prefer it filled and frosted with rum-flavored whipped cream. Have all ingredients at room temperature.

2⅔ cups sifted pastry or cake flour	½ cup milk
2 tablespoons baking powder	⅔ cup butter or margarine
¼ teaspoon salt	1⅓ cups superfine granulated sugar
¼ teaspoon baking soda	3 large eggs, separated
½ cup rum or ½ cup water and 1 tablespoon rum flavoring	1 teaspoon vanilla extract

Sift the flour with the baking powder, salt, and soda. Set aside. Combine rum or water and rum flavoring and milk. Cream the butter or margarine, gradually adding the sugar and creaming until light. Add the egg yolks and vanilla and beat until light. Add the sifted dry ingredients to the creamed mixture alternately with the liquid ingredients, beginning and ending with dry ingredients. Beat the egg whites until stiff and fold into the batter. Turn into 2 9-inch round layer pans that have been buttered and floured. Bake in a 350° F. oven for 30 to 35 minutes, or until cake tests done. Cool in pans for 5 minutes before turning out onto racks to cool.

JEWISH HONEY CAKE

This rich honey cake keeps almost indefinitely, and is at its best when cut into very thin slices and served with whipped butter. If you must frost it, make a thin, powdered sugar frosting with orange juice and drizzle it over the cake and down the sides.

3½ cups sifted pastry or cake flour
2 teaspoons baking soda
½ teaspoon salt
1 teaspoon cinnamon
½ teaspoon each: cloves, ginger, and nutmeg
3 large eggs
1 cup sugar
1 pound (1⅓ cups) dark honey (buckwheat is good)
½ cup salad oil (not olive oil)
1 cup tea or coffee (medium strength)
1 tablespoon each: grated lemon and orange rind
½ cup golden raisins
½ to 1 cup walnut halves, or blanched, slivered almonds
1 tablespoon flour

Sift the dry ingredients together and set aside. Beat the eggs until very light and thick. Beat in the sugar gradually, beating until it no longer feels grainy. Drizzle in the honey and beat until well blended. Combine the oil and the tea or coffee. Stir in the grated rinds. Add the sifted dry ingredients to the egg mixture alternately with the oil mixture, beginning and ending with the dry ingredients. Beat until smooth. Combine the raisins, nuts, and the remaining tablespoon of flour. Stir together, and then fold into the batter. Turn batter into a buttered 10-inch tube pan that has been lined with waxed paper and buttered again. Bake in a 350° F. oven for 1 hour and 10 minutes, or until cake tests done. Cool in the pan for 10 minutes before turning out on a rack. Cool thoroughly. Then wrap the cake in aluminum foil and store at room temperature. This cake improves with age.

NOTE. If desired, cake may be baked in 2 buttered and lined loaf pans. Bake in a 325° F. oven for 1 hour and 15 to 30 minutes.

MARGUERITE CAKE

This old-fashioned cake was very popular during World War I and is certainly still worthwhile. Have all ingredients at room temperature.

1¾ cups sifted pastry or cake flour
1 teaspoon baking soda
½ cup butter or margarine
1 cup brown sugar
3 tablespoons molasses or sorghum
¼ cup buttermilk or sour milk
3 large egg whites

Sift the flour with the baking soda. Cream the butter or margarine until it is thick. Gradually beat in the sugar, beating until mixture is light and fluffy. Now beat in the molasses just until blended. Add the sifted dry ingredients to the creamed mixture alternately with the buttermilk or sour milk, beginning and ending with dry ingredients. Beat the egg whites until stiff and carefully fold into the batter. Turn into 2 8-inch round layer pans that have been buttered and floured. Bake in a 350° F. oven for 25 to 30 minutes, or until cake tests done. Cool in pans for 5 minutes before turning out onto racks. Fill with RAISIN FILLING (page 95), and top with whipped cream, or frost with NUTMEG FROSTING (page 88).

BUTTERY EGG-WHITE CAKE

This cake may at first remind you of an angle food cake, but the addition of melted butter gives a melt-in-the-mouth buttery flavor. Have all ingredients at room temperature.

1 cup sifted pastry or cake
    flour
1 teaspoon baking powder
1 cup (about 8) egg whites
1 cup superfine granulated
    sugar
¼ teaspoon salt

1 teaspoon vanilla extract, or
    1 teaspoon grated lemon
    rind, or 1 tablespoon grated
    orange rind
½ cup butter, melted and
    cooled to room temperature

Sift the flour with the baking powder and set aside. Beat the egg whites until foamy, gradually add the sugar, and beat until whites are stiff and glossy. Then beat in the salt and the flavoring used. Fold the flour, a little at a time, into the beaten whites. Then fold in the melted and cooled butter, being very careful to blend the butter completely *into* the batter. Turn batter into a 10-inch tube pan or Bundt pan that has been buttered and sprinkled with sugar. Bake in a 350° F. oven for 1 hour, or until cake tests done. Cool in pan for 10 minutes before turning out onto a rack to cool completely. Dust with sifted powdered sugar, but do not frost.

ICE WATER WHITE CAKE

The lady who gave me this excellent recipe called it "Sweet Water Mountain Cake." We find that it makes a very good tiered cake. If multiplied five times, the recipe will make a 4-tier cake, with a 4-inch, an 8-inch, a 10-inch, and a 12-inch layer. It also makes very good cupcakes, and a good loaf cake. With the exception of the water, which should be ice cold, all ingredients should be at room temperature.

3¼ cups sifted pastry or cake
    flour
½ teaspoon salt
4 teaspoons baking powder
½ cup butter or margarine
2 cups superfine granulated
    sugar

1½ cups ice water
1 teaspoon vanilla extract
¼ teaspoon almond extract
    (optional)
½ cup (about 4) egg whites

Sift the flour with the salt and baking powder. Cream the butter or margarine and gradually add 1½ cups of the sugar. Beat until mixture is light and fluffy. Combine ice water and flavorings. Add sifted dry ingredients to the creamed mixture alternately with the ice water, beginning and ending with dry ingredients. Beat until smooth, but do not overbeat. In another bowl, beat the egg whites until foamy, gradually beat in the remaining ½ cup sugar, and beat until stiff and glossy. Very carefully fold this meringue into the batter, folding just until no traces of white can be seen. Turn batter into 3 8-inch round layer pans that have been buttered and floured. Bake in a 350° F. oven for 25 to 30 minutes, or until cake tests done. Cool in pans for 5 minutes before turning out onto racks. Fill and frost as desired.

GOLD CAKE

This makes a moist, lush cake that utilizes all the egg yolks left over from cake decorating, or meringues, or an angel food cake. Have ingredients at room temperature except where otherwise specified.

2¼ cups sifted pastry or cake flour
2 teaspoons baking powder
¼ teaspoon salt
¾ cup (about 10) egg yolks
2 cups superfine granulated sugar
1 cup scalded milk, hot
1 teaspoon vanilla extract
1 teaspoon grated lemon rind, or 1 tablespoon grated lime, orange, or tangerine rind
½ cup melted butter

Combine the flour, baking powder, and salt. Sift and set aside. Combine egg yolks and sugar and beat, with an electric mixer, until thick and light. Combine milk and flavorings. Pour hot milk mixture, all at once, into the yolk-sugar mixture, beating with the electric mixer at low speed, until ingredients are thoroughly blended. Carefully fold the flour mixture, a little at a time, into the yolk mixture. Now, most carefully and preferably using a wire whisk, fold in the melted butter. Do not beat. Turn the batter into 2 9-inch round layer cake pans that have been buttered and floured. Tap the pans lightly on the counter top and then bake in a 350° F. oven for 25 to 30 minutes, or until cake tests done. Cool in pans for 5 minutes before turning out onto racks. Cool thoroughly and fill and frost as desired.

MAYONNAISE CAKE

The recipe for this simple and tasty cake has for years had the following story associated with it: A lady who was having dinner in an elegant New York hotel was so impressed by this cake that she requested the recipe. The chef gave it to her, along with a bill for $100, which her lawyer advised her to pay. She called it "The $100 Cake" and gave the recipe freely.

2 cups sifted pastry or cake flour
1 cup sugar
¼ cup cocoa
2 teaspoons baking soda
¼ teaspoon salt
1 cup cold water

1 cup commercial whole-egg mayonnaise (for best results do not use commercial salad dressing or homemade mayonnaise)
1 teaspoon vanilla extract

Sift the dry ingredients into a bowl. Combine water, mayonnaise, and vanilla. Blend well, and then stir into the sifted dry ingredients. Blend ingredients thoroughly. Turn batter into a buttered 7 x 11-inch or 8 x 12-inch pan. Bake in a 350° F. oven for 35 minutes, or until cake tests done.

DATE-NUT MAYONNAISE CAKE.   Add to the batter 1 teaspoon cinnamon, 1 cup chopped, pitted dates, and 1 cup chopped walnuts. Bake in a 9 by 13-inch pan.

PRUNE-NUT MAYONNAISE CAKE.   Use a 1-pound jar of pitted, cooked prunes, drained and cut up. Substitute the cold prune liquid for the water and add 1 cup chopped nuts. Very good, and very appealing to the children.

"Content the stomach, and the stomach will content you."
THOMAS WALKER

SAUERKRAUT SURPRISE CAKE

This recipe is supposed to have been invented by German immigrants to this country. Whoever first developed it, I envy their courage. It is, however, a moist delicious cake with absolutely no sauerkraut flavor. The pieces of snipped sauerkraut resemble coconut. Have all ingredients at room temperature.

2¼ cups sifted pastry or cake flour
1 teaspoon baking powder
1 teaspoon baking soda
¼ teaspoon salt
½ cup cocoa (Dutch cocoa preferred)

⅔ cup sauerkraut
⅔ cup butter or margarine
1½ cups sugar
3 large eggs
1 teaspoon vanilla extract
1 cup water

Sift the flour with the baking powder, soda, salt, and cocoa. Set aside. Rinse and drain the sauerkraut. Snip it into smaller pieces with kitchen scissors. Cream the butter or margarine until fluffy. Gradually add the sugar and cream until light. Add the eggs, 1 at a time, and beat in well. Add the vanilla and blend. Now stir in the flour mixture alternately with the water, beginning and ending with dry ingredients. Fold in the sauerkraut last. Turn batter into 2 8-inch round layer pans that have been buttered and floured. Tap pans lightly on a counter top to release excess air. Bake in a 350° F. oven for 30 to 35 minutes, or until cake tests done. Cool in pans for 5 minutes before turning out onto racks to cool. The SOUR CREAM CHOCOLATE FROSTING (page 93) is excellent with this cake.

WACKY CAKE

This cake was first presented to the delighted housewife sometime during the 1950's. You don't even need a bowl. Everything is mixed directly in the pan the cake is baked in. With the exception of the cold water, have ingredients at room temperature.

1½ cups sifted pastry or cake
     flour
1 cup sugar
3 tablespoons cocoa (Dutch
     preferred)
1 teaspoon baking soda
¼ teaspoon salt

⅓ cup melted butter or
     margarine, or salad oil (not
     olive oil)
1 tablespoon vinegar
1 teaspoon vanilla extract
1 cup cold water

Sift the flour with the sugar, cocoa, baking soda, and salt directly into
an 8-inch square pan that has been buttered and lightly floured. Make
3 holes in the flour mixture. Into 1 hole pour the oil, into another the
vinegar, and the vanilla goes into the third hole. Pour the cold water
over all, and using a fork, blend the mixture vigorously. When blended,
bake in a 350° F. oven for 25 to 30 minutes, or until cake tests done.
Cool in the pan and frost as desired.

TOMATO SOUP CAKE

Sometimes called "Mystery Cake," this cake is different and *good*. The
fruits and nuts may be varied according to individual taste and con-
venience. Have ingredients at room temperature.

2 cups sifted all-purpose flour
1 teaspoon baking soda
2 teaspoons baking powder
½ teaspoon salt
1 teaspoon cinnamon
1 teaspoon nutmeg or allspice
½ cup butter or margarine
1 cup sugar

1 can (10½ ounces)
     condensed tomato soup
1½ cups raisins or chopped
     pitted dates
1 to 1½ cups candied fruits
     or fruit mix
1 cup chopped nuts

Sift the flour with the baking soda, baking powder, salt, and spices.
Set aside. Cream the butter or margarine with the sugar until fluffy.
Fold the sifted flour mixture into the creamed mixture alternately
with the tomato soup, beginning and ending with dry ingredients. Fold
the fruits and nuts in last. Turn batter into a buttered and floured 9-
inch tube pan or mini-Bundt pan and bake in a 350° F. oven for 45
to 55 minutes, or until cake tests done. Cool in the pan 10 minutes
before turning out onto a rack. Frost with any white frosting, or
simply dust the still-warm cake with sifted powdered sugar.

CLASSIC 1-2-3-4 CAKE

The title of this old-fashioned, basic, and superb cake is derived from the quantities of the ingredients—1 cup butter, 2 cups sugar, 3 cups flour, and 4 eggs—a recipe that any busy housewife can keep right in her head. Some old cookbooks call for the same ingredients, only using 1 cup egg whites instead of the 4 whole eggs. It works either way, and the variation is as good as the original. Have all ingredients at room temperature.

3 cups sifted pastry or cake flour
1 tablespoon baking powder
½ teaspoon salt
1 cup butter or margarine
2 cups superfine granulated sugar
1 teaspoon vanilla extract, or

1 teaspoon grated lemon rind, or 1 tablespoon rose water and ½ teaspoon almond extract, or 2 tablespoons grated orange rind
4 large eggs
¾ cup milk or orange juice

Sift the flour with the baking powder and salt. Set aside. Cream the butter or margarine until light, gradually beat in the sugar, and beat until light and fluffy. Add the flavoring desired and the eggs, 1 at a time. Beat each egg in thoroughly. Add the sifted dry ingredients to the creamed mixture alternately with the milk or orange juice, beginning and ending with the dry ingredients. Batter should be smooth, but do not overbeat. Turn into buttered and floured pans: 2 9-inch round layer pans, or 3 8-inch round layer pans, or 1 10-inch tube pan or Bundt pan. Tap the pans on the counter top to release excess air. For layers, bake in a 375° F. oven 25 to 30, minutes or until cake tests done. Cool in pans for 5 minutes before turning out onto racks to cool. If baking in the tube pan or Bundt pan, bake in a 350° F. oven for 1 hour, or until cake is done.

BOURBON CAKE. Make cake as directed using the grated orange rind and orange juice. Bake in a tube pan or Bundt pan. When cake is baked, cool for 5 minutes, then pour BOURBON GLAZE (page 20) over cake and finish cooling in the pan.

BOURBON GLAZE.   Combine ¼ cup butter, ⅔ cup sugar and ½ cup fine bourbon whisky. Heat over direct heat until sugar is melted. Pour over cake while hot.

OLD-FASHIONED JAM CAKE

Old in the tradition of the South is this delicious, fruity cake. It has the good keeping qualities which make it especially nice for the holidays. We prefer using a blackberry or raspberry jam, but have on occasion used blueberry, strawberry, fig, apricot and others. Have all ingredients at room temperature.

1 cup butter or margarine	2 teaspoons cinnamon
2 cups sugar (part may be brown)	1 teaspoon nutmeg
	½ teaspoon cloves
4 large eggs	½ teaspoon ginger or allspice
3 cups sifted pastry or cake flour	1 cup buttermilk or sour milk
	1 teaspoon vanilla extract
1 teaspoon baking soda	1 cup jam or preserves

Cream the butter and sugar until light and fluffy. Beat in the eggs, one at a time, beating until blended. Sift the dry ingredients and stir into the creamed mixture alternately with the buttermilk or sour milk, beginning and ending with dry ingredients. Stir the vanilla into the jam or preserves and fold this into the batter, quickly but carefully. Turn the batter into a well-buttered 10-inch tube pan or Bundt pan. Bake in a 300° F. oven for 15 minutes, then raise the heat to 350° F. and bake for another 45 minutes. Test the cake carefully before removing from the oven to make certain that it is done. Cool in the pan for 10 to 15 minutes before turning out onto a rack. Sift powdered sugar over the cake while it is still warm.

VARIATIONS

1. Coffee may replace half of the buttermilk or sour milk.

2. Reduce butter to ¾ cup, omit the buttermilk, and use ¾ to 1 cup of commercial sour cream.

3. Cake may be baked in 2 10-inch square pans, buttered and lined with waxed paper. Bake in a 350° F. oven for 35 to 40 minutes.

4. Add 1 cup each: raisins, chopped nuts, and coconut. Excellent.

5. Because it is a sturdy cake, it is ideal for tiered cakes. Double the recipe will make 2 10-inch round layers, plus 1 6-inch square pan that is 3 inches deep. Bake the layers at 350° F. for approximately 40 to 45 minutes. The square pan requires a slightly longer baking time. Cool in the pans for 10 minutes before turning out onto racks.

TENNESSEE JAM CAKE. To make this delicious holiday treat, reduce sugar to 1 cup, use 5 large eggs and increase the baking soda to 1 tablespoon. Use a total of 3 cups jam or preserves, part blackberry, part strawberry, and part fig. Add 1 cup of chopped walnuts or pecans. Bake as in basic recipe. This cake will keep for a month.

CAKES WITH
FRUIT AND NUTS

ALMA ELDRIDGE'S TEXAS APPLE CAKE

This fine apple-nut cake is of the quick-mix type made with oil. I bake it in a Bundt pan and dust the warm cake with sifted powdered sugar.

3 cups sifted pastry or cake flour

1 teaspoon baking soda

1 teaspoon salt

1 or 2 teaspoons cinnamon

1¼ cups salad oil (not olive oil)

2 cups sugar (part may be brown sugar)

1 large egg

3 cups grated apple

2 teaspoons vanilla extract

1 cup chopped walnuts

Sift the flour with the baking soda, salt, and cinnamon. Set aside. Beat the oil with the sugar and egg until creamed. Fold the sifted flour into the creamed mixture alternately with the chopped apple and vanilla, beginning and ending with dry ingredients. Add the chopped nuts last. Turn into a buttered 10-inch tube pan or Bundt pan, and bake in a 325° F. oven about 1 hour and 10 to 15 minutes. Cool in the pan 10 minutes before turning out onto a rack to cool completely.

APRICOT NECTAR CAKE

If you like an apricot flavor, you will especially like this cake. Have all ingredients at room temperature.

2½ cups sifted pastry or cake flour

1 tablespoon baking powder

½ teaspoon salt

⅔ cup butter or margarine

1¾ cups superfine granulated sugar

1 teaspoon grated lemon rind

2 large eggs

2 extra egg yolks

¼ cup water

1 cup apricot nectar

Combine flour, baking powder, and salt. Sift into a bowl and set aside. Cream the butter or margarine with the sugar until light and fluffy. Add the lemon rind, whole eggs, and extra yolks and beat until mixture is light. Combine water and nectar. Add the sifted dry ingredients to the creamed mixture alternately with the liquid ingredients, beginning and ending with dry ingredients. Batter should be smooth, but do not overbeat. Turn batter into 3 9-inch round layer pans that have been buttered and floured. Tap pans lightly on the counter top to release excess air, and bake in a 350° F. oven for 25 to 30 minutes, or until cake tests done. Cool in pans for 5 minutes before turning out onto racks. Fill layers with APRICOT FILLING (page 96) and drizzle the top with APRICOT GLAZE (page 99), or frost with any boiled frosting.

BANANA-DATE CAKE

We call this "Picnic Cake" at our house. It carries well, stays moist, and is a must for picnics. I sometimes double the recipe and bake it in 2 9-inch square pans. I then fill it and frost it with whipped cream. Have all ingredients at room temperature.

2 cups sifted pastry or cake flour	2 large eggs, separated
1 teaspoon baking soda	1 teaspoon vanilla extract
½ teaspoon salt	½ cup buttermilk or sour milk
½ cup butter or margarine	1 cup mashed bananas
1 cup brown sugar	½ cup chopped, pitted dates
½ cup granulated sugar	½ cup chopped walnuts

Sift the flour with the baking soda and salt. Set aside. Cream the butter or margarine until light and then gradually add the sugars, beating until mixture is light and fluffy. Beat in the egg yolks and vanilla. Combine the buttermilk or sour milk with the mashed bananas. Add the sifted dry ingredients to the creamed mixture alternately with the liquid mixture, beginning and ending with dry ingredients. Blend in the dates and nuts. Beat the egg whites until stiff and fold them in last. Turn batter into a 9-inch square pan that has been buttered and floured. Bake in a 350° F. oven for 45 minutes, or until cake tests done. Cool on a rack, in the pan.

YOGURT CAKE

For this fine cake you may use the smooth, custard-firm yogurt or commercial sour cream. Have ingredients at room temperature.

3 cups sifted pastry or cake flour

1 teaspoon baking soda

1 teaspoon baking powder

1 cup sweet butter

2 cups superfine granulated sugar

4 large eggs

2 teaspoons grated lemon rind

1 teaspoon vanilla extract

1 cup yogurt or sour cream

1 cup blueberries (optional)

Sift the flour with the baking soda and baking powder. Set aside. Cream the butter until very light. Gradually add the sugar, beating all the time, and beat until light and fluffy. Beat in the eggs, 1 at a time, and then the flavorings. Fold in the sifted flour mixture alternately with the yogurt or sour cream, beginning and ending with dry ingredients. If you use the blueberries, fold them in at the very last. Turn batter into a buttered and floured 10-inch tube pan, or Bundt pan. Bake in a 350° F. oven for 1 hour and 10 to 12 minutes. Cool in the pan for 10 minutes before turning out onto a rack. Dust with sifted powdered sugar. If you use the blueberries, serve the cake slices topped with BLUEBERRY SAUCE (page 101).

UPSIDE-DOWN CAKE

This is a fine-textured cake, as simple to make and as delicious to the taste as any cake should be. Any fruit or any combination of fruits and/or nuts may be used with excellent results. I have used the traditional pineapple, cherries, apricots, peaches, and pears, as well as the less traditional papayas, mangoes, various berries, and cranberries. Have all ingredients at room temperature.

⅓ cup butter or margarine

1 cup brown sugar

3 or 4 cups whole berries, or sliced fresh or canned fruit

2 cups sifted pastry or cake flour

2 teaspoons baking powder

2 large eggs

1½ cups granulated or brown sugar

1 cup heavy cream, unwhipped

Butter a 9 by 13 by 2-inch baking dish. Melt the butter or margarine and pour into the baking dish. Sprinkle with the brown sugar and arrange the fruit in the pan. Set aside. Sift the flour with the baking powder. Beat the eggs with the 1½ cups sugar until light. Stir in the sifted flour mixture and then the heavy cream. Turn this batter into the pan, being careful not to disarrange the fruit. Bake in a 350° F. oven for 25 minutes, then reduce heat to 325° F. and bake for another 20 to 25 minutes, or until done. Remove from oven and cool for 5 minutes. Then carefully turn the cake out onto a serving dish. Serve with a dollop of whipped cream or with ice cream.

CRANBERRY UPSIDE-DOWN CAKE. If you use fresh cranberries, cook them first in about ½ cup light corn syrup, just until they pop. Then follow basic recipe.

PUERTO RICAN COCONUT CAKE

The use of coconut milk makes this a superb cake. Have all ingredients at room temperature.

2¾ cups sifted pastry or cake flour
4 teaspoons baking powder
½ teaspoon salt
¾ cup butter or margarine
1½ cups superfine granulated sugar
1 cup coconut milk or milk
1 teaspoon vanilla extract
½ teaspoon almond extract (optional)
4 large egg whites

Sift together the flour, baking powder, and salt and set aside. Cream the butter or margarine. Gradually add 1 cup of the sugar and cream until light and fluffy. Combine coconut milk or milk and flavorings. Add the sifted dry ingredients to the creamed mixture alternately with the milk mixture, beginning and ending with dry ingredients. In a small bowl, beat the egg whites until foamy. Gradually add the remaining ½ cup of sugar and beat until stiff and glossy. Carefully fold the meringue into the batter, folding just until there are no patches of white. Turn batter into 3 8-inch round layer pans that have been buttered and floured. Bake in a 350° F. oven for 25 to 30 minutes, or until layers test done. Cool in pans for 5 minutes before turning out onto racks.

Cool thoroughly. Fill with UNCOOKED COCONUT FILLING (page 97), and frost with COCONUT FROSTING (page 87).

COCONUT MERINGUE CAKE

This is a new and delicious version of the old meringue cake. Have all ingredients at room temperature.

¾ cup sifted pastry or cake flour
1 teaspoon baking powder
3 large eggs, separated
½ cup superfine granulated sugar
¼ cup milk
1 teaspoon grated lemon rind or 1 tablespoon grated orange rind

MERINGUE
½ cup sugar
½ cup flaked or grated coconut
1 teaspoon vanilla extract

Sift the flour with the baking powder and set aside. Separate the eggs, reserving whites for the meringue. Beat yolks with the sugar until thick. Combine the milk and lemon or orange rind. Add the dry ingredients to the yolk mixture alternately with the liquid ingredients, beginning and ending with the dry ingredients, and beating just until well blended. Pour batter into a buttered and floured 8-inch round layer pan. To make the MERINGUE, beat the egg whites until foamy, gradually add the sugar and beat until whites form stiff peaks. Fold in the coconut and vanilla. Spread meringue over the batter. Bake in a 350° F. oven for 10 minutes, then reduce heat to 325° F. and bake another 10 to 15 minutes. Cool and serve in pan.

DATE CAKE

This is an excellent, easy-to-make cake. Have all ingredients at room temperature.

2 cups sifted pastry or cake
flour
1 teaspoon baking soda
½ teaspoon salt
½ teaspoon nutmeg
1 teaspoon cinnamon
½ teaspoon allspice or cloves
1½ cups sugar

1 cup salad oil (not olive oil)
3 large eggs
1 cup buttermilk or sour milk
1 teaspoon vanilla extract, or
2 teaspoons grated lemon
rind
1 cup chopped nuts
1 cup chopped, pitted dates

Sift the flour with the baking soda, salt, and spices. Set aside. Combine the sugar, oil, and eggs and beat until smooth. Add the sifted dry ingredients to the sugar mixture alternately with the buttermilk or sour milk, beginning and ending with dry ingredients. Stir in the flavoring, nuts, and dates. Blend. Pour into a buttered and floured 9 by 13-inch pan. Bake in a 300° F. oven for 55 to 60 minutes, or until cake tests done. Cool in the pan, on a rack. Best spread with BUTTERMILK ICING (page 89), which complements the flavor.

FALLEN DATE-NUT CAKE

This cake cannot wait from the last mixing stage to the pans, or the bubbles from the beaten eggs, which in baking carry the scant flour mixture to the top to form the crust, will rise in the waiting time and the top will only brown, with no crust. The cake, which is very good, is made in several ways throughout the Coachella Valley. Some cooks simply bake it at 300° F. until it falls, and do not concern themselves about the careful directions given here. But then the cake cannot be turned out of the pan. Have all ingredients at room temperature.

1 pound chopped, pitted dates
½ pound chopped walnuts
1 cup sifted pastry or cake
flour
1 teaspoon baking powder

5 large eggs
1 cup sugar
2 teaspoons vanilla extract, or
1 tablespoon grated lemon
rind

Combine the dates and nuts. Sift the flour with the baking powder and then sift them again over the dates and nuts. Stir to blend. Beat the eggs thoroughly. This is very important and they should be beaten, with an electric mixer, for about 5 minutes. Then add the sugar and the flavoring used and beat until the mixture is no longer grainy. Pour this over the date mixture and mix just to blend. Be careful not to overmix. Immediately pour into a buttered and waxed paper-lined 9 by 13-inch pan. Bake in a 350° F. oven for 28 to 30 minutes. Top will be tan or a very light brown and puffy-looking. When you remove the cake from the oven it will drop slightly. Be especially careful not to overbake the cake.

While the cake is still quite warm, place a piece of waxed paper over the top of the pan, and a board over it. Flip the whole thing over, so that the cake is on the waxed-papered board. Carefully lift the pan, and then peel the waxed paper off the cake. The bottom should be browned. If raw in spots, the cake is still good, but the next time you make it bake it another minute or so longer. Now place another piece of waxed paper over the cake, and another board, and flip it again so that it is right side up. The cake is so fragile that these troublesome-sounding directions are quite necessary. When the cake is cool, cut it into bars or squares, and serve topped with a dollop of whipped cream.

FRUIT COCKTAIL CAKE

This delicious cake is so simple a child can make it. Some recipes call for draining the fruit, but I think that using the syrup makes a superior cake.

1 large egg	1-pound can fruit cocktail,
1 cup sugar (white or brown)	syrup included
1 cup sifted flour	½ cup brown sugar
1 teaspoon baking soda	½ cup chopped walnuts, or
	blanched, slivered almonds

Beat the egg. Add the 1 cup sugar and blend thoroughly. Sift the flour and baking soda and stir into the egg-sugar mixture. Now add the fruit cocktail and syrup. Blend. Pour into a buttered and floured 9-inch square pan. Combine the ½ cup brown sugar and the nuts and sprinkle over the top. Bake in a 350° F. oven for 30 minutes. Cut into squares to serve.

NOTE. Make recipe as above, using 2 large eggs, 1½ cups sugar, 2 teaspoons baking soda, 2 cups flour and 2 cans fruit cocktail with the syrup drained from one can. Turn batter into a well-buttered 9-inch tube pan or mini-Bundt pan. Bake in a 300° F. oven for 1 hour. Cool cake in the pan for 15 minutes before turning out onto a rack. Drizzle with a simple powdered-sugar glaze or frost with any coconut frosting and sprinkle with chopped nuts. This makes an exceptional cake, moist and flavorful, and will keep for several days.

FAVORITE ORANGE CAKE

We fill this with ORANGE CHEESE (page 251) and frost it with ORANGE MOUNTAIN FROSTING (page 87). But sometimes I bake it in a tube pan and use a simple glaze. Delicious and tender either way. Have all ingredients at room temperature.

2½ cups sifted pastry or cake
  flour
1 tablespoon baking powder
½ teaspoon salt
½ cup butter or margarine
1½ cups superfine granulated
  sugar

2 tablespoons grated orange
  rind
1 cup orange juice
½ cup (about 4) egg whites

Sift the flour with the baking powder and salt and set aside. Cream the butter or margarine, gradually adding the sugar and beating until light and fluffy. Add the orange rind and blend in. Add the sifted flour mixture to the creamed mixture alternately with the orange juice, beginning and ending with dry ingredients and beating until smooth. Beat the egg whites until very stiff and fold into the batter very carefully, folding just until there are no remaining patches of white. Turn batter into 3 8-inch round layer pans that have been buttered and floured. Bake in a 350° F. oven for 25 minutes, or until cake tests done. Cool in pans for 5 minutes before turning out onto rack. Fill and frost as suggested above.

NOTE. If desired, use a 9-inch tube pan or mini-Bundt pan, buttered and floured. Bake in a 350° F. oven for 1 hour, testing carefully before removing cake from oven as it may require another 5 or 10 minutes. Cool in pan 10 minutes before turning out onto racks.

SOUR CREAM ORANGE CAKE

This delicious cake is made even more moist by the addition of a hot syrup spooned over the cake. Have all ingredients at room temperature.

2 cups sifted pastry or cake flour	1 cup superfine granulated sugar
1 teaspoon baking powder	3 large eggs, separated
1 teaspoon baking soda	1 tablespoon grated orange rind
¼ teaspoon salt	1 teaspoon grated lemon rind
1 cup butter or margarine	1 cup commercial sour cream

Sift the flour with the baking powder, baking soda, and salt. Set aside. Cream the butter or margarine until it is fluffy, then gradually add the sugar and beat until light. Now beat in the egg yolks and the flavorings and blend well. Stir the sifted dry ingredients into the creamed mixture alternately with the sour cream, beginning and ending with dry ingredients. Beat the egg whites until stiff and carefully fold into the batter, folding just until there are no remaining patches of white. Turn batter into a buttered and floured 9-inch tube pan, or mini-Bundt pan. Bake in a 325° F. oven for 1 hour or until cake tests done. Cool in pan 10 minutes. Then turn cake out onto a round plate with a rim.

ORANGE SYRUP.   Combine ½ cup orange juice and 2 tablespoons lemon juice (or ⅓ cup each of orange juice and an orange liqueur, such as Triple Sec or Grand Marnier) with ½ cup sugar. Bring to a boil and simmer 3 or 4 minutes. Slowly spoon the hot syrup over the cake, allowing time for it to soak in.

CARROT-PINEAPPLE CAKE

This is a quickly made, virtually failure-proof cake that keeps well and is especially liked by the children for an after-school snack. Have all ingredients at room temperature.

3 cups sifted pastry or cake flour
1 teaspoon baking powder
1 teaspoon baking soda
1 teaspoon cinnamon (optional)
2 cups sugar

1½ cups salad oil (not olive oil)
3 large eggs
2 teaspoons vanilla extract
1 small can crushed pineapple, not drained
2 cups grated fresh carrots
1 cup chopped nuts

Combine flour, baking powder, soda, and cinnamon, if used. Sift into a bowl and set aside. Combine sugar, oil, and eggs. Beat to blend. Add vanilla and blend in. Add the sifted dry ingredients and blend in but do not overmix. Lastly, fold in the pineapple, carrots, and nuts. Turn batter into a buttered 10-inch tube pan or a Bundt pan. Bake in a 325° F. oven for 1 hour and 20 minutes, or until cake tests done. Cool in pan for 10 minutes before turning out onto rack to cool.

PINEAPPLE LAYER CAKE

This makes a large, luscious cake, fine for a party. The recipe is easily halved, using ¾ cup + 2 tablespoons sugar, and 2½ teaspoons baking powder. This cake is rich, so I don't use a regular frosting, but prefer whipped cream between the layers and on top. Have all ingredients at room temperature.

4½ cups sifted pastry or cake flour

1¾ cups superfine granulated sugar

5 teaspoons baking powder

½ teaspoon salt

1 cup butter or margarine

4 large eggs

2 cups crushed pineapple, undrained

½ cup milk

2 teaspoons vanilla extract

Combine flour, sugar, baking powder, and salt. Sift into a bowl. Make a well in the center, and into this well put the remaining ingredients. Using an electric mixer (a must with this cake), beat, at slow speed, for 3 or 4 minutes, scraping the bowl as you go along. Turn the batter into 2 buttered and floured 9-inch square pans. Tap pans on counter top to release excess air. Bake in a 350° F. oven for 30 to 35 minutes, or until cake tests done. Cool in pans for 5 minutes before turning out onto racks.

RAISIN LAYER CAKE

This is a modern version of an old-fashioned cake, baked in layers and frosted. Have all ingredients at room temperature.

1 cup golden or dark raisins

2¼ cups sifted flour

2½ teaspoons baking powder

1 teaspoon salt

1 teaspoon cream of tartar

⅔ cup butter or margarine

1½ cups sugar

1 teaspoon vanilla extract

3 large eggs, separated

1 cup milk

Chop raisins coarsely with a knife that is frequently dipped in hot water to keep the raisins from sticking to it. Sift the flour with the baking powder, salt, and cream of tartar. Set aside. Cream the butter or margarine, gradually adding 1¼ cups of the sugar and beating until light and fluffy. Add the vanilla and egg yolks to the creamed mixture, and beat in thoroughly. Add the flour mixture to the creamed mixture alternately with the milk, beginning and ending with dry ingredients. Batter should be smooth. Stir in the raisins. Beat the egg whites until foamy, gradually add the remaining ¼ cup sugar, and continue beating until mixture forms a medium-stiff meringue. Fold into the batter, folding just until there are no patches of white. Turn batter into 2 buttered and floured 8- or 9-inch round layer pans. Bake in a 350° F.

oven for 30 to 35 minutes, or until done. Cool in pans for 5 minutes before turning out onto racks.

NOTE.   If desired, you may substitute ½ cup brown sugar for ½ cup granulated sugar. Add 1 teaspoon cinnamon and ¼ teaspoon each of nutmeg and cloves to the sifted flour.

FRESH STRAWBERRY CAKE

This unusual cake has strawberries in the batter and in the frosting. It's an easy, one-bowl cake that makes a fine summertime treat. Have all ingredients at room temperature.

2¼ cups sifted pastry or cake flour

¼ teaspoon salt

2½ teaspoons baking powder

½ cup butter or margarine

1½ cups superfine granulated sugar

2 large eggs

1 teaspoon vanilla extract

¾ cup fresh, crushed, unsweetened strawberries

Sift the flour with the salt and baking powder. Combine butter or margarine, sugar, eggs, and vanilla in a bowl. Beat with an electric mixer for a total of 3 minutes, scraping the sides of the bowl once or twice. Then add the flour mixture alternately with the strawberries. Blend into the creamed mixture and then beat for 2 minutes. Turn batter into 2 8-inch round layer pans that have been buttered, lined with waxed paper and buttered again. Tap pans on counter to release excess air, and bake in a 350° F. oven for 25 to 30 minutes, or until cake tests done. Cool in pans for 5 minutes, before turning out onto racks. Remove waxed paper carefully while layers are still warm. When cool, frost with UNCOOKED FRUIT WHIP, using fresh strawberries (page 98), or with whipped cream and sliced strawberries.

SOUR CREAM NUT CAKE

This is a fine cake that can be baked either in a tube pan or in an oblong pan. Have all ingredients at room temperature.

2 cups sifted pastry or cake flour

1 teaspoon baking soda

1 teaspoon baking powder

¼ teaspoon salt

½ cup butter or margarine

1 cup sugar

3 large eggs, separated

2 tablespoons grated lemon rind

1 cup commercial sour cream

1 cup semisweet chocolate chips

1 cup chopped nuts

LEMON SAUCE (see following recipe)

Sift the flour with the baking soda, baking powder, and salt. Set aside. Cream the butter or margarine with the sugar until light and fluffy. Beat in the egg yolks, 1 at a time. Add the lemon rind and stir through the mixture. Add the sifted flour mixture to the creamed mixture alternately with the sour cream, beginning and ending with dry ingredients. Batter should be smooth. Beat the egg whites until stiff and fold through the batter. Combine chocolate chips and nuts and fold into the batter. Turn into a buttered and floured 10-inch tube pan or Bundt pan. Bake in a 350° F. oven for 50 minutes, or until cake tests done. Cool in pan for 10 minutes before turning out onto a rack to cool. Baste with LEMON SAUCE while cake is hot.

NOTE.   If desired, bake in a 9 by 13-inch pan in a 350° F. oven for 35 to 40 minutes. Pour LEMON SAUCE over the hot cakes, cool, and serve in the pan.

LEMON SAUCE.   Combine and bring to a boil ½ cup sugar, 2 tablespoons lemon juice and 2 tablespoons orange liqueur or orange juice.

WALNUT CAKE

This fine cake keeps well, and makes a superior company dessert. Have ingredients at room temperature.

3½ cups sifted pastry or cake flour

½ teaspoon salt

1½ cups butter or margarine

2 cups superfine granulated sugar

6 large eggs, separated

½ cup milk

½ cup Madeira wine, brandy, Cognac, or whisky

1 teaspoon vanilla extract

2 cups coarsely chopped walnuts

1 teaspoon cream of tarter

Sift the flour with the salt and set aside. Cream the butter or margarine until light and gradually beat in the sugar until the mixture is smooth. Beat in the egg yolks. Combine the milk, wine or liquor, and vanilla. Add this to the creamed mixture alternately with the sifted flour mixture, beginning and ending with dry ingredients. Then fold in the chopped nuts. Beat the egg whites until foamy, sprinkle the cream of tartar over them, and continue beating until they hold stiff peaks. Fold this meringue into the batter gently but thoroughly, folding only until there are no remaining patches of white. Butter a 10-inch tube pan, line with *brown* paper, and butter the paper. Turn the batter into the prepared pan and bake in a 275° F. oven for 2½ to 3 hours, or until cake tests done. Cool the cake in the pan 30 minutes before turning it out. Dust cake with sifted powdered sugar while it is still warm.

AIR-RAISED CAKES

ANGEL FOOD CAKE

All recipes for angel food cake are basically the same, but the methods of preparation are varied and wondrous. Here are several items of special importance in making any air-raised cake such as the Angel Food.

1. Best results are obtained by using a tube pan with a removable bottom and straight sides.

2. Egg whites *must* be at room temperature, but the eggs should be separated just upon removing from the refrigerator. Leftover whites from a previous baking day will not make a good angel food cake.

3. Superfine granulated (not powdered or confectioners') sugar is best in all cakes but is especially important to a good angel food cake.

4. It is best to fold the flour mixture into the beaten egg whites by hand, using a rapid but gentle movement. If you rely on an electric mixer at this point, it is apt to break down the mass of air bubbles upon which the cake volume depends.

5. All air-raised cakes (angel food, sponge, and chiffon) must be cooled in the pan, with the pan inverted over a rack or an inverted funnel. If the cake is removed from the pan before it is completely cooled, it will collapse upon itself.

1 cup sifted pastry or cake flour	½ teaspoon salt
1½ cups superfine granulated sugar	1½ teaspoons vanilla extract or grated lemon rind, or a combination of these or other flavorings
⅓ cup cold water	
1½ cups (about 12) egg whites	1½ teaspoons cream of tarter

First, heat the oven to 425° F. and place the tube pan in the oven to heat. Now sift the flour with ¼ cup of the sugar at least 3 times, preferably 5 times. Set aside. In a large bowl combine the cold water, egg whites, salt, flavoring used, and cream of tartar. Beat, with an electric mixer, until stiff. Then, very gradually, beat in the remaining 1¼ cups sugar and continue beating until mixture is stiff and glossy. Now, very carefully, sprinkle a little (about ¼ cup at a time) of the sifted flour mixture over the egg whites and fold in. Continue until all has been folded into the beaten whites. Turn batter into the *hot* angel food pan, being very careful not to burn yourself, and place it in the 425° F. oven. Bake at this temperature for 15 minutes. Then turn the heat *off*, and leave the cake in the oven for another 15 minutes. Remove from the oven and invert to cool.

ANGEL FOOD CUPCAKES.   Follow the recipe and turn into approximately 16 unbuttered muffin cups. Bake in a 375° F. oven for about 20 minutes, or until done. To frost, swirl in WHITE MOUNTAIN FROSTING (page 87) and coat with chopped nuts or flaked coconut, or sprinkle with grated orange rind.

ROSE GERANIUM ANGEL FOOD CAKE. Wash and carefully dry 12 large rose geranium leaves (the herb rose geranium) and lay them on the bottom of the tube pan before adding the batter. The delightful fragrance permeates the cake.

CUSTARD ANGEL FOOD CAKE

1 cup sifted pastry or cake flour
¼ teaspoon salt
8 large eggs, separated
1¼ cups superfine granulated sugar

½ cup water
1 teaspoon cream of tartar
1 teaspoon flavoring (vanilla extract, lemon juice, orange juice, or grated citrus rind)

Sift the flour with the salt at least 4 times and set aside. Separate the eggs and let come to room temperature while you make the syrup. Combine the sugar and water in a saucepan. Let come to a boil and boil until mixture reaches the long thread stage (230° F. on a candy thermometer). Beat the egg yolks until they are very thick and pale. Continue beating while you pour in the hot syrup. Beat until mixture is quite thick. Gradually fold the flour, ¼ cup at a time, into the egg yolk mixture. Beat the egg whites until foamy, sprinkle the cream of tartar over them, and continue beating until very stiff. Fold the whites and the flavoring used into the egg yolk mixture carefully, to keep the mixture airy and light. Turn the batter into an ungreased 10-inch tube pan. Cut through the batter several times with a table knife to break any large air bubbles. Bake in a 300° F. oven for 1½ hours, or until cake tests done. Invert pan on a rack or an inverted funnel, and allow cake to cool completely before removing from pan.

*"There is nothing in the way of fruit
half so good as baked apples."*
JANE AUSTIN

MOCK ANGEL FOOD CAKE

This cake is firmer than an angel food cake and does not crush or crumble as easily as a true angel food. It has a good flavor and keeps well. Have all ingredients at room temperature.

2 cups sifted pastry or cake flour

2 cups superfine granulated sugar

2½ teaspoons baking powder

½ teaspoon salt

1 cup water, milk, or orange juice

2 teaspoons vanilla extract, or 1 tablespoon grated orange rind, or a combination of these or other flavorings

1 cup (about 8) egg whites

1 teaspoon cream of tarter

Combine flour, sugar, baking powder, and salt. Sift together at least 3 times. Bring the liquid to a boil and pour over the sifted dry ingredients. Beat with an electric mixer until batter is smooth. Set aside to cool to room temperature. When ready to use, stir in the flavoring used. Beat the egg whites until foamy, sprinkle the cream of tartar over the whites, and continue beating until the whites form stiff peaks. Fold the beaten whites into the batter until there are no remaining patches of white. Turn into an ungreased 10-inch tube pan, or a Teflon-coated Bundt pan. Bake in a 300° F. oven for 20 minutes, raise heat to 350° F., and continue baking another 20 to 25 minutes, or until cake springs back when top is lightly touched. Invert to cool.

AN AMERICAN TRIFLE

This rich dessert, made with a baked angel food cake, is fine for company. If desired, you may use CHOCOLATE CREAM FILLING (page

96) or CREAM FROSTING (page 86). First, break up an angel food cake into bite-sized pieces and set aside. Then make the following gelatin mixture.

1 envelope unflavored gelatin	½ cup sherry or Madeira wine
3 tablespoons water	
4 large eggs, separated	2½ cups heavy cream
1 cup sugar	

Soften the gelatin in the water in a custard cup. Place the cup in a pan of very hot water to dissolve the gelatin. Beat the egg yolks until light, gradually adding ½ cup of the sugar. Add the wine and place in the top part of a double boiler. Cook over hot, not boiling, water until mixture thickens. Stir constantly. Cool. Beat the egg whites until stiff, gradually adding the remaining ½ cup of sugar. Whip 2 cups of the heavy cream until stiff, and fold into the beaten whites. Then add the dissolved gelatin and the cooled yolk mixture.

Layer the custard and the cake pieces in a large tube pan or ring mold. The top and bottom layers should be cake. Chill for at least 12 hours, preferably for 24 hours. Then turn out of the pan or mold. Whip the remaining ½ cup of cream until thick, sweetening it with 1 or 2 tablespoons sugar. Use this to gild the lily.

FILLED ANGEL FOOD CAKE

This makes an especially delicious surprise cake. Use any of the types of angel food cake listed. First, slice a layer of cake from the top and set it aside to use later. Then pull out enough of the cake to leave a nice hollow in the center. There must be enough cake on the sides, however, to hold in the filling without leaking. Now fill this hollow with any of the following: sweetened whipped cream with sliced bananas, small, whole strawberries, or other sliced fruit, CHOCOLATE CREAM FILLING (page 96), CREAM WHIP (page 92), UNCOOKED FRUIT WHIP (page 98), or LEMON-LIME CREAM FILLING (page 95). When cake is filled, arrange the reserved layer over the filling. Chill thoroughly before serving. You may, if desired, top the cake with a glaze or with whipped cream.

CHIFFON LAYER CAKE

This inexpensive cake can be baked in layer pans, or in a 9 x 13-inch pan. We use WHIPPED BUTTER FROSTING (page 92) with this cake. Have all ingredients at room temperature.

1¾ cups sifted pastry or cake flour
1½ cups superfine granulated sugar
¾ teaspoon baking soda
½ teaspoon salt

2 large eggs, separated
⅓ cup salad oil (not olive oil)
1 cup buttermilk or sour milk
2 squares unsweetened chocolate, melted
1 teaspoon vanilla extract

Sift the flour with 1 cup of the sugar, the baking soda, and salt. Set aside. Beat the egg whites until foamy, gradually beat in the remaining ½ cup of sugar, and beat until meringue is stiff and glossy. Combine the salad oil and ½ cup of the buttermilk or sour milk. Beat this into the flour mixture and beat for 1 minute with an electric mixer. Add the remaining ½ cup buttermilk or sour milk, egg yolks, melted chocolate, and vanilla and beat for 1 minute, scraping the sides of the bowl constantly. Fold the meringue into the batter, folding just until there are no remaining patches of white. Turn batter into 2 buttered and floured 9-inch round layer pans, or 1 buttered and floured 9 by 13-inch pan. Bake in a 350° F. oven 30 to 35 minutes for the layers, 40 to 45 minutes for the oblong pan, or until cake tests done. Cool layers in pans for 5 minutes before turning out onto racks. Cool the oblong cake in the pan. Frost as desired.

PERFECT SPONGE CAKE

In the making of all air-raised cakes (sponge cakes, chiffon cakes, and angel food cakes), it is especially important that the ingredients be at room temperature. Room temperature egg whites beat to a greater volume than do cold whites, and this has a definite effect on the volume of your cake. And I do not go along with the new idea of not beating the egg yolks. I feel that not beating the yolks results in a heavier, more compact cake. I never frost these cakes, but prefer them either drizzled with a glaze or cut and served with a sauce.

1 cup sifted pastry or cake flour	2 tablespoons grated orange rind (optional)
7 large eggs, separated	5 tablespoons orange juice
1½ cups superfine granulated sugar, sifted 3 times	1 teaspoon vanilla extract
	½ teaspoon cream of tartar
	½ teaspoon salt

Sift the flour 3 times and set it aside. Beat the egg yolks until very thick and fluffy, gradually add ¾ cup of the sugar, and continue beating until you can feel no graininess. Add the grated rind, if used, the juice, and vanilla to the yolks and beat in. Now beat the egg whites until foamy, add the cream of tartar and the salt, and beat until the whites hold a soft peak. Add the remaining ¾ cup of sugar, beating until mixture is stiff. Fold the flour into the egg yolk mixture, folding carefully until no white shows. Now fold this mixture carefully into the beaten whites. Do not overmix. Turn into a 10-inch tube pan. The pan should not be buttered and should be perfectly dry. Cut through the batter with a knife to release any air bubbles. But don't do this too enthusiastically or the cake will not raise properly. You just want to break the large bubbles. Bake the cake in a 325° F. oven for 1 hour. Invert the pan to cool and allow the cake to cool completely in the pan. Air-raised cakes will collapse if turned out of the pan before they are completely cooled.

VARIATIONS

1. Omit the orange rind and use 1 teaspoon grated lemon rind. Use 2 tablespoons orange juice and 3 tablespoons lemon juice.

2. Omit the grated rind and fruit juice. Use ¼ cup hot coffee or water and beat into the beaten egg yolks. If desired, you may add 1 or 2 teaspoons of instant coffee.

3. Omit orange rind and use 1 teaspoon grated lemon rind. Use pineapple juice in place of orange juice.

CHOCOLATE RUM SPONGE CAKE

Chocolate was brought to the United States in 1755 when the New England traders traded rum for cacao beans on their trips to the West Indies. Both ingredients are combined in this delicious cake. Have ingredients at room temperature.

1 cup sifted pastry or cake flour	¾ cup milk
1 teaspoon baking powder	¼ cup rum
¼ teaspoon salt	1 teaspoon vanilla extract
4 squares unsweetened chocolate	4 large eggs, separated
	2 cups superfine granulated sugar

Sift the flour with the baking powder and salt and set aside. Combine the chocolate, milk, rum, and vanilla. Cook over low heat, stirring, until chocolate is melted and mixture is blended. Remove from heat and cool to room temperature. Beat the egg yolks with the sugar until mixture is pale and thick. Stir the sifted flour into the yolk mixture alternately with the melted chocolate mixture. Beat the egg whites until they hold stiff peaks and then fold them into the batter. Turn the batter into 2 8- or 9-inch *ungreased* round layer cake pans. Bake in a 350° F. oven for 30 to 35 minutes, or until cake tests done. Cool in the pans 10 minutes, then invert onto cake racks and remove from pans. Cool cakes completely before frosting.

EGG YOLK SPONGE CAKE

This makes an exceptionally tall, glamorous-looking cake that is especially delicious served as suggested below. Except where specified, have ingredients at room temperature.

2¾ cups sifted flour	1 tablespoon grated lemon rind
2¾ teaspoons baking powder	2 cups superfine granulated sugar
½ teaspoon salt	
1 cup (about 12) egg yolks	1 cup hot water or milk

Sift the flour with the baking powder and salt at least 3 times. Set aside. Beat the egg yolks with the lemon rind until thick. Add the sugar and hot water or milk alternately, beating until thick and smooth after each addition. Fold in the flour mixture, about ¾ cup at a time. Fold gently just until there are no remaining patches of white. Pour into an unbuttered 10-inch tube pan. Bake in a 350° F. oven for 1 hour. Invert pan to cool, and cool thoroughly before removing from pan.

BANANA SPONGE CAKE.   Omit water and use 1½ cups of mashed bananas instead.

NOTE.   Egg Yolk Sponge Cake becomes a most glamorous dessert when served with a mixture of ¾ cup apricot preserves, ¼ cup Kirsch, and 3 cups sliced fresh strawberries and topped with a CUSTARD SAUCE (page 102).

COLONIAL TIPSY CAKE

This was considered to be the finest dessert to grace the holiday tables in the Old South. It is similar to the English Trifle, and we would like to see it return to the modern holiday table. It certainly makes a most impressive and beautiful dessert. Make the cake at least a day before needed. I use the EGG YOLK SPONGE CAKE (page 42), but any slightly dry cake layers can be used. Some people make a delicious variation by spreading the layers with berries, sprinkling with rum or sherry, pouring a rich custard over all and then garnishing with whipped cream and blanched, slivered almonds. Here is how I make it. Use a deep serving dish.

½ pound almonds, shelled
and blanched
3 to 4 cups boiled custard

1 cup good sherry (some
prefer much more)
1 cup heavy cream
1 tablespoon sugar

Put the Egg Yolk Sponge Cake in a serving dish with sides. Stud the cake with the whole, blanched almonds. Carefully spoon the wine over the cake, allowing as much to soak in as possible. Fill the center of the cake with the custard and pour what remains over the cake, letting it run down the sides. Then whip the heavy cream until thick, sweetening it with the sugar. Use this to garnish the cake.

ICE CREAM CAKE

For this delicious summer dessert use an angel food cake or a sponge cake. Cut the cake into several layers as thick or as thin as you wish. Spread each layer with ice cream (any flavor) that has been softened just enough to spread. The ice cream should be spread about ½ inch thick. Put the layers together neatly, wrap the cake, and place in the freezer until ready to serve.

When ready to serve, remove cake from the freezer and let stand while you make the frosting. Whip 1½ cups heavy cream until thick, sweetening the cream with 2 tablespoons sugar. Frost top and sides of the cake with the whipped cream. Cut immediately and serve.

If desired, the cake may be served with any appropriate sauce, or with fresh fruit or berries. Sliced, slightly sweetened fresh peaches or mangoes are especially good.

GOLD ANGEL FOOD CAKE

Not a true angel food, nonetheless this is a moist, delicious cake, light as a thistle. We prefer the cake drizzled with a glaze, the type used depending on the flavoring used in the cake. Sprinkle the glaze with chopped nuts. With the exception of the ice water, have all ingredients at room temperature.

1 cup superfine granulated sugar	¼ teaspoon salt
1 cup sifted pastry or cake flour	½ teaspoon cream of tartar
½ teaspoon baking powder	1 teaspoon vanilla extract
1 cup (about 12) egg yolks	1 teaspoon grated lemon rind, or 1 or 2 tablespoons grated orange or tangerine rind (optional)
½ cup ice water	

Combine the sugar, flour, and baking powder and sift together at least 3 times, and preferably 4 or 5 times. Set aside. Combine egg yolks, ice water, salt, cream of tartar, vanilla, and rinds, if used. Beat, with an electric mixer, until very thick and light. This will take about 5 minutes. Then, a little at a time, sift the flour mixture over the egg yolk mixture and carefully fold in, folding only until there are no remaining patches of white. Turn the batter into an *ungreased* 10-inch pan. Bake in a 275° F. oven for 30 minutes, then raise oven temperature to 325° F. and continue baking for another 30 minutes, or until cake tests done. Invert pan to cool thoroughly.

CHEESECAKES

Our American cheesecakes are a rich relative of the German *Käseku-chen,* brought to these shores by the Pennsylvania Dutch. The original American cheesecake was made with fresh, homemade cheese. The modern housewife makes it even richer by using cream cheese, more eggs, and heavy cream to make a cake of universal appeal. Always bake cheesecakes at a low temperature and, if possible, cool the cake in the oven with the door open for at least an hour before removing it. This prevents the cake from settling too much. Following are two recipes for crusts for cheesecakes and three recipes for glazes. If you like to glaze the cake, spoon the glaze on the cooled cake and then chill thoroughly before serving.

ZWIEBACK CRUMB CRUST

¼ cup butter or margarine, melted	2 tablespoons sugar
1 cup zwieback crumbs	½ teaspoon cinnamon (optional)

Combine all the ingredients and press onto the bottom and sides of a spring-form pan, reserving some of the mixture to sprinkle over the top of the cake. Chill before pouring in the filling.

COOKY CRUST

2 cups sifted flour	1 large egg
½ cup sugar	1 or 2 tablespoons brandy,
½ cup butter or margarine	Cognac, or rum (optional)

Sift the flour into a bowl. Add the rest of the ingredients and work the
dough with the fingertips to make a smooth paste. Form into a ball
and chill for 1 hour before rolling to fit the spring-form pan.

CHERRY GLAZE

1 can sour pie cherries	¼ teaspoon almond or vanilla
⅓ cup sugar	extract (optional)
2 tablespoons cornstarch	

Drain the cherries, reserving the liquid. Add water to make 1 cup
liquid. Combine liquid with the sugar and cornstarch and blend until
smooth. The blender is ideal for this. Add the flavoring, if used. Cook
over direct heat until the mixture thickens. Cool and add a little red
food coloring, if desired. Arrange the cherries on the cooled cheesecake. Carefully spoon the cooled syrup over the cherries. Chill before
serving.

FRUIT GLAZE

This is easily made with any desired canned fruit syrup. You may use
it plain or spoon it over small pieces of fruit that have been arranged
on the cooled cake. First cook the syrup over direct heat until it is
noticeably reduced and thickened. To each ½ cup of thickened syrup
add 1 teaspoon cornstarch and 1 tablespoon sugar, blending to a smooth
glaze.

STRAWBERRY GLAZE

5 or 6 cups washed, hulled
strawberries
3 tablespoons cornstarch
½ cup sugar

⅓ cup water
1 tablespoon lemon juice
1 tablespoon butter

Reserve 3 or 4 cups of the berries to arrange on the cooled cake. Take 2 cups of the berries and whirl them in the blender until smooth. Add the cornstarch and sugar and whirl for a minute longer. Add the water and cook the mixture over direct heat, stirring, until thickened. Stir in the lemon juice and butter. Cool before spooning over the berries. Chill.

NEW YORK BAKERY CHEESECAKE

This light-textured, creamy cheesecake is the type often sold in Jewish bakeries. Serve it with a glaze, if desired. We prefer it with sliced, sugared strawberries ladled over the slices. Have all ingredients at room temperature.

COOKY CRUST (page 46;
optional)
1½ pounds hoop cheese or
cream cheese
6 large eggs, separated'
1⅓ cups sugar

2 tablespoons flour
1¾ cups commercial sour
cream
2 teaspoons grated lemon rind
2 teaspoons lemon juice
1½ teaspoons vanilla extract

If you use the cooky crust, make it as directed, line a 9-inch spring-form pan with the crust, and chill again before pouring in the filling. If you do not wish to use the cooky crust, you may simply butter the pan and sprinkle it with graham cracker crumbs. Shake the pan to coat the butter with the crumbs and shake out any excess.

Combine cheese and egg yolks and beat with an electric mixer until completely blended and perfectly smooth. Any lumps in the filling will mar the texture of the cake. When cheese is perfectly smooth add, beating all the time, 1 cup of the sugar, the flour, sour cream, and flavorings. Beat until light and smooth. Then beat the egg whites until they form soft peaks. Beat in the remaining ⅓ cup sugar and beat until the whites form stiff peaks. Fold egg whites into cheese mixture and pour into the prepared pan. Bake in a 325° F. oven for 70 to 75 minutes. Turn off the oven heat and let cake cool in the oven with the door open.

BAKER'S CHEESECAKE

For this luscious cake we'll start from scratch and make baker's cheese! Baker's cheese is a cottage cheese, but with a drier, softer curd. It is also called "pot cheese," "farmer's cheese," and "Dutch *smierkäse*." It makes a truly fine cheescake.

BAKER'S CHEESE

4 quarts (1 gallon) pasteurized skim (non-fat) milk	¼ cup cultured buttermilk (commercial buttermilk)
	1 rennet tablet dissolved in 1 tablespoon cold water

Put the skim milk in a large pan and heat, using a very low heat, just until it starts to simmer. (About 170° F. if you are using a candy thermometer.) Remove from heat and cool to about 70° F. Then stir in the buttermilk and the dissolved rennet tablet. Mix thoroughly. Let stand in a warm kitchen, undisturbed, until the clabber or curd is firm, with a noticeable whey (liquid) separation. This will take from 10 to 14 hours. Line a large colander with several thicknesses of cheesecloth or a clean muslin bag and pour the cheese into the cloth. Cover with several thicknesses of cheesecloth, or close the bag, and let the cheese drain thoroughly. Save the whey to make LEMON OR LIME WHEY PIE (page 235), or to use in bread-making. When the cheese has drained sufficiently you should have about 3 cups of a non-sticky cheese. You may add a teaspoon of salt and several tablespoons of cream to make a tasty cheese to eat plain. Or use it to make cheesecake.

THE CAKE

COOKY CRUST (page 46) or
   CRUMB CRUST (page 45)
2 cups unsalted baker's cheese
⅓ cup sugar
1 teaspoon grated lemon rind
¼ teaspoon salt

4 large eggs, separated
¼ cup sifted flour
1 cup heavy cream
¼ teaspoon cream of tartar
¼ cup sugar

Line a 9-inch spring-form pan with desired crust and chill. If using crumb crust, reserve ⅓ cup to sprinkle on top of cake. Combine cheese, the ⅓ cup sugar, lemon rind, salt, and egg yolks. Beat, with an electric mixer, until thoroughly blended and perfectly smooth. Add the flour and cream and blend until smooth. Beat the egg whites until frothy, add the cream of tartar and continue beating. Add the ¼ cup sugar a little at a time and beat until egg whites hold stiff peaks. Gently fold into the cheese mixture. Pour into the pan and, if crumb crust is used, sprinkle the reserved crumbs on top. Bake in a 300° F. oven for 1 hour. Turn off oven heat and leave the cake in the oven, with the door *closed,* for another hour. Chill before serving.

WHIPPED CREAM CHEESECAKE

Have all ingredients at room temperature except the heavy cream, which should be well chilled to whip properly.

graham cracker crumbs
4 cups large-curd cottage
   cheese
6 large eggs
½ cup flour

1⅓ cups sugar
2 tablespoons lemon juice
2 teaspoons grated lemon rind
1 teaspoon vanilla extract
1 to 1½ cups heavy cream

Prepare a 9- or 10-inch spring-form pan by buttering it and then sprinkling it generously with graham cracker crumbs. Shake the pan to coat the butter with the crumbs to form a thin crust. Shake out any excess. Chill before filling.

Whirl the cottage cheese in the blender until smooth. Pour ½ the blended cheese into a mixing bowl. Add the eggs and flour to the cheese left in the blender. Whirl until smooth. Pour this mixture into the mixing bowl and stir all together to blend thoroughly. Add the sugar, juice, and flavorings. Blend. Whip the cream until thick and fold this into the cheese mixture. Pour the batter into the chilled pan. Bake in a 350° F. oven for 1 hour and 10 to 20 minutes or until there is a soft spot in the center that is no more than 2 or 3 inches in diameter. Turn off oven heat and cool the cake in the oven with the door open. Chill before serving.

MOCK CHEESECAKE

9-inch graham cracker pie shell, unbaked and well chilled
4 egg yolks
1 can condensed milk
1 tablespoon grated lemon rind
⅓ to ½ cup lemon juice
4 egg whites

Combine egg yolks, condensed milk, lemon rind, and juice. Beat thoroughly. Beat egg whites until stiff. Fold into yolk mixture. Pour into well-chilled pie shell. Sprinkle top with a spoonful of graham cracker crumbs. Bake in a 375° F. oven for 25 minutes. Open oven door and allow pie to cool in the oven for 25 to 30 minutes.

NOTE. Some good cooks add 1 teaspoon vanilla extract and ¼ teaspoon nutmeg. If desired, lime juice and rind may replace the lemon juice and rind.

POUND CAKES

Traditional recipes for pound cake call for a pound each of flour, sugar, butter, and eggs, with no leavening other than the well-beaten eggs.

As always, the housewife took the basic recipe and proceeded to change it, searching for the particular method that would guarantee a perfect cake. Some creamed the butter with the sugar; others felt that creaming the butter and working the flour into it before adding the sugar and eggs resulted in a finer-textured cake. Some added the eggs whole, while other cooks separated the eggs and beat the whites to a fine stiffness before incorporating them into the cake batter. To make a lighter cake the Colonial housewife often used more whites than yolks and added some brandy or Cognac.

If the Colonial housewife desired more than the delicate butter flavor, she used grated lemon rind, mace, nutmeg, or rose water. Sometimes she lined the bottom of the well-buttered baking pan with rose geranium leaves (the herb) before adding the batter. The delicate fragrance permeated the cake.

As noted in carefully handwritten cookbooks, the creative housewife used the pound cake as a base for other fine cakes. To make a fine "almond cake" required only the addition of a pound of blanched and slivered almonds. For a "citron cake," she added a pound or two of diced citron to the recipe for almond cake. A popular English "seed cake" simply required the addition of a tablespoon of caraway seeds. To make an opulent "fruit cake," she added pounds of currants, raisins, chopped nuts, and candied fruits, and some brandy. Spices were either omitted entirely or used in profusion. To further change the character of the cake she sometimes used brown sugar in place of the granulated sugar. However varied, the base was the traditional pound cake.

Whichever recipe you prefer, and whatever method is used, the following will be helpful:

. All ingredients must be at room temperature.

. Use only the finest butter. The use of margarine or vegetable shortenings is not recommended in pound cakes

. The beating of the eggs is very important If you use whole eggs, beat them until very thick and yellow. If you separate the eggs, beat the whites until very stiff.

To any recipe that requires no leavening, you may safely add a teaspoon of baking powder.

5. The pan must be well-buttered. If desired, the pan can then be coated with finely grated, chopped, or slivered nuts. The nuts can be combined with grated lemon or orange rind. This mixture bakes into the cake and adds greatly to its appeal.

6. Pound cakes benefit from a longer, slower baking period. Any recipe that calls for a 350° F. baking temperature can safely be baked, for a longer time, at 325° F. This will often keep the top of the cake from cracking, a common complaint in making pound cakes.

7. Cool the cakes in the pans for 15 to 20 minutes before turning out onto a rack. Cool thoroughly and preferably wait 24 hours before cutting.

8. Wrapped carefully and stored in an air-tight container, pound cakes will keep for several weeks. They can be frozen successfully.

BUTTERMILK POUND CAKE

This cake is unusual in that it uses buttermilk. It has a fine flavor and texture. All ingredients must be at room temperature.

3 cups sifted pastry or cake flour
½ teaspoon baking soda
½ teaspoon baking powder
½ teaspoon salt
1 cup butter
2 cups superfine granulated sugar

4 large eggs
1 teaspoon vanilla extract
1 teaspoon lemon extract or grated lemon rind (optional)
1 cup buttermilk (or sour milk)
sifted powdered sugar

Sift the dry ingredients into a bowl and set aside. Cream the butter and the sugar until light and fluffy. Add the eggs, 1 at a time, and beat in. Combine flavorings and buttermilk. Add liquid ingredients and sifted

y ingredients to the creamed mixture alternately, beginning and end-
g with dry ingredients. Turn batter into a well-buttered 10-inch tube
an or Bundt pan, and bake in a 350° F. oven for 1 hour and 10
inutes. Test the cake at the end of an hour. If it is done, the sides
ill have pulled away from the pan a little and the top will spring
ack when touched with the finger. Cool in the pan for 10 to 15 minutes
fore turning out onto a rack. Dust with sifted powdered sugar while
ke is still warm.

BUTTERCRUST POUND CAKE

e think that all pound cakes are delicious, and this one won't disap-
int the cook. If a cast aluminium Bundt pan is used, the crust will be
en better, eliminating the need for any topping. The cake is made
a very old method of creaming the butter with the *flour* rather
an with the sugar. All ingredients must be at room temperature.

1¾ cups butter
4 cups (1 pound) sifted pastry
or cake flour
8 large eggs
2 cups superfine granulated
sugar
¼ teaspoon salt
1 teaspoon baking powder

1 teaspoon vanilla extract
1 teaspoon lemon extract or
grated lemon rind
(optional)
1 tablespoon sherry, rum,
brandy, or 2 teaspoons rose
water (not extract)

ream the butter until light and fluffy. Sift the flour again, and work
e sifted flour into the butter until the mixture is of a fine, mealy
xture. In a separate bowl, beat the eggs, adding the sugar gradually.
at thoroughly. Add the egg mixture to the flour mixture along with
e remaining ingredients. Beat with an electric mixer, at medium
eed, for 5 minutes. Turn into a well-buttered 10-inch tube pan or
undt pan. Bake in a 250° F. oven for 40 minutes, then raise the
mperature to 325° F. and continue baking another 40 minutes. Cool
ke on a rack 15 minutes before turning out of pan. Cool thoroughly
fore storing.

CREAM CHEESE POUND CAKE

Some call this a pound cake because it is baked in a tube pan. Whether it is considered such or not, it is a tender, well-flavored cake and lends itself well to varied flavorings. I bake it in a Bundt pan that is well coated with finely chopped nuts. Have all ingredients at room temperature.

2¼ cups pastry or cake flour
2 teaspoons baking powder
½ pound cream cheese
½ pound butter or margarine
1½ cups sugar
4 large eggs

1 teaspoon vanilla extract
1 teaspoon grated lemon rind
1 or 2 tablespoons rum,
    brandy, or Cognac
powdered sugar

Sift the flour with the baking powder and set aside. Cream the cheese and butter until well blended. Add the sugar and beat until light. Beat in the eggs and flavorings. Add the flour mixture last, blending it in carefully. Turn batter into a buttered 10-inch tube pan or Bundt pan and bake in a 325° F. oven for 75 to 80 minutes, or until cake tests done. Cool in pan for 5 minutes before turning out onto a rack to finish cooling. Dust with powdered sugar while warm.

NOTE. If desired you may use 1 tablespoon grated orange rind and 2 tablespoons orange juice in place of the lemon rind and liquor.

WHIPPED-CREAM POUND CAKE

I consider this one of my finest and most treasured recipes, partly for its exceptional flavor and light texture, and partly because it lends itself so well to variation. When I make it into layers, I use LEMON CHEESE (page 250) between the layers and top the cake with whipped cream.

1½ cups sifted pastry or cake
    flour
2 teaspoons baking powder
¼ teaspoon salt
1 cup whipping cream

1 cup superfine granulated
    sugar
2 large eggs, beaten
1 teaspoon vanilla extract or
    ½ teaspoon almond extract

ift the flour, baking powder, and salt into a bowl and set aside. Whip
he cream until thickened, but not stiff enough to hold a peak. Fold
he sugar into the whipped cream, then the beaten eggs and vanilla
r almond extract. Add the dry ingredients, folding in carefully and
lending only until smooth. Never overmix. Now turn the batter into
loaf pan that has been buttered and dusted with granulated sugar.
Bake in a 350° F. oven for 55 minutes, or until the cake starts to
ull away from the sides of the pan. Cool on a rack for 10 minutes
efore turning out of pan.

VARIATIONS

. Slice the cake and serve topped with whipped cream, LEMON CHEESE
page 250), or crushed fresh fruit in season.

. The ingredients may be halved again, using 2¼ cups flour, 3 tea-
poons baking powder, etc., to make a higher, fluffier cake. It may need
o be baked slightly longer.

. Batter may be baked in 2 8-inch round layer pans, at 350° F. for
5 minutes.

. Double the recipe and bake the batter in 3 8-inch round layer
ans, or 2 9-inch round layer pans, or in a 10-inch tube pan. Bake
he layers at 350° F. for approximately 25 minutes, the tube pan for
pproximately 1 hour.

. In place of the flavorings suggested in the recipe, you may use
rom 1 to 3 teaspoons grated lemon rind, or 2 tablespoons rum.

. If the cake is baked in layers, fill layers with whipped cream into
vhich has been folded sliced fresh fruit. Top with more, or dust the
op layer with sifted powdered sugar.

VIRGINIA POUND CAKE

This traditional recipe probably originated in England. Have all ingredients at room temperature.

4 cups (1 pound) sifted pastry or cake flour	1 or 2 teaspoons vanilla extract or grated lemon rind
1 pound butter	
12 large eggs, separated	½ teaspoon mace or nutmeg (optional)
2 cups (1 pound) superfine granulated sugar	

Sift the flour again and set aside. Cream the butter until it is very light and fluffy. Gradually add the flour, about ½ cup at a time, and beat until mixture is a smooth paste. Combine egg yolks and sugar and beat until thick and light. Add the flavorings to the yolk-sugar mixture, and gradually beat in the creamed butter and flour. Now, with clean beaters, beat the egg whites until they hold stiff peaks, and then fold into the combined mixtures. Fold quickly but carefully, so as not to lose too much air. Now turn the batter into a well-buttered 10-inch tube pan or Bundt pan, and bake in a 325° F. oven for 1 hour and 15 minutes. Test carefully before removing from oven. Cool in pan for 15 minutes before turning out onto a rack.

VARIATIONS

1. Half of the recipe may be made and baked in a 9-inch tube pan, or a mini-Bundt pan. Bake at 325° F. about 50 minutes.

2. Follow the basic recipe, and add 3 tablespoons of any of the following: lemon juice, orange juice, rose water, brandy, rum, Cognac, whisky, Madeira wine. Beat into the yolk-sugar mixture.

COCONUT CAKE. Colonial recipes called for the grated meat of 1 or 2 whole coconuts. But 1 or 2 cups flaked or grated coconut will do and the further addition of 1 or 2 tablespoons grated orange rind makes a luscious "Ambrosia Cake."

GINGER CAKE. Follow basic recipe. Add 1 teaspoon ground ginger and the juice and grated rind of 1 large lemon.

NUT CAKE. Follow basic recipe. Stir into the butter-flour mixture 3 or 4 cups pecan halves or chopped walnuts, or a combination of nuts. This may be combined with variation #2.

RAISIN CAKE. Follow basic recipe. Soak 3 or 4 cups golden or dark raisins in ⅓ cup brandy or Cognac. Drain, and add to the butter-flour mixture.

EXTRA-RICH. Follow basic recipe, adding 1 cup sugar to yolk-sugar mixture, and stirring 2 teaspoons baking powder into the butter-flour mixture.

HAWAIIAN CAKE. Follow basic recipe. Stir 2 or 3 cups chopped macadamia nuts into the butter-flour mixture.

FAVORITE WHITE POUND CAKE

A rich throwback to more opulent times, but if you sometimes make the GOLD CAKE (page 15), this recipe provides a delicious use for the leftover whites. Have all ingredients at room temperature before starting.

½ pound butter
2 cups (1 pound) superfine granulated sugar
4 cups (1 pound) sifted cake or pastry flour
1 or 2 teaspoons baking powder

½ cup heavy cream
2 cups (about 16) egg whites, unbeaten
1 teaspoon grated lemon rind
1 teaspoon vanilla extract

Cream the butter and sugar until very light and fluffy. Sift the flour and baking powder (use the larger amount of baking powder if you wish a lighter cake). Add the sifted dry ingredients to the creamed mixture alternately with the heavy cream, beginning and ending with dry ingredients. The mixture at this point will be very stiff. Now add the unbeaten egg whites and the flavorings. Beat, with an electric mixer, for 5 to 7 minutes. Turn batter into a well-buttered 10-inch tube pan or Bundt pan. Bake in a 325° F. oven for 20 minutes, then raise heat to 350° F. and continue baking another 30 to 40 minutes, or until cake tests done. Cool in pan for 15 minutes before turning out onto rack.

NOTE. If desired, you may substitute ½ cup egg yolks for the heavy cream. Beat in half (1 cup) of the egg whites as directed above. Beat the remaining cup of egg whites until very stiff and fold into the batter. Bake as directed. This makes a somewhat heavier but very flavorful cake.

HISTORICAL CAKES

Most of our historical cakes have long been "famous name" cakes, and the sound of the name alone brings a twinge of recognition and nostalgia. Even if we have never eaten one, we recognize such names as "Scripture Cake," "General Robert E. Lee's Cake," "Lane Cake," "the Watermelon Cake," and others. Some, such as the "Jeff Davis Cake" and the "James K. Polk Cake," have faded completely from memory.

Because the instructions on the cakes that have come down to us through the old, handwritten cookbooks were so vague, most of the "famous name" cakes have, in the last generation, been reconstructed using modern measurements and methods. No longer are we told, as in a Colonial recipe for a wedding cake, to "take 40 eggs, separate them, and beat to a fine froth."

One of the most popular Colonial recipes, especially throughout the New England states, was the following one.

"Dame, get up and bake your pies,
Bake your pies, bake your pies,
Dame, get up and bake your pies
On Christmas day in the morning."
FOLK SONG

SCRIPTURE CAKE

3½ cups First Kings 4:22
(flour)
½ teaspoon Leviticus 2:13
(salt)
2 teaspoons First Corinthians
5:6 (baking powder)
First Kings 10:2 (spices)
1 cup Judges 5:25 (butter)
2 cups Jeremiah 6:20 (sugar)
6 Isaiah 10:14 (eggs)

1 cup Genesis 24:25 (water)
1 large spoon Exodus 16:34
(honey)
2 cups First Samuel 31:12
(raisins)
2 cups First Samuel 31:12
(dried figs)
1 cup Genesis 43:11
(almonds)

All of the old-time recipe books then said to follow Solomon's advice for making good boys, as stated in the first clause of Proverbs 23:14 ("Thou shalt beat him with a rod").

Sift the flour with the salt, baking powder, and spices and set aside. Cream the butter with the sugar, adding the eggs 1 at a time and beating in thoroughly. Now add the flour mixture alternately with the water, beginning and ending with dry ingredients. Stir in the honey and then at the very last fold in the chopped fruit and nuts. Turn the batter into a buttered and floured 10-inch tube pan or Bundt pan. Bake in a 350° F. oven for 1 hour and 10 minutes, or until cake tests done. Cool in pan for 10 minutes before turning out onto a rack to cool completely.

BOSTON CREAM PIE

As with "Washington Pie," this is not a pie but a custard-filled cake, topped either with powdered sugar or a thin chocolate icing. Actually the cake generally used was a simple one-egg cake, but we prefer this recipe for an old-fashioned "Hot Milk Cake." With the exception of the milk, have all ingredients at room temperature.

2 cups sifted pastry or cake
flour
2 teaspoons baking powder
½ teaspoon salt
1 cup scalded milk, hot
2 tablespoons butter or

margarine
4 large eggs
2 cups superfine granulated
sugar
1 teaspoon vanilla extract
CUSTARD FILLING (see below)

Sift the flour with the baking powder and salt. Set aside. Melt the butter or margarine in the hot milk. Beat the eggs until very light, and gradually beat in the sugar and vanilla. Add the hot milk mixture, beating constantly. Then add the flour mixture and beat just until batter is smooth. Turn batter into 2 9-inch round layer pans that have been buttered and floured. Tap pans lightly on counter top to release excess air. Bake in a 350° F. oven for 25 to 30 minutes, or until cake tests done. Cool in pans for 5 minutes before turning out onto racks. Cool completely before filling.

CUSTARD FILLING.   Scald 1 cup half and half. Combine ¼ cup sugar, ¼ cup flour, and ¼ teaspoon salt. Stir to blend and then stir into the scalded milk, beating until smooth. Beat 1 large egg and very carefully add the hot half and half mixture. Turn into a double boiler and cook, over hot water, stirring constantly, until smooth and thickened. Remove from heat and add ½ teaspoon vanilla extract. Cool completely before using to fill layers. Dust the top layer with sifted powdered sugar, or drizzle with CHOCOLATE GLAZE (page 99) or COCOA GLAZE (page 100).

WASHINGTON PIE.   Make cake as for Boston Cream Pie, only omit custard filling and use instead a current or raspberry jam or jelly between layers. Dust top layer with sifted powdered sugar.

HARTFORD ELECTION CAKE

At one time the only holidays observed throughout the New England States were Thanksgiving Day, Militia Day, and Election Day. As a treat, voters were served slices of this heavily liquored yeast cake.

The original recipe was supposed to have been developed in the 18th century, and was first published in Amelia Simmon's 1800 edition of *American Cookery*. First you must make a raised yeast dough and then, in the second step, you work other ingredients into it. Frugal Colonial housewives used several cups of any bread dough on hand. We'll start from the beginning. Have ingredients, except where otherwise specified, at room temperature.

YEAST DOUGH

1 cup diced raw potato (peeled)
1 cup milk, scalded
1 teaspoon salt
2 tablespoons sugar
2 tablespoons butter or margarine
1 cake yeast
1 large egg
3½ to 4 cups sifted flour

ADDITIONS

¾ cup butter or margarine
1 large egg
1¼ cups light brown sugar
½ cup brandy or bourbon
1 cup dark or light raisins
1 cup candied fruits (optional)
1 cup sifted flour
1 teaspoon cinnamon
½ teaspoon nutmeg
½ teaspoon cloves

Cook the potato in water to cover until tender. Drain, mash and set aside. Pour the scalded milk into a large bowl and add the salt, sugar, and butter or margarine. Stir until butter is melted. Then stir in the mashed potato. When lukewarm, stir in the yeast. Now add 1 egg and enough of the flour to make medium soft dough that is workable. Turn out onto a lightly floured bread board and knead, adding just enough flour to make a smooth dough. Place in a buttered bowl, cover and let rise until doubled. When dough has doubled, punch it down.

Now we are ready for the Additions. The ¾ cup of butter or margarine should be very soft, but not melted. Work this into the dough and then add the egg, brown sugar, and brandy or bourbon. Coat the raisins and the fruits, if used, with the flour and add to the dough along with any remaining flour and the spices. Work very well, so that the dough is not streaky. It will, however, be soft. Turn into a well-buttered 10-inch tube pan or a Bundt pan. Cover and let rise until doubled. Bake in a 325° F. oven for 50 to 60 minutes. Cool in the pan for 10 minutes before turning out onto rack. When completely cooled, frost with BUTTERMILK ICING (page 89).

ROBERT E. LEE'S CAKE

This is one of the most famous of historical cakes. The original recipe tells us, very simply, to "take 12 eggs, their full weight in sugar, half their weight in flour, and bake in pans." Which leads us to believe that early-day cooks, besides being expert in cookery, were expert in mind-reading as well! Traditionally, the cake was put together with a lemon and orange filling made by combining the fruit juices with sugar. We prefer a LEMON CHEESE (page 250) between layers and any boiled frosting well sprinkled with lemon and/or orange rind. All ingredients should be at room temperature.

2 cups sifted pastry or cake flour
½ teaspoon salt
1½ teaspoons baking powder (optional)
10 large eggs, separated

2 cups superfine granulated sugar
1 teaspoon lemon juice
1 tablespoon orange juice
1 teaspoon grated lemon rind

Combine the flour, salt, and baking powder (old-time recipes, even when brought up to date, omitted *any* baking powder, but it may be used) and sift. Set aside. Beat the egg yolks until very thick and light. Gradually beat in the sugar, a few spoonfuls at a time, beating until mixture is smooth and yellow. Stir in the juices and the rind. Now beat the egg whites until very stiff. Fold the beaten whites into the yolk mixture alternately with the flour mixture. Blend only until smooth. Spoon into buttered and floured 9-inch round layer pans, using 3 pans if you wish thicker layers, and 4 pans for thinner layers. Bake in a 325° F. oven for 20 to 25 minutes, or until layers test done. Loosen the edges, and cool in the pans for 5 minutes before turning out onto racks.

"A man all virtue—like a pie all spice—will not please."
FOLK SAYING

CLEVELAND WHITE CAKE

This is named, not for the city, but rather for President Grover Cleveland, whose favorite cake it is supposed to have been. It appears in all the cookbooks of the era, usually under the practical name, "Cornstarch Cake." It was baked in layers, and usually filled and frosted with a plain white or chocolate frosting. But we much prefer it baked in a Bundt pan and served plain. All ingredients should be at room temperature.

1 cup butter
3 cups superfine granulated sugar
1 cup milk
1½ cups (about 12) egg whites
1 tablespoon baking powder

1 cup cornstarch
3 cups sifted pastry or cake flour
1 tablespoon vanilla extract
1 teaspoon grated lemon rind (optional)

Cream butter and sugar until light and fluffy. Beat in the milk, just until thoroughly blended. Beat the egg whites until very stiff and carefully fold into the creamed mixture. Now, sift the dry ingredients together and very carefully, about ½ cup at a time, sprinkle over the batter and fold in. Be very careful so that you do not force the air out. At the last, sprinkle the vanilla and grated rind, if used, over the batter and fold in. Now turn the batter into 3 9-inch round layer pans that have been buttered and floured. Do not tap these pans, as you do not want the air forced out in this cake. Bake in a 350° F. oven for 25 to 30 minutes, or until done. Cool in the pans for 10 minutes before turning out to cool on a rack. If you bake the cake in a 10-inch tube pan or a Bundt pan, bake it at 350° F. for 1 hour and 10 to 20 minutes.

LADY BALTIMORE CAKE

As there are fads in clothes, there are also fads in foods. And this cake, after publication of Owen Wister's 1906 novel *Lady Baltimore,* in which it was carefully described, was certainly the most "in" cake of the day. Have all ingredients at room temperature.

3 cups sifted pastry or cake flour
1 tablespoon baking powder
¼ teaspoon salt
⅔ cup butter or margarine
1¾ cups superfine granulated sugar

1 cup milk
1 teaspoon almond extract or 2 teaspoons rose water
5 large egg whites

Sift the flour with the baking powder and salt and set aside. Cream the butter or margarine, adding the sugar gradually and beating until mixture is light and fluffy. Combine milk and flavoring. Add the flour mixture to the creamed mixture alternately with the milk, beginning and ending with dry ingredients. Blend until batter is smooth. Beat the egg whites until very stiff and fold in last, folding just until there are no remaining patches of white. Turn batter into 3 buttered and floured 9-inch round layer pans. Bake in a 350° F. oven for 25 to 30 minutes, or until cake tests done. Cool in pans for 5 minutes before turning out onto racks.

FILLING AND FROSTING. Make WHITE MOUNTAIN FROSTING (page 87). Divide into 2 parts. Into one part fold 1 cup golden raisins, 1 cup chopped, dried figs, and 2 cups chopped pecans or walnuts (traditionally these are soaked in sherry or brandy for several hours or overnight, and then drained). Use this to fill the layers. Use the remaining half of the frosting to frost the top and sides of the cake. If desired, the top of the cake may be sprinkled with more chopped nuts.

NOTE. Some old recipes call for a simple syrup, made by simmering until thick 1 cup sugar, ½ cup water and ½ teaspoon flavoring, to be spooned over the hot cake layers. The layers are then cooled thoroughly before being filled and frosted. We found that while this definitely made a more moist cake, with excellent keeping qualities, it was also entirely too sweet for modern tastes.

LANE CAKE

Several Southern states lay claim to originating this luscious cake. This and the "Rocky Mountain Cake" are the same, except that the "Rocky Mountain Cake" is filled with a plain white frosting. Have all ingredients at room temperature.

3¼ cups sifted pastry or cake flour
¼ teaspoon salt
3½ teaspoons baking powder
1 cup butter or margarine

2 cups superfine granulated sugar
1 teaspoon vanilla extract
1 cup milk
1 cup (about 8) egg whites

Sift the flour with the salt and baking powder and set aside. Cream the butter or margarine, adding the sugar gradually, and beating until very light and fluffy. Add the vanilla and blend in. Add the flour mixture to the creamed mixture alternately with the milk, beginning and ending with dry ingredients and beating until batter is smooth. Beat the egg whites until very stiff and carefully fold into the batter, folding only until there are no remaining patches of whites. Turn batter into 3 buttered and floured 9-inch round layer pans. Bake in a 375° F. oven for 30 to 35 minutes, or until cake tests done. Cool in pans for 5 minutes before turning out onto racks. Fill with LANE CAKE FILLING (page 94), and frost with the WHITE MOUNTAIN FROSTING (page 87) or any other boiled frosting or plain white frosting.

WATERMELON CAKE

This is an old-time recipe that sadly has been long forgotten. To achieve the proper decorative effect you must carefully spoon the dough into a tube pan (old-time cooks used loaf pans) so that the white dough virtually surrounds the pink dough. It must be made in 2 separate mixtures, so it isn't a quickly made cake. Any frosting can be used. Have all ingredients at room temperature.

WHITE MIXTURE	PINK MIXTURE
2 cups sifted pastry or cake flour	2 cups sifted pastry or cake flour
½ teaspoon baking soda	½ teaspoon baking soda
½ cup butter or margarine	½ cup butter or margarine
2 cups superfine granulated sugar	1½ cups superfine granulated sugar
½ cup buttermilk or sour milk	4 large egg yolks
4 large egg whites	½ cup buttermilk or sour milk
½ teaspoon vanilla extract or grated lemon rind	pink vegetable coloring
	½ teaspoon rose *extract* (optional)
	1 cup dark whole raisins

First make the white mixture thus: sift the flour with the soda. Cream the butter or margarine with the sugar until light. Add the sifted dry ingredients to the creamed mixture alternately with the buttermilk or sour milk, beginning and ending with dry ingredients. Beat the egg whites until stiff and fold into the batter along with the flavoring. Set aside while you make the pink mixture.

Now make the pink mixture. Sift the flour with the soda. Cream the butter or margarine with the sugar until light. Beat in the egg yolks. Add the flour mixture to the creamed mixture alternately with the buttermilk or sour milk, beginning and ending with dry ingredients. Now beat in the vegetable coloring and the rose extract, if used, just until the batter is colored. Be careful not to overbeat. Fold the raisins into the batter last.

Butter and flour a 10-inch tube pan or Bundt pan. Now carefully spoon half of the white mixture into the pan. Spoon the entire amount of pink mixture over the white batter. Do not pour it into the pan as it will have a tendency to peek through the white batter. Now spoon the remaining white mixture over the pink batter. Bake in a 350° F. oven for 1 hour, or until cake tests done. A cake tester or toothpick inserted into the center of the cake should come out clean. When cake is done cool it in the pan for 10 minutes before turning out onto a rack to cool.

SALT-PORK CAKE

This old cake recipe was called by many names: "Farm Cake," "Come-To-Meeting Cake," and "Pork Cake." But under any name it was, very simply, a cake using the ingredients on hand in any household. The salt pork, used in place of other shortening, adds no flavor of its own. With the exception of the boiling liquid, have all ingredients at room temperature.

4 cups sifted pastry or cake flour
2 teaspoons baking soda
1 teaspoon cinnamon
½ teaspoon cloves
1 cup boiling water or coffee
1 cup salt pork that has been rinsed, dried with a towel, and then finely diced or ground

1 cup sorghum molasses
1 cup light brown sugar
2 large eggs, separated
1 cup dark or light raisins
1 cup chopped, pitted dates
½ cup currants
½ cup chopped walnuts
1 teaspoon vanilla extract

Sift the flour with the baking soda and spices. Set aside. Pour the boiling liquid over the salt pork and stir thoroughly. Add the molasses and brown sugar and blend. Cool. Add the egg yolks and blend. Combine fruits and nuts and coat with ½ cup of the sifted flour mixture. Stir the remaining flour mixture into the liquid mixture and then add the floured fruits and nuts. Last, beat the egg whites until stiff and add to the batter along with the vanilla. Turn batter into 2 buttered and floured loaf pans. Bake in a 275° F. oven for 1½ to 2 hours, or until cake tests done. Cool in pans for 10 minutes before turning out onto racks. Frost or not, as desired.

MISSISSIPPI POTATO CAKE

This fine old recipe was one of the many listed in the large cake section of an old handwritten cookbook that belonged to the grandmother of a friend. With the exception of the potatoes, which must be hot, all ingredients should be at room temperature.

2 cups sifted pastry or cake flour

1 tablespoon baking powder

1 teaspoon cinnamon

½ teaspoon nutmeg (optional)

½ teaspoon salt

¼ cup cocoa (Dutch cocoa is preferable)

¾ cup butter or margarine

2 cups sugar

4 large eggs, separated

1 teaspoon vanilla extract

⅔ cup milk

1 cup hot, unseasoned, mashed potatoes

1 cup chopped nuts

sifted powdered sugar

Sift flour with baking powder, spices, salt, and cocoa. Set aside. Cream the butter or margarine, adding the sugar gradually and beating until mixture is light and fluffy. Add the egg yolks and beat in until thoroughly blended. Combine vanilla and milk. Fold the sifted dry ingredients and the milk into the creamed mixture alternately, beginning and ending with dry ingredients. Then stir in the potatoes, blending thoroughly. Beat the egg whites until stiff, and fold into the batter along with the chopped nuts. Turn batter into a buttered and floured loaf pan and bake in a 350° F. oven for 50 minutes, or until cake tests done. Cool in pan for 5 minutes before turning out on rack to cool. Sprinkle with sifted powdered sugar.

NOTE. If desired, batter may be baked in 2 9-inch round layer pans that have been buttered and floured. Bake at 350° F. about 25 minutes.

SPICE CAKES

OATMEAL SPICE CAKE

Spice cakes, using ingredients likely to be found in every kitchen, are simple to make and seem to be especially loved by children. Have ingredients at room temperature.

1 cup old-fashioned rolled oats
1 cup dark or golden raisins
1½ cups boiling water
1½ cups sifted flour
1 teaspoon baking soda
1 teaspoon cinnamon
½ teaspoon nutmeg

¼ teaspoon cloves
½ cup butter or margarine
1½ cups sugar (granulated, brown, or a mixture)
2 large eggs
1 teaspoon vanilla extract

Combine oats and raisins. Pour boiling water over them and set aside. Sift the flour with the baking soda and spices. Cream the butter or margarine with the sugar, beating until light and fluffy. Add the eggs and vanilla, and beat until blended. Now, add the sifted flour mixture to the creamed mixture alternately with the cooled oat-raisin mixture (do not drain), beginning and ending with dry ingredients. Blend well. Turn into a buttered and floured 8 by 12–inch baking pan. Bake in a 350° F. oven for 35 to 40 minutes, or until done.

NOTE. If desired, cake may be baked in prepared muffin tins in a 375° F. oven for 20 minutes.

OATMEAL COCOA CAKE. Omit spices in recipe and add ½ cup cocoa. Cake remains moist and tasty for several days.

PERSIMMON SPICE CAKE

A moist, delicious cake with good keeping qualities. Have all ingredients at room temperature.

1¾ cups sifted pastry or cake flour
1 teaspoon cinnamon
½ teaspoon nutmeg or cloves
2 teaspoons baking soda
2 tablespoons lemon or orange juice
½ cup light raisins or chopped, pitted dates

1 cup sugar
½ cup butter or margarine
1 large egg
1 cup persimmon pulp
½ cup chopped nuts
¼ cup candied fruit peel

Combine flour, spices, and soda. Sift into a bowl and set aside. Pour the fruit juice over the raisins or dates and stir. Set aside. Cream the

sugar and butter or margarine until light. Add the egg and beat in.
Stir the persimmon pulp, which has been either pureed in a strainer
or whirled in the blender, into the creamed mixture. Stir the sifted dry
ingredients into the creamed mixture, and then add the raisin-juice
mixture, the nuts, and the candied peel. Turn batter into a buttered
and floured 7 by 11–inch baking dish. Bake in a 300° F. oven for 1
hour and 15 minutes, or until cake tests done. Cool on rack and serve
from the pan.

PRUNE SPICE CAKE

This is another cake which is made more useful because of the variations. The lady who gave me the recipe has been making this cake
weekly for fifty years. Have all ingredients at room temperature.

2 cups sifted pastry or cake flour	1 cup chopped, cooked prunes, drained
1 cup sugar	1 cup prune syrup
¼ teaspoon salt	2 large eggs, separated
1 teaspoon baking soda	¼ cup melted butter
½ teaspoon allspice	1 teaspoon vanilla extract
2 teaspoons cinnamon	

Sift together, into a mixing bowl, the flour, sugar, salt, baking soda,
and spices. Stir in the prunes and then the prune syrup. Add the egg
yolks, melted butter, and vanilla extract and blend thoroughly. Beat
the egg whites until stiff and fold into the batter. Turn batter into
2 buttered and floured 8-inch round layer pans. Bake in a 350° F.
oven for 30 to 35 minutes, or until cake tests done. Cool in pans for
5 minutes before turning out onto racks.

NOTE.   Batter may be baked in prepared muffin tins. Bake in 350° F.
oven for 20 minutes, or until done. Makes approximately 16 muffins.

APPLESAUCE SPICE CAKE.   Instead of prunes, use 1 cup canned
applesauce. Substitute ¾ cup buttermilk for the prune syrup.

BANANA SPICE CAKE. Instead of prunes, use 1 cup of mashed bananas. Substitute ¾ cup buttermilk for the prune syrup.

SOUR CREAM SPICE CAKE

This excellent spice cake is especially useful because it has two variations. Have all ingredients at room temperature.

¼ pound butter or margarine	1 teaspoon baking soda
2 cups light or dark brown sugar	2 teaspoons cinnamon
3 large eggs	1 teaspoon ginger
2¼ cups sifted pastry or cake flour	¼ teaspoon nutmeg
¼ teaspoon salt	¼ teaspoon cloves
	1 cup commercial sour cream

Cream the butter or margarine, gradually adding the brown sugar. Add the eggs, 1 at a time, beating well after each addition. Sift the dry ingredients together and stir into the creamed mixture alternately with the sour cream. Turn batter into 2 8-inch round layer pans that have been buttered and floured. Tap pans on counter top to release excess air in the batter. Bake in a 350° F. oven for 25 to 30 minutes, or until cake is done. Cool in pans for 5 minutes, before turning out onto racks. The NUTMEG FROSTING (page 88) is especially nice with this cake.

VARIATIONS

1. Follow above recipe only use ½ pound of butter and substitute 1 cup buttermilk for the sour cream.

2. For an old-fashioned "Rum Spice Cake," follow basic recipe, adding 1 cup golden raisins and 1 tablespoon dark rum. Fill with RUM FILLING (page 89), and frost with any plain frosting.

CHOCOLATE CAKES

CHOCOLATE CREAM CHEESE CAKE

This excellent cake has cream cheese in the batter, and it keeps very well. Have all ingredients at room temperature.

2 cups sifted pastry or cake flour	½ cup butter or margarine
1 teaspoon baking powder	½ pound cream cheese
½ teaspoon baking soda	1½ cups superfine granulated sugar
¼ teaspoon salt	2 large eggs
4-ounce package sweet cooking chocolate	1 teaspoon vanilla extract
	½ cup milk

Sift flour with baking powder, soda, and salt. Set aside. Melt the chocolate. Combine butter or margarine and cream cheese and cream together. Gradually add the sugar, beating until light and fluffy. Add the eggs, 1 at a time, and the vanilla. Beat until blended. Now add the melted chocolate and blend in. Add the sifted dry ingredients alternately with the milk, beginning and ending with dry ingredients, and beating until smooth. Pour batter into 2 9-inch round layer pans that have been buttered and floured. Tap pans on counter top to release excess air in the batter. Bake in a 350° F. oven for 30 to 35 minutes, or until cake tests done. Cool in pans for 5 minutes before turning out onto racks. CREAM CHEESE CHOCOLATE FILLING OR FROSTING (page 93) is especially good with this.

CHOCOLATE HONEY CAKE

Mildly honey-flavored, this good keeper stores well. Have all ingredients at room temperature.

2 cups sifted pastry or cake flour
½ teaspoon salt
½ teaspoon baking soda
1½ teaspoons baking powder
⅓ cup mild flavored honey
⅔ cup milk

¼ cup water or orange juice
4-ounce package sweet cooking chocolate
½ cup butter or margarine
1 cup mild flavored honey
2 large eggs, or 4 yolks
1 teaspoon vanilla extract

Combine flour, salt, baking soda, and baking powder. Sift into a bowl and set aside. Combine the ⅓ cup honey, milk, water or orange juice, and chocolate in a small saucepan. Heat, stirring, over low heat until the chocolate is melted and the ingredients are thoroughly blended. Cool to room temperature. Cream the butter or margarine until fluffy and then, while still beating, add the 1 cup honey in a thin stream, beating until mixture is light. Beat in the eggs or yolks and vanilla and blend well. Now add the sifted dry ingredients and the chocolate mixture alternately, beginning and ending with dry ingredients. Blend until batter is smooth, but do not overmix. Turn batter into 2 9-inch round layer pans that have been buttered and floured. Tap the pans on the counter top to release excess air. Bake in a 350° F. oven for 30 to 35 minutes, or until cake tests done. Cool in the pans for 5 minutes before turning out onto racks.

SOUR CREAM CHOCOLATE CAKE

This cake remains moist and tender for a week and is easily made. With the exception of the boiling water, all ingredients should be at room temperature.

½ cup cocoa (Dutch cocoa preferable)
¾ cup boiling water
2 cups sifted pastry or cake flour
½ teaspoon baking soda

1 cup commercial sour cream
½ cup butter or margarine
2 cups sugar
1 teaspoon vanilla extract
3 large egg whites

Dissolve the cocoa in the water and set aside to cool. Sift the flour with the baking soda and set aside. Stir the sour cream into the cooled cocoa mixture and blend. Cream the butter or margarine and gradually add the sugar until mixture is light and fluffy. Add the vanilla and blend. Now, add the flour mixture to the creamed mixture alternately with the cocoa mixture, beginning and ending with the dry ingredients. Beat until batter is smooth. Beat the egg whites until stiff and fold into the batter last. Turn batter into a buttered and floured 9 by 13–inch pan and bake in a 300° F. oven for 1 hour, or until cake tests done. Cool in the pan, on a rack.

SWEET CHOCOLATE CAKE

This delicious cake has become very popular in recent years. We like the richer taste brought about by using brown sugar. With the exception of the boiling water, all ingredients should be at room temperature.

4-ounce package sweet cooking chocolate
½ cup boiling water
2½ cups sifted pastry or cake flour
1 teaspoon baking soda

½ teaspoon salt
1 cup butter or margarine
2 cups white or brown sugar
4 large eggs, separated
1 teaspoon vanilla extract
1 cup buttermilk or sour milk

Melt the chocolate in the boiling water and cool. Sift the flour with the baking soda and salt and set aside. Cream the butter or margarine, adding the sugar gradually and beating until light and fluffy. Add the egg yolks and vanilla and beat until blended. Stir in the cooled chocolate mixture and blend well. Now add the dry ingredients to the creamed mixture alternately with the buttermilk or sour milk, beginning and ending with dry ingredients. Beat after each addition until batter is smooth. Beat the egg whites until stiff and fold into the batter last. Pour batter into 3 8-inch round layer pans that have been buttered and floured. Bake in a 350° F. oven for 35 to 40 minutes, or until done. Cool in pans for 5 minutes before turning out on racks.

NOTE. Batter may be baked in a buttered and floured 9 by 13–inch pan, at 350° F. for 50 minutes. Serve from the pan.

WELLESLEY FUDGE CAKE

Some recipes for this famous cake with the deep chocolate taste call for granulated sugar, but I prefer to use brown sugar. Except for the boiling water, have all ingredients at room temperature.

4 squares unsweetened chocolate
⅔ cup boiling water
2⅔ cups sifted pastry or cake flour
1¼ teaspoons baking soda
1½ teaspoons baking powder
¼ teaspoon salt

⅔ cup butter or margarine
2⅔ cups brown sugar
3 large egg yolks
1 large egg
⅔ cup thick buttermilk or sour milk
1½ teaspoons vanilla extract

Melt the chocolate in the boiling water. Sift the flour with the baking soda, baking powder, and salt and set aside. Cream the butter or margarine, gradually adding the sugar and creaming until thick and light. Add the egg yolks and the whole egg to the creamed mixture, 1 at a time, and beat in. Now beat in the melted chocolate. Combine the buttermilk or sour milk and vanilla. Add the flour mixture to the creamed mixture alternately with the buttermilk or sour milk, beginning and ending with dry ingredients. Beat until smooth but do not overbeat. Turn batter into 2 8-inch square pans that have been buttered and floured. Tap pans on counter top to release excess air. Bake in a 350° F. oven for 30 to 35 minutes, or until cake tests done. Cool in pans for 5 minutes before turning out onto racks. Frost, when cool, with FUDGE FROSTING (page 89).

ICE WATER CHOCOLATE CAKE

This cake is tender, delicate, and tall, as delicious to look at as to eat. The old, handwritten cookbooks specified sweet well water or mountain spring water, but plain ice water will do just fine (but make certain it is icy). Except for the ice water, all ingredients should be at room temperature.

3 cups sifted pastry or cake flour

1½ teaspoons baking soda

½ teaspoon salt

¾ cup butter or margarine

2¼ cups superfine granulated sugar

3 large eggs

3 squares unsweetened chocolate, melted

1 or 2 teaspoons vanilla extract

1½ cups ice water

Sift the flour with the baking soda and salt and set aside. Cream the butter or margarine until very light. Gradually add the sugar and cream until mixture is thick and fluffy. Add the eggs, 1 at a time, and beat in thoroughly. Now blend in the melted chocolate and the vanilla. Add the sifted dry ingredients alternately with the ice water, beginning and ending with dry ingredients. Mix only until batter is smooth. Turn into 3 8-inch round layer pans that have been buttered and floured. Tap the pans lightly on the counter top to remove excess air, and then bake in a 350° F. oven for 30 to 35 minutes, or until done. Cool in the pans for 5 minutes before turning out onto racks. Cool thoroughly before filling and frosting. The DATE FILLING (page 97) and any chocolate frosting go very well with this.

CUP CAKES AND JELLY ROLLS

Cupcakes and jelly rolls make a pleasant change from the more usual layer cake, and are often much easier to serve, especially to a large group. Any cake recipe, including those for pound cakes, can be baked in muffin tins to make cupcakes. Bake in a 350° F. oven, generally for 15 to 20 minutes, although this depends on the type of cake. For example, a pound cake or a heavy jam cake requires a longer baking time.

The directions for making cupcakes are the same as for layer cakes. Room-temperature ingredients and a preheated oven are most important. The importance of proper creaming and careful folding in of ingredients is not lessened. Be careful that the muffin tins are well buttered, or sprayed with Pam, or lined with paper liners. The finished cupcakes can be dusted with sifted powdered sugar or cocoa, or a combination of the two. Or they may be swirled in a WHITE MOUNTAIN FROSTING (page 87), or spread with a BUTTER CREAM (page 90), or even intricately decorated. If you occasionally decorate cupcakes, I've found it best to bake them in paper liners and then only the top need be frosted and decorated.

The following recipe is a very old one, delicately fragrant and delightfully surprising.

ROSE LEAF CUPCAKES

Have all ingredients at room temperature.

1 cup fragrant rose petals	1 cup butter or margarine
3 cups sifted pastry or cake flour	2 cups superfine granulated sugar
1 tablespoon baking powder	5 large eggs
½ teaspoon salt	1 teaspoon grated lemon rind

The rose petals may be snipped into smaller pieces with kitchen scissors or left whole, but be certain that they are clean and dry. Combine flour, baking powder, and salt. Sift several times and set aside. Cream the butter or margarine until light. Gradually add the sugar and beat until fluffy. Add the eggs, 1 at a time, and beat until smooth after each. Add the lemon rind and then carefully fold in the flour mixture and the rose petals. If mixture is too thick, thin with a little milk. Turn batter into paper-lined muffin tins, filling no more than ⅔ full. Bake in a 350° F. oven for 15 to 20 minutes. Cool on rack.

SPONGE CAKE SHORTCAKES

Old-time cooks always made a sweet biscuit for strawberry shortcakes, and many of them consider our modern taste for sponge cake bases as pure heresy. But if you prefer the sponge-cake type of base, this is a good recipe. Have ingredients at room temperature.

1 cup sifted pastry or cake
flour
1 teaspoon baking powder
¼ teaspoon salt
2 large eggs, separated

1 cup superfine granulated
sugar
½ cup cold water
1 teaspoon grated lemon rind

Combine flour with baking powder and salt. Sift several times. Beat the egg whites until stiff. Beat the yolks just to blend them. Now gradually fold the yolks into the beaten whites, then fold in the sugar and the sifted flour mixture. Combine the water and grated rind and fold into the batter last. Spoon into buttered and floured Mary Ann pans. Bake in a 350° F. oven for 20 minutes. Makes 8 shortcakes.

COTTAGE-CHEESE CUPCAKES

These are as modern as the "Rose-leaf Cupcakes" are old and they are so simple and sure-fire that they make an excellent cupcake for beginning cooks. Both my daughters (the younger only nine years old) learned how to bake with this recipe. Have all ingredients at room temperature.

2 cups sifted pastry or cake
flour
1 teaspoon baking soda
½ teaspoon salt
½ cup butter or margarine
2 cups light brown sugar

2 teaspoons grated lemon rind
1 teaspoon vanilla extract
1 large egg
2 cups creamed cottage cheese
1 cup raisins or nuts, or a
combination of both

Sift the flour with the baking soda and salt. Set aside. Cream the butter or margarine until light. Gradually add 1 cup of the brown sugar and continue creaming until fluffy. Add flavorings and the egg and beat thoroughly. Now stir in the cottage cheese and the remaining cup of sugar. Stir until very well blended. Then work in the flour mixture and the raisins and/or chopped nuts. Batter should be well blended, but not overbeaten. Turn into 2 dozen buttered or paper-lined muffin cups. Bake in a 350° F. oven for 25 to 30 minutes, or until done. Cool in pans for 5 minutes, and then turn out onto racks. Frost or not as desired.

BASIC SPONGE ROLL

This superb cake roll requires no leavening other than the air that is beaten into the eggs. The eggs must be at room temperature, or a little warmer, and then beaten with the sugar for at least 10 minutes, or until thickened, tripled in bulk, and full of air.

6 large eggs
1 cup superfine granulated sugar
1¼ cups sifted pastry or cake flour

1 teaspoon vanilla extract, or grated lemon rind, lime rind, or 2 teaspoons grated orange or tangerine rind

First, butter a 12 by 18 by 1-inch jelly-roll pan, line it with waxed paper and butter the paper. Place the eggs in a large bowl and, if possible, place the bowl over a container of hot water. Stir to keep the eggs from cooking on the bottom. Add the sugar, and let rest over the hot water until the mixture is a little warmer than room temperature. Then beat, with an electric mixer, for 10 minutes. Sift the flour, measure, then sift again over the egg mixture a little at a time. Carefully fold the flour and the flavoring used into the eggs and sugar, being careful not to disturb the air bubbles too much. Then spread the batter in the prepared pan. Bake in a 350° F. oven for 18 to 20 minutes. The top of the roll will spring back when touched lightly. As soon as you take the roll out of the oven, turn it out onto a clean dish towel and peel off the waxed paper. Roll the cake and let it cool thoroughly before unrolling and filling. Use any desired filling. Dust the roll with powdered sugar or frost with any desired frosting.

NOTE. To make a fine cake, turn the roll out of the pan as directed above, and peel off the waxed paper. Do not roll, but cut the cake exactly in the middle, making 2 squares. Let it cool thoroughly. Then put the layers together with any red jam or jelly between the layers. Spread the top with a thin layer of apricot jam and dust with sifted powdered sugar. Let set for several hours before serving, otherwise the top layer might slide off the bottom layer.

CHOCOLATE JELLY ROLL

The most fabulous of all chocolate rolls, this is actually a simple soufflé mixture that is baked and then allowed to fall. It is expensive but virtually failure-proof. If it cracks (and it will) in the rolling, you can mask the mistakes with sifted cocoa, or a mixture of cocoa and powdered sugar. For company, I put two of them together and mask the seam with cocoa. One roll will serve no more than 8. Have all ingredients at room temperature.

6 ounces semisweet chocolate chips
3 tablespoons strong coffee, tea, rum, or brandy
1 teaspoon vanilla extract
6 large eggs, separated
¾ cup sugar
sweetened whipped cream
unsweetened cocoa, or a mixture of cocoa and sifted powdered sugar

Use a 10 by 15–inch jelly-roll pan. Butter it, line it with waxed paper, and butter the paper. Melt the chocolate chips, over low heat, with the liquid and the vanilla. Stir to blend, and let cool slightly. Beat the egg whites until foamy, add the sugar, a tablespoon or 2 at a time, and continue beating until mixture is stiff and glossy. Beat the egg yolks enough to thicken them a little, and then beat in the melted chocolate mixture. Fold the beaten egg whites into the egg yolk mixture very carefully, so that you do not lose the air in the beaten whites. Spread this evenly in the jelly-roll pan. Bake in a 350° F. oven for 15 to 18 minutes, or until the top is firm. A cake tester will come out clean. Remove from the oven and cool in the pan, covered by a clean linen towel that has been sprinkled with water. After about 30 minutes, carefully turn the roll out onto a strip of waxed paper that is a little longer than the pan. Carefully peel off the waxed paper that the roll has been baked on. Spread the jelly roll with sweetened whipped cream, and, lifting one end of the waxed paper that the roll has been turned out on, roll it up. The last roll should deposit it onto a platter or serving dish. Now dust it generously with sifted cocoa and/or powdered sugar, and store in the refrigerator until serving time.

FRUITED CREAM ROLL. Fold sliced bananas or fresh strawberries into the whipped cream before spreading on roll.

LARGER CHOCOLATE ROLL. To make enough to fill a 12 by 18 by 1-inch jelly-roll pan, use 8 large eggs, 1 cup sugar, ½ pound semisweet chocolate chips, or sweet chocolate, and ⅓ cup water, coffee, or rum. Make as above. This makes enough to serve 12.

GOLD JELLY ROLL

This jelly roll always comes out tender and good. I sometimes fill it with any preserves on hand, at other times I use both preserves and whipped cream. With the exception of the boiling water, have all ingredients at room temperature.

1 cup sifted pastry or cake flour	1 cup superfine granulated sugar
2 teaspoons baking powder	1 teaspoon vanilla extract or grated lemon or orange rind
¼ teaspoon salt	
1 cup (about 12) egg yolks	⅓ cup *boiling* water

Sift the flour with the baking powder and salt. Set aside. Beat the egg yolks with an electric mixer for about 5 minutes, or until thick. Add the sugar gradually and continue beating. Sprinkle a few tablespoons of the flour mixture over the beaten yolks and fold in. Continue until all the flour is used. Now, at the very last, sprinkle the flavoring used and the boiling water over the batter and quickly fold in. When batter is thoroughly blended, turn it into a buttered and floured 10 by 15-inch jelly-roll pan. Bake in a 350° F. oven for 15 to 20 minutes, or until cake tests done. The top will spring back when lightly touched. Turn the cake out onto a damp linen cloth that has been sprinkled with powdered sugar. Spread with filling desired and, lifting one end of the towel, roll the cake up. Cool on rack. If whipped cream is used, serve the cake while warm.

PINEAPPLE JELLY ROLL

This exceptionally good jelly roll is baked *over* the filling. We sometimes serve the slices topped by a dollop of whipped cream, and
sometimes with a custard sauce. It's good plain, also. Have all ingredients at room temperature.

No. 2½ can crushed
　pineapple, drained
½ cup brown sugar
¾ cup sifted pastry or cake
　flour
1 teaspoon baking powder

½ teaspoon salt
4 large eggs, separated
¾ cup sugar
1 teaspoon vanilla extract
½ teaspoon grated lemon
　rind (optional)

Butter a 10 by 15-inch jelly-roll pan generously. Spread the drained
pineapple over the pan and sprinkle with the brown sugar.

Sift the flour with the baking powder and salt and set aside. Beat
the egg whites until foamy, then gradually add ½ cup of the sugar
and continue beating until stiff. Beat the yolks with the remaining
¼ cup sugar until thick and light. Fold the yolks into the beaten
whites. Add the vanilla and lemon rind, if used. Sprinkle the sifted
flour mixture over the egg mixture, a little at a time, and fold in.
Spread this batter over the pineapple as evenly as possible. Bake in a
375° F. oven for 18 to 20 minutes, or until cake tests done. Turn
the cake, pineapple side up, out onto a damp linen towel that has been
sprinkled with powdered sugar. Roll the cake by lifting one end of the
towel, and let the cake cool in the towel. Serve as suggested above.

HIGH-ALTITUDE
CAKE BAKING

As all cake recipes differ in their balance of ingredients, there can be
no readjustment of ingredients that will guarantee success on the first

try. You will have to experiment to find out which adjustment will work best for you, so begin with the lesser adjustment for each ingredient.

A friend who lived for many years in Denver, Colorado, gave me two fine recipes and the following suggestions for successful baking at higher altitudes:

1. Grease the pans, line them with waxed paper, and grease the paper. This is especially important, as cakes baked at higher altitudes have a greater tendency to stick.

2. Raise the baking temperature 25° F.

3. At altitudes of 3,000 to 4,000 feet, *increase* the baking powder by ¼ teaspoon for each teaspoon called for. At altitudes over 5,000 feet, *decrease* the baking powder by ¼ teaspoon for each teaspoon called for.

4. At altitudes of 3,000 to 4,000 feet, no change in the sugar is necessary. At altitudes of 5,000 to 6,000 feet, *decrease* the sugar by 2 tablespoons for each cup called for. At altitudes of 6,000 feet and over, *decrease* the sugar by 3 to 4 tablespoons for each cup called for.

5. At altitudes of 3,000 to 4,000 feet, *decrease* the liquid by 1 tablespoon for each cup called for. At altitudes of 5,000 feet and over, *increase* the liquid by 2 to 4 tablespoons for each cup called for.

For further material on high-altitude baking, some of it free, write to the following sources:

Colorado Agricultural Experiment Station
Colorado A. and M. College
Fort Collins, Colorado

University of Wyoming Agricultural Experiment Station
Laramie, Wyoming

U. S. Department of Agriculture
Washington 25, D. C.

HIGH-ALTITUDE FUDGE CAKE

1½ cups sifted all-purpose
   flour
¾ cup sugar
¾ teaspoon baking powder
½ teaspoon salt
¼ teaspoon baking soda
⅓ cup butter or margarine

2 large eggs
½ cup milk
1½ squares unsweetened
   chocolate, melted
2 tablespoons milk
¼ to ½ cup chopped nuts

Sift the flour with the sugar, baking powder, salt, and baking soda into a mixing bowl. Make a well in the center and into the well put the butter or margarine, eggs, and the ½ cup milk. Beat with an electric mixer, at medium speed, for 4 minutes or by hand until perfectly smooth. Then stir in the melted chocolate just until blended. Add the 2 tablespoons milk and mix gently until batter is smooth. Fold in the nuts last. Turn batter into 2 8- or 9-inch round layer pans, buttered and papered. Bake in a 375° F. oven for 20 to 25 minutes. Cool in pans for 5 minutes before turning out onto racks.

HIGH-ALTITUDE POUND CAKE

3½ cups sifted all-purpose
   flour
½ teaspoon salt
1 teaspoon baking powder
1 cup butter or margarine
2 cups sugar

6 large eggs
3 or 4 tablespoons heavy
   cream
½ of a small can evaporated
   milk

Sift the flour with the salt and baking powder. Cream the butter or margarine until fluffy. Add the sugar gradually and beat well. Beat in 1 egg until blended, and then ½ cup of the sifted flour mixture. Then

eat in another egg, and another ½ cup flour mixture. Continue until
ll are added. Stir in the remaining ½ cup flour mixture, and then the
ombined liquids. Beat just until blended. Pour into a buttered 10-inch
ibe pan or Bundt pan. Bake in a 300° F. oven for 15 minutes, then
aise heat to 350° F. and bake another 45 minutes.

IOTE.   These 2 recipes have been adjusted for use at up to 6,000
et. At higher altitudes, make any further adjustment according to
ie information in HIGH-ALTITUDE CAKE BAKING (page 82).

*Let me have the necessary means, a kitchen amply stored, and you shall
*e that like enchantment I will spread around a charm as powerful as
e siren's voice."

HEGESANDER

2. *Frostings, Fillings, Glazes, Sauces*

COOKED FROSTINGS

CREAM FROSTING

This is especially good on angel food or sponge cakes. Enough for one 10-inch tube cake.

1 envelope unflavored gelatin	¾ cup sugar
½ cup water	1 cup heavy cream
1 cup half and half	1 cup slivered, blanched
4 large egg yolks	almonds or other nuts

Soften the gelatin in the water. Heat the half and half in a double boiler over hot, but not boiling, water. Beat the egg yolks with the sugar and stir into the hot half and half. Cook, stirring, until thickened. Stir in the softened gelatin and remove from the heat. Stir until gelatin is dissolved. Cool to room temperature. Whip the heavy cream until thick and fold into the cooled mixture. Cool until thick enough to spread. Spread on cake and sprinkle lavishly with nuts.

WHITE MOUNTAIN FROSTING

A boiled frosting that spreads and mounds beautifully. Enough to fill and frost an 8- or 9-inch round layer cake or a tube cake.

2 cups sugar
1 cup water
pinch salt
1 tablespoon lemon juice

2 large egg whites
½ to 1 teaspoon vanilla extract

Combine sugar, water, salt, and lemon juice in a saucepan, and stir just to blend. Cook over medium heat until the mixture reaches the long thread stage (230° F. to 235° F. on a candy thermometer). Beat the egg whites until stiff enough to form peaks. Pour the syrup over the beaten whites in a thin stream, *beating constantly*. Beat until frosting holds its shape. Then add the vanilla.

COCONUT FROSTING. To the recipe add 1 tablespoon grated orange rind. Frost cake and sprinkle lavishly with grated coconut.

ORANGE MOUNTAIN FROSTING

Makes enough to fill and frost a 9-inch round layer cake.

2 large egg whites
1 cup sugar
⅛ teaspoon cream of tartar
¼ cup orange juice

1 tablespoon grated orange rind
2 tablespoons light corn syrup

Combine all the ingredients in the top of a double boiler and blend. Place over *boiling* water and beat with an electric mixer until the frosting holds nice peaks when the mixer is lifted. Remove from heat and continue beating until frosting holds a definite shape and is cool.

COOKED CREAM FROSTING

I never use this frosting on a cake that the recipe isn't requested. For cake decorators, it makes a good base for decoration. To make it white use an uncolored shortening in place of the butter. Makes enough to fill and frost two 9-inch round layers.

1 cup milk	1 cup sifted powdered sugar
¼ cup flour	1½ teaspoons vanilla extract
½ pound butter or margarine	or grated lemon rind

Combine the milk and flour and blend until smooth. I whirl it in the blender. Cook over low heat, stirring all the time, until as thick as a pudding. Set aside to cool to room temperature. Cream the butter until light and fluffy. Add the cooled pudding, and blend thoroughly. Gradually beat in the sugar and flavoring used. Beat with an electric mixer until of spreading consistency, about 10 to 15 minutes.

SOUR CREAM FROSTING

This makes enough to frost the top and sides of a 9-inch round layer cake.

1 cup granulated sugar	1 cup commercial sour cream
1 cup light brown sugar	1 teaspoon vanilla extract

Combine the two sugars and the sour cream in a saucepan. Cook over medium heat, stirring, until mixture reaches the soft ball stage (236° F.) Remove from heat and cool to barely lukewarm. Add the vanilla and beat with an electric mixer until frosting is of spreading consistency. If necessary, thin it with a few drops of milk or liqueur.

NUTMEG FROSTING. Follow basic recipe, omitting vanilla and adding ¼ to ½ teaspoon ground nutmeg.

RUM FILLING. Follow basic recipe, omitting vanilla and adding 2 tablespoons dark rum and ¼ to ¾ cup chopped pecans.

FUDGE FROSTING

½ cup evaporated milk
½ cup sugar
2 tablespoons butter

1 cup semisweet chocolate chips
2 tablespoons light corn syrup

Combine in a saucepan the evaporated milk, sugar, and butter. Bring to a full boil over direct heat, stirring constantly. Boil for 5 minutes. Remove from heat and immediately stir in the chocolate chips and the corn syrup. Beat until blended. Cool until thick enough to spread, about 15 to 20 minutes. Enough to fill and frost an 8-inch round layer cake.

BUTTERMILK ICING

1 cup sugar
½ cup buttermilk
½ teaspoon baking soda

½ teaspoon vanilla extract or
1 teaspoon grated lemon rind
½ cup butter or margarine

Combine all the ingredients in a saucepan and stir to blend. Cook over medium heat, stirring constantly, until mixture reaches the soft-ball stage (230° F. on a candy thermometer). Remove from heat and cool for 5 minutes. Then beat with an electric mixer until icing starts to thicken. Spread on cake immediately.

'Tis not the quantity of the food, but the cheerfulness of the guests, which makes the feast."

LORD CLARENDON

UNCOOKED FROSTINGS

BUTTER CREAM FROSTING

The true butter cream frosting is European in origin and consists of a sugar syrup poured over egg yolks and then beaten into softened butter of the finest quality. What the American housewife calls a butter cream is a simple mixture of beaten butter and powdered sugar, flavored according to taste. The use of white shortenings (which are necessary only in frostings that are to be colored and used in decorating) makes it impossible to achieve the delicacy of flavor that is ideally desired. If you use butter or a good margarine, and beat to a fine cream before adding the sifted powdered sugar and flavoring, you can have a fine topping for any cake. The slightly raw taste of powdered sugar is easily eliminated by letting the frosting stand in a bowl over hot water for 15 minutes and then beating again until cool and thick enough to be spread. Or you can cover the taste by adding any desired flavoring. When spreading the butter cream over the cake, you can make peaks with the rounded part of a spoon, or you can make it perfectly smooth by going over the frosting with a knife that has been dipped in hot water. The water won't hurt the frosting.

½ pound butter or margarine	1 teaspoon vanilla extract, or
1 pound sifted powdered	grated lemon or orange rind,
sugar	or 2 teaspoons rum, or ¼
	teaspoon almond extract

Beat the softened butter until it has the consistency of whipped cream Gradually beat in the sifted powdered sugar. The mixture should be beaten until it is fine and smooth. Add flavoring to taste.

NOTE.   If the frosting needs to be thinned, you may use cream or any desired fruit juice or liqueur. If you use orange juice, the addition of an egg yolk makes a fine color.

RUM BUTTER CREAM.   Simply add 1 or 2 tablespoons rum, or as much as your taste dictates.

RICH CHOCOLATE FROSTING

2 cups semisweet chocolate
   chips
  ½ cup butter or margarine
1 cup powdered sugar

2 large eggs
1½ teaspoons vanilla extract
  or 2 tablespoons rum

Melt the chocolate chips in the top of a double boiler over hot, not boiling, water. When melted, remove from heat and let stand at room temperature for 1 hour. Cream the butter or margarine with the powdered sugar. Add the eggs and flavoring used and beat in. Then add the chocolate and beat until of spreading consistency. Makes enough to fill and frost a 9-inch round layer cake.

CHOCOLATE BUTTER CREAM

In this creamy frosting you can use unsweetened chocolate or cocoa. Makes enough to fill and frost an 8-inch round layer cake.

½ cup butter or margarine
2½ cups powdered sugar
1 large egg or 2 egg yolks

3 squares melted unsweetened
  chocolate or ⅓ cup cocoa
1 teaspoon vanilla extract or 1
  tablespoon rum

Cream the butter or margarine. Add the powdered sugar. Beat in the egg, chocolate or cocoa, and flavoring. Thin, if necessary, with cream or rum.

CREAM WHIP

This makes enough to fill and frost an 8- or 9-inch round layer cake.

1 cup heavy cream
⅓ cup brown sugar

1 teaspoon vanilla extract or 1 tablespoon rum

Combine ingredients and chill for 30 minutes. Then whip until stiff.

COCOA CREAM WHIP. Follow the recipe, omitting the brown sugar and adding 2 tablespoons each of cocoa and sifted powdered sugar.

DECORATING BUTTER CREAM

This is a very good frosting for decorating purposes. The use of the egg white makes a thin crust on the flowers and borders, and this helps them to hold their shapes. I always chill the flowers before putting them on the cake. If you can obtain the colorless vanilla, you can have a perfectly white frosting which will take a truer color. This is the only time I recommend the use of colorless vegetable shortenings.

2 cups shortening
4 cups sifted powdered sugar
pinch of salt
flavoring to taste

¼ cup cornstarch (to be used only during hot weather)
1 or 2 large egg whites

Cream the shortening until almost like whipped cream. Gradually add the sugar, salt, flavoring, and cornstarch, if used. Beat thoroughly. Beat in 1 egg white and if icing is too stiff, beat in another. If the icing is too soft, add more sifted powdered sugar. This keeps well, and does not need to be stored in the refrigerator unless the weather is hot.

WHIPPED BUTTER FROSTING

This delicious frosting has the consistency of whipped cream. It can be refrigerated for several days. Allow it to come to room temperature before using. Makes enough to fill and frost two 8-inch round layers.

1 cup butter or margarine
1 cup sugar
⅔ cup warm milk

1 teaspoon vanilla extract or grated lemon or orange rind, or 1 square unsweetened chocolate, melted

Beat the butter or margarine until it is well creamed. Add the sugar and blend. Pour the milk in slowly, beating all the while. Add the flavoring used and continue beating for at least 5 minutes. The frosting will become thick and creamy.

SOUR CREAM CHOCOLATE FROSTING

This is a superb frosting. Makes enough to fill and frost two 9-inch round layers, or a 10-inch tube cake.

9 ounces semisweet chocolate chips
⅓ cup butter or margarine
¾ cup commercial sour cream

1 teaspoon vanilla extract
¼ teaspoon salt
3½ to 4½ cups sifted powdered sugar

Combine chocolate chips and butter or margarine in the top of a double boiler and melt over hot, not boiling, water. Remove from heat and cool slightly. Blend in the sour cream, vanilla, and salt. Gradually beat in enough of the powdered sugar to make an easy-to-spread frosting.

CREAM CHEESE CHOCOLATE FILLING
OR FROSTING

This superb filling-frosting can be used to fill and frost cakes and also to fill hollowed-out angel food or sponge cakes. It can be frozen, but thaw it before using. Enough to generously fill and frost a 9-inch round layer cake.

1 cup semisweet chocolate chips	1 teaspoon vanilla extract or 1 tablespoon rum
⅔ cup white or brown sugar	1 egg yolk
4 ounces cream cheese	1 or 1½ cups heavy cream, whipped

Melt the chocolate over hot, not boiling, water. Cream the sugar, cream cheese, and flavoring used. Add the egg yolk and beat in. Then pour in the melted chocolate, beating all the while. Last, beat the cream until thick and fold into the chocolate mixture. Chill several hours or until thick enough to spread.

FILLINGS

LANE CAKE FILLING

Have ingredients at room temperature. This rich filling can be used to fill almost any white or yellow cake.

8 large egg yolks	½ to 1 cup candied cherries, quartered (optional)
1 cup sugar	
½ cup butter or margarine	1 to 1½ cups chopped pecans
1 cup dark or light raisins	½ cup brandy or bourbon
1 cup coconut	1 teaspoon vanilla extract

Beat the egg yolks until light and thickened. Add the sugar and continue beating until mixture no longer feels grainy. Melt the butter or margarine in the top of a double boiler, and then stir in the yolk-sugar mixture. Cook over hot water, stirring, until mixture thickens. Remove from heat and stir in the remaining ingredients. Cool thoroughly before using.

RAISIN FILLING

3 large egg yolks
¾ cup milk
¾ cup brown sugar
1 cup dark or light raisins

2 tablespoons butter or
   margarine
2 teaspoons vanilla extract

Beat the egg yolks with the milk. Add the sugar, raisins, and butter or margarine. Cook over medium heat, stirring constantly, until mixture is thickened. Stir in the vanilla and chill the filling. When ready to use it should mound slightly when dropped from a spoon.

LEMON-LIME CREAM FILLING

3 large egg yolks
½ cup sugar
¼ cup lemon or lime juice

1½ cups heavy cream
2 teaspoons grated lemon or
   lime rind

Combine egg yolks, sugar, and juice in the top of a double boiler. Cook, stirring constantly, over hot, not boiling, water until mixture is very thick, about 15 to 20 minutes. Cool thoroughly. Whip the cream with the grated rind and fold into the cooled yolk mixture.

COCONUT PECAN FILLING

This also makes a marvelous filling for jelly rolls.

1 cup evaporated milk
2 or 3 large egg yolks
½ cup butter or margarine
1 cup sugar

1 teaspoon vanilla extract
1 cup flaked coconut
1 cup chopped pecans

Combine milk, egg yolks, softened butter or margarine, sugar, and vanilla in a saucepan. Stir to blend thoroughly. Cook, stirring, over medium heat until mixture thickens, about 12 minutes. Remove from heat and add coconut and pecans. Cool to spreading consistency, beating occasionally. Use to fill cake layers and to spread on the top layer also. Do not attempt to make this adhere to the sides of a cake.

CHOCOLATE CREAM FILLING

This may be used to fill *and* frost, and is especially good on angel food or sponge cakes.

1 envelope unflavored gelatin	4 large egg whites
¼ cup water	½ cup sugar
1 cup semisweet chocolate chips	1 cup heavy cream
1 cup milk or half and half	1 teaspoon vanilla extract

Soften the gelatin in the water. Combine chocolate chips and milk or half and half in the top of a double boiler. Heat over hot, not boiling, water until chips are melted. Stir until smooth. Add the gelatin and stir until gelatin is dissolved. Cool slightly. Beat the egg whites until foamy, gradually adding sugar and beating until stiff. Fold into the chocolate mixture. Whip the cream until thick and add the vanilla. Fold into chocolate mixture. Cool until thick enough to use.

APRICOT FILLING

¼ cup cornstarch	1 tablespoon lemon juice
¼ teaspoon salt	3 tablespoons butter or margarine
2 cups apricot nectar	

Combine cornstarch, salt, apricot nectar, and lemon juice. Blend until smooth or whirl in the blender for a second or two. Cook over low heat, stirring, until thickened, about 5 minutes. Stir in the butter or margarine and cool completely before using.

CHOCOLATE FROSTING OR FILLING

1 cup semisweet chocolate
    chips
16 large marshmallows

½ cup milk
1 cup heavy cream, whipped

Combine chocolate chips, marshmallows, and milk in the top of a double boiler over hot, not boiling, water. Stir until melted. Remove from heat and chill. When ready to use, fold into the whipped cream.

DATE FILLING

1 to 1½ cups pitted, chopped
    dates
1 tablespoon lemon juice or
    rind

⅓ to ½ cup water or fruit
    juice, such as orange or
    apricot

Combine ingredients and cook over low heat, stirring, until thick enough to spread.

UNCOOKED COCONUT FILLING

½ cup coconut milk or heavy
    cream
¼ cup sifted powdered sugar

2 large egg whites
1½ cups grated coconut

Combine coconut milk or cream and sugar and chill for several hours. Beat the egg whites until stiff. Add the milk mixture and continue beating. Fold in coconut.

UNCOOKED FRUIT WHIP

This simple whip can be used between cake layers, and also to top the cake.

2 fresh peaches, peeled and   1 cup sugar
   stoned, or 1 cup strawberries   1 large egg white ·

Mash the fruit to a nice pulp. Add sugar and egg white and beat until light and thick. Use immediately.

UNCOOKED RUM FILLING

This filling should be spread about ½ inch thick between the layers of a white cake. Then put the cake together and frost with whipped cream flavored with more rum. Chill thoroughly before serving.

⅔ cup butter (no substitute)   ⅓ to ½ cup rum
2½ cups sifted powdered
   sugar

Beat the butter to a fine smooth cream. Gradually add the powdered sugar and the rum. Beat until soft and smooth. Chill until filling is of spreading consistency.

GLAZES

A glaze is a thin icing that is spooned over the top of the cake or over a frosting. It is usually made with a cup of sifted powdered sugar blended with 1 or 2 tablespoons melted butter and thinned with fruit juice or liqueur until it can be drizzled from a spoon.

APRICOT GLAZE. Use apricot nectar and a teaspoon of grated orange rind to thin the sugar.

ORANGE GLAZE. Thin the powdered sugar with orange juice or a combination of the juice and an orange liqueur, and 2 teaspoons grated orange rind.

LEMON GLAZE. Made the same way as orange glaze, using lemon juice and rind.

STRAWBERRY GLAZE. An unusual glaze. Use crushed strawberries with 1 cup powdered sugar, 2 tablespoons melted butter, ½ teaspoon vanilla extract and enough crushed berries to thin the mixture.

APRICOT LIQUEUR GLAZE

This is the finest of all glazes. Use it on tube cakes, layer cakes that have been filled with whipped cream, and also on fruit cakes.

1 cup apricot preserves	2 tablespoons any desired liqueur

Whirl the preserves in the blender to make a purée. Add the liqueur and heat, over direct heat, to the boiling point. Cool slightly, but use while still warm.

CHOCOLATE GLAZE

¼ pound sweet chocolate	1¼ cups sifted powdered sugar
3 tablespoons water or rum	
1 tablespoon butter	1 teaspoon vanilla extract

Break the chocolate into pieces. Combine with the liquid and butter in a saucepan. Cook over low heat until the chocolate and butter are melted. Combine with rest of ingredients and stir to blend. Cool before using.

COCOA GLAZE

This is an easy glaze that can be varied, if desired, by using liquids other than water.

¼ cup cocoa (Dutch preferred)
1¼ cups sifted powdered sugar

¼ cup butter or margarine
2 tablespoons water, rum, or orange juice

Combine cocoa and sugar. Heat the butter or margarine with the liquid until butter is melted. Pour over sugar mixture and blend.

SAUCES FOR CAKES

All cakes, but especially pound cakes, sponge cakes, and angel food cakes, are different and delicious when served with a sauce. The simplest and one of the most satisfying ways of "saucing" a cake is to ladle slightly sweetened, sliced fresh fruit over the cake and top with heavy sweet cream or a custard sauce. Peaches are very popular and fresh strawberries, crushed just enough to release the juices, are probably the most popular. But don't overlook the mangoes and papayas that are appearing in markets all over the country. Peel and slice them, then sweeten slightly and add barely a teaspoon of lime juice before ladling onto the cake. Top with whipped cream. If your family has never tasted these exotic fruits, it's a good way to introduce them.

Since cakes served with a sauce should not be frosted, they are often a boon for the busy housewife who entertains a great deal. I make pound cakes by the half dozen and freeze the extras. Then, when I'm expecting company I make the sauce while the cake thaws.

APRICOT SAUCE

2 cups puréed apricots
2 tablespoons lemon or
    orange juice

1 tablespoon rum, Cognac, or
    apricot brandy
1 teaspoon grated lemon or
    orange rind

Combine ingredients and let stand for 20 minutes before using. This sauce is especially good with pound cakes.

BLUEBERRY SAUCE

1 package frozen sweetened
    blueberries
1 stick cinnamon

2 teaspoons lemon juice
½ cup sugar

Combine ingredients and simmer over direct heat, stirring occasionally, until thickened, about 15 to 20 minutes. Remove cinnamon stick. Serve the sauce either hot or lukewarm

WHITE CUSTARD SAUCE

This is a slightly unusual custard sauce and very delicious.

2 cups heavy cream
¼ cup sugar
½ cup (about 4) egg whites

½ teaspoon almond extract or
    other flavoring

Combine 1 cup of the cream and the sugar in the top of a double boiler. Scald over hot water. The cream should be very hot. Combine the egg whites and the remaining cup of cream and beat until thoroughly blended. Beat a little of the hot cream into the egg-white mixture then add this, gradually, to the rest of the hot cream. Cook and stir over boiling water until the custard is thick enough to coat a spoon. Cool before stirring in the flavoring. Chill before using.

CUSTARD SAUCE

1 cup milk
½ cup heavy cream
1-inch piece of vanilla bean or
  1 teaspoon vanilla extract

⅓ cup sugar
4 egg yolks
½ teaspoon grated lemon
  rind

Combine the milk, cream, and vanilla bean in a saucepan. Bring the mixture to a boil over direct heat. Remove from heat immediately and cool for 20 minutes. Remove the vanilla bean, if used. Add vanilla extract, if used. Gradually beat the sugar into the egg yolks and beat until pale. Stir the milk mixture into the beaten yolks and then add the lemon rind. Cook, stirring constantly, over direct heat until mixture coats a spoon. Cool. Chill thoroughly before serving.

RASPBERRY PEACH SAUCE

1 cup raspberries
1 cup sliced peaches or
  mangoes

¼ cup sugar
1 tablespoon brandy or rum

Combine ingredients. Let stand about 20 minutes before using. This sauce is especially good with pound cakes.

SOUR CREAM SAUCE

1 tablespoon granulated or
  brown sugar
1 cup commercial sour cream

1 cup sliced fruit or berries
toasted chopped nuts

Combine sugar, sour cream, and fruit and blend. Ladle onto cake and sprinkle with toasted chopped nuts.

SYRUP SAUCE

This is a simple and very, very old sauce for cakes and gingerbread. Use maple sugar if you can.

¼ cup water	3 or 4 eggs
¼ to ⅓ cup maple sugar or brown sugar	pinch of salt
	½ teaspoon vanilla extract

Combine water and sugar and bring to a boil. Combine the eggs, salt, and vanilla and blend with a fork. Very quickly, stirring constantly to keep syrup from boiling over, whip the eggs into the syrup and stir until spongy. Serve at once.

WHIPPED CREAM SAUCE

1 cup heavy cream	⅓ cup melted butter or margarine
1 large egg	1 tablespoon rum or Cognac
¼ to ⅓ cup sugar	

Beat the heavy cream until thick. Combine the egg, sugar, and melted butter or margarine. Beat until thoroughly blended. Then fold this into the whipped cream. Chill thoroughly before adding the rum.

FRUITED WHIPPED CREAM

1 cup heavy cream	2 to 3 tablespoons dark rum
canned fruit, well drained (guavas and mangoes are especially nice)	

Whip the cream until thick. Add the fruit and rum. Serve immediately.

MINCEMEAT SAUCE FOR POUND CAKES

The handy jar of mincemeat, either commercial or homemade, provides an excellent holiday sauce for cakes.

2 cups mincemeat (any kind)
½ cup Madeira or port, or apple, orange, or pineapple juice

1 or 2 tablespoons brandy or rum (optional)

Combine ingredients and let stand for a while so that flavors may blend. Ladle a small amount of this rich sauce on slices of cake.

SUGARED FLOWERS

These are lovely on cakes. If you store them carefully, they will keep for up to a week. Use roses, nasturtiums, violets, rose geranium leaves, lemon leaves, or mint leaves. Pick the flowers with a stem which may, if desired, be cut off later. The stem makes it easier to sugar the flowers. Clean the petals very carefully, mainly for cosmetic reasons, as most people do not eat the sugared flowers. Use the following ingredients. It is impossible to give exact amounts.

1 or 2 egg whites

superfine granulated sugar (not powdered or confectioners')

Beat the egg white just until foamy, preferably using a fork. With a small, soft brush, brush both sides of the petals with egg white. Make certain that all parts are coated. Then sprinkle with the sugar, using enough to make a good coating, but not so much as to destroy the shape of the flower. Set on waxed paper to dry. Store carefully.

3. Cookies

The American cookie was originally brought to these shores by the English, Scotch, and Dutch immigrants. Our simple "butter cookies" still bear the strong imprint of the English "tea cakes" and the Scotch shortbread.

The Southern Colonial housewife took great pride in her cookies, almost always called simply "tea cakes." These were often flavored with nothing more than the finest butter, sometimes with the addition of a few drops of rose water. But in other regions the housewife experimented with the addition of various ingredients to the basic butter-cooky dough. In the New England states especially, she preferred brown sugar or molasses and added nuts and dried fruits to the dough. She indulged a penchant for whimsical names by giving the cookies such names as Snickerdoodles, Cry Babies, Rocks, Brambles, and Hermits.

In an effort to let nothing go to waste, the early housewife experimented with fats other than butter and then added spices to cover the taste of lard, bear fat, and something called cotter-beef fat. She used honey and molasses when regular sugar was scarce, but the cooky crock, kept by the kitchen door, was always full.

It is doubtful whether any sure count of the hundreds upon hundreds of cooky recipes could ever be made or whether any one book could hold the recipes for all of the various types of cooky. But since most cooky recipes are simply variations of a basic theme, you can, by following the suggestions given with many of the recipes in this chapter, have enough cookies to keep any cooky jar full to overflowing.

GENERAL INFORMATION

1. For fine cookies always use quality ingredients. The delicate butter-type cookies, to be as good as they should be, must be made with butter (or at the very least a really fine margarine).

2. The butter should be creamed until light and fluffy, as for cakes, and then the sugar beaten in.

3. For delicate butter-type cookies, the superfine granulated sugar is best, but regular granulated sugar can be used.

4. When brown sugar is used, it must be firmly packed for measuring.

5. When baking powder is called for, use double-acting baking powder.

6. For macaroon-type cookies, liner papers for the cooky sheets save much wear and tear on the nerves.

7. For delicate butter-type cookies, it is best to use butter to grease the cookie sheets. For other cookies, margarine or oil can be used.

8. Always cool cookies on racks.

9. Always *preheat* the oven to the required temperature.

10. The old-time cooky crock, made of stone, was ideal for storing moist cookies. Lacking this, use any airtight container and add a piece of fresh bread, an apple, or an orange to keep moist cookies moist.

11. Crisp cookies are best kept in a container with a loose-fitting lid. If they lose their crispness, they can be recrispened by heating them in a 275° F. oven for 5 minutes.

12. With the exception of macaroon-type cookies, all cookies freeze well either baked or unbaked.

BAR COOKIES

Bar cookies are an American invention. They are simply a cross between a cooky and a cake. They can be frosted, rolled in sifted powdered sugar, or served plain.

BROWNIES I

The brownie must be America's favorite cooky. Even young girls, if they can't cook anything else, learn to make brownies. Recipes for brownies range from the simple to the luxurious.

1 cup sugar	1 cup sifted flour
2 squares unsweetened chocolate	1 or 2 teaspoons vanilla extract
½ cup butter	1 cup chopped nuts
2 large eggs	

Combine chocolate, butter, and sugar in the top of a double boiler. Cook, stirring constantly, over hot water until mixture is melted and blended. Remove from heat. Beat the eggs, and then pour the melted chocolate mixture slowly over the eggs, beating all the time. Add flour, vanilla, and nuts. Blend thoroughly. Turn into a buttered 8-inch square pan. Bake in a 350° F. oven for 20 to 25 minutes. Cut into squares while warm.

NOTE.   Recipe is easily doubled and baked in a large pan. For "Applesauce Brownies" add ½ cup applesauce and ¼ teaspoon baking soda to the basic recipe.

BROWNIES II

These are our favorites.

1 cup sifted flour
1 teaspoon baking powder
½ cup butter, melted
12 tablespoons cocoa (Dutch cocoa is preferred) or 4 squares unsweetened chocolate, melted

4 large eggs
2 cups sugar
½ teaspoon salt
2 teaspoons vanilla extract
1 cup chopped walnuts

Sift the flour with the baking powder. Combine the melted butter with the cocoa or melted chocolate. Add to the eggs and beat to a smooth cream with the sugar, salt, and vanilla. Then add the flour mixture and the chopped nuts. Blend all ingredients. Turn into a buttered 9 by 13 by 2-inch pan. Bake in a 325° F. oven for 35 to 40 minutes. While still warm, spread with BROWNIE FROSTING (page 154).

NOTE.   For thinner brownies, halve the recipe again, using ¾ cup butter, 6 large eggs, etc., and bake in a 10 by 15 by 1-inch jelly roll pan. Bake in a 375° F. oven for 20 to 25 minutes.

MERINGUE BROWNIES

These aren't true brownies, but they're very good.

2 cups sifted flour
¼ teaspoon salt
¼ teaspoon baking soda
1 teaspoon baking powder
½ cup butter or margarine
2 large eggs, separated
½ cup granulated sugar
½ cup light brown sugar
1 tablespoon cold water
1 teaspoon vanilla extract
1½ cups semisweet chocolate chips
1 cup granulated or light brown sugar

Sift the flour with the salt, baking soda, and baking powder. Set aside. Cream the butter or margarine with the egg yolks, the ½ cup granulated sugar and the ½ cup brown sugar. Add the cold water and vanilla. Add the sifted dry ingredients and blend. Turn batter into a buttered 9 by 13 by 2–inch pan, and sprinkle the chocolate chips over the batter. Beat the egg whites until foamy, and then gradually beat in the 1 cup granulated or light brown sugar. Beat until mixture forms stiff peaks. Spread over the chocolate chips. Sprinkle with chopped nuts, if desired. Bake in a 375° F. oven for about 25 minutes.

BROWNIE BONBONS

These are baked in muffin pans with very small cups, and the shape makes them particularly appealing.

1 cup semisweet chocolate chips
⅓ cup butter or margarine
½ cup sifted flour
½ teaspoon baking powder
⅛ teaspoon salt
½ cup sugar
2 large eggs
1 teaspoon vanilla extract
¾ cup slivered Brazil nuts or chopped filberts

Place chocolate chips and butter or margarine in the top of a double boiler, over hot water. Stir and heat until melted. Sift the flour with the baking powder and salt. Set aside. When the chocolate is melted, remove mixture from heat and blend with the sugar. Add the eggs, beating all the time to keep the eggs from coagulating. Stir in the vanilla, the flour mixture and nuts. Turn into well-buttered muffin pans, with cups that measure about 1¼ inches across and are slightly less than 1 inch deep. Bake in a 375° F. oven for 10 minutes. Cool in pans for 5 minutes before turning out. Makes 2 to 3 dozen.

MERINGUE NUT BARS

This is a delicious, fairly easy-to-make, bar cookie. Any jam might be used, but we prefer apricot or peach. If you use a marmalade, such as orange or tangerine, use an orange liqueur such as Curaçao or Triple Sec in the meringue topping.

2½ cups sifted flour
5 large eggs, separated
⅓ cup sugar
1 cup butter or margarine, softened
2 teaspoons vanilla extract
preserves, jam, or marmalade

1 cup sugar
2 teaspoons vanilla extract or 1 tablespoon bourbon, brandy, or liqueur
3 cups walnuts or pecans, finely chopped

Sift the flour into a large bowl. Make a well in the center and in the well put the egg yolks, the ⅓ cup sugar, the butter or margarine and 2 teaspoons vanilla extract. Use your fingers and blend ingredients to make a smooth paste. Press the paste into the bottom of a buttered 10 by 15–inch jelly-roll pan. Spread the dough with a layer of preserves, as thin or thick as you prefer. Now, beat the egg whites until they form soft peaks. Gradually beat in the 1 cup sugar, beating until the mixture forms stiff peaks. Fold in the flavoring and then the chopped nuts. Spread this meringue over the preserves. Bake in a 350° F. oven for 35 to 40 minutes. Remove from oven and cool on a rack. When cool, cut into strips or bars.

HAWAIIAN MERINGUE BARS. Follow recipe, using pineapple preserves and chopped macadamia nuts.

BROWN SUGAR SQUARES

Some call these "Blonde Brownies." They are delicious.

2½ cups sifted flour
1 teaspoon salt
2 teaspoons baking powder
5 large eggs
1 teaspoon vanilla extract
 (optional)

1 pound brown sugar
1 cup heavy cream
½ cup butter, melted
1 to 1½ cups chopped nuts
1 cup semisweet chocolate
 chips (optional)

Combine the flour, salt, and baking powder. Sift and set aside. Beat the eggs until foamy. Add the vanilla, if used, sugar, cream, and melted butter. Beat to blend. Add the sifted dry ingredients, chopped nuts, and chocolate chips, if used, and blend. Turn batter into a buttered and floured 10 by 15 by 1–inch jelly-roll pan. Bake in a 350° F. oven for 20 to 30 minutes. Cool in the pan and cut into squares when cool. Frost or not as desired.

NOTE. If you do not have heavy cream, use ½ cup milk and increase the butter to 1 cup. To vary the basic recipe you may use butterscotch chips instead of chocolate chips. Or you may use instead of the chips ½ cup each of chopped pitted dates and flaked coconut.

SPICY CARROT BARS

This spicy, flavorful cooky makes a good after-school snack for the children.

1¼ cups sifted flour
1 teaspoon cinnamon
1 teaspoon baking powder
½ cup butter or margarine
1 cup sugar
2 large eggs

¼ teaspoon salt
¾ cup grated raw carrots
¾ cup shredded coconut
¾ cup chopped walnuts
¼ cup hot water or orange
 juice

Sift the flour with the cinnamon and baking powder. Cream the butter or margarine with the sugar, eggs, and salt until smooth and light. Stir in the carrots, coconut, and chopped nuts. Then add the sifted flour mixture alternately with the hot water or orange juice. Blend well. Turn into a buttered 9 by 13 by 2–inch baking pan. Bake in a 375° F. oven for about 25 minutes. Cool on a rack and cut into bars or squares while warm. Dust with sifted powdered sugar if desired.

COCONUT NUT BARS

This makes a rich, two-layer cooky, well liked by everyone. The pastry can be used for other cookies and tarts.

PASTRY
½ cup butter or margarine
⅓ cup sugar
1 large egg, or 2 egg yolks
1¼ cups sifted flour

FILLING

3 large eggs
1½ cups light brown sugar

1 teaspoon vanilla extract
1 teaspoon grated lemon rind
  (optional)
3 tablespoons flour
¾ teaspoon baking powder
½ teaspoon salt
¾ cup shredded coconut
1½ cups chopped pecans,
  filberts, Brazil nuts,
  almonds, walnuts, or
  macadamia nuts

First make the pastry. Soften the butter or margarine and cream it with the sugar and egg or yolks. Then work in the flour. Using your hands, pat the dough in the bottom of a buttered 9 by 13 by 2–inch pan. Bake the pastry in a 350° F. oven for 15 minutes.

Meanwhile, make the filling by beating the eggs with the brown sugar and vanilla. Stir in the lemon rind, if used, and the flour, baking powder, and salt. Blend well. Add the coconut and nuts last. Spread the filling over the baked pastry and bake for another 20 to 25 minutes, or until filling is browned and done. Cool slightly and cut into 36 to 40 squares.

NOTE.   If desired, you may use ¾ cup chopped nuts and ¾ cup semisweet chocolate chips. Or you could omit the coconut and use 2 cups chopped nuts.

DATE BARS

These sweet bars are good rolled in powdered sugar, or frosted with a chocolate or mocha icing, or with a thin glaze flavored with orange juice and rind.

2 cups sifted flour
1 teaspoon baking powder
1 teaspoon baking soda
¼ teaspoon salt
½ cup melted butter or margarine

4 large eggs
2 cups light or dark brown sugar
2 cups chopped pitted dates
2 cups chopped walnuts, or 1 cup shredded coconut and 1 cup chopped walnuts

Sift the flour with the baking powder, baking soda, and salt. Combine the melted butter or margarine with the eggs and sugar and beat until thoroughly blended. Then stir in the sifted flour mixture and last the chopped fruit and nuts. Spread the batter in a buttered 9 by 13 by 2-inch pan. Bake in a 350° F. oven for 40 minutes. Cool in the pan and cut into squares or bars. Makes 24 to 36 squares or bars.

FROSTED CHRISTMAS BARS

These are moist and rich, fine for the holiday season. Make the pastry and bake as directed in COCONUT NUT BARS (p. 112). Add the following filling.

4 large eggs
1¾ cups light brown sugar
½ cup sifted flour
1 teaspoon baking powder
¼ teaspoon salt

1 cup raisins or chopped pitted dates
1 cup chopped walnuts or pecans
1 cup candied fruit mix or quartered candied cherries

Beat the eggs with the sugar. Stir in the flour, baking powder, and salt. Add the chopped fruits and nuts and blend ingredients thoroughly. Pour this over the baked pastry. Bake in a 325° F. oven for about

30 minutes. Spread with LEMON GLAZE (p. 99) and decorate with more nuts and candied fruits. Cut into 36 bars. If desired, these can also be served plain.

MACAROON BARS AND CAKES

These delicious macaroons can be baked as cookies, bars, or tiny cupcakes. If you wish to make bars, first make and bake the pastry as directed for COCONUT NUT BARS (page 112).

½ cup (about 4) egg whites
1 cup sugar
½ teaspoon vanilla extract or grated lemon rind (optional)

1½ cups shredded (or macaroon) coconut
1 tablespoon flour

Beat the egg whites until foamy. Gradually beat in ½ cup of the sugar, beating only until the mixture forms soft peaks. Fold in the vanilla or lemon rind, if used. Combine the remaining ½ cup sugar, coconut, and flour. Fold into the egg white mixture. Bake as follows:

COOKIES.   Line cookie sheets with silicone-treated parchment paper. Drop dough by teaspoons onto cookie sheets, leaving space for the cookies to spread. Bake in a 350° F. oven about 15 to 20 minutes, or until golden brown and dry on the surface.

CUPCAKES.   Use paper liners in the muffin pans. Fill almost, but not quite, full. Bake in a 350° F. oven about 20 to 25 minutes, or until golden brown and dry on the surface.

MACAROON BARS.   Make and bake the pastry as directed for COCONUT NUT BARS (p. 112). Spread macaroon mixture carefully over the baked pastry. Bake in a 350° F. oven for approximately 25 to 30 minutes, or until golden brown. Cool before cutting into bars. Use a very sharp knife to make the bars neat.

Any of the variations makes about 2 dozen cookies.

ORIENTALS

he Orient never saw these cookies. They are an easy-to-make, delicious
oky, a variation of shortbread.

2 cups butter or margarine,
  softened
2 to 4 tablespoons instant
  coffee
½ teaspoon salt
½ teaspoon almond extract
  (optional)

1 teaspoon vanilla extract
  (optional)
2 cups white or brown sugar
4 cups sifted flour
2 cups semisweet chocolate
  chips, or butterscotch pieces
slivered, blanched almonds
  (optional)

eat the butter or margarine until creamed. Then add the instant
offee, salt, and flavorings, if used, and beat in. Gradually add the
gar and continue beating until light and fluffy. With clean hands,
ork in all the flour and the chocolate chips. Spread the mixture in an
buttered 10 by 15 by 1–inch jelly-roll pan. Sprinkle the dough with
vered blanched almonds if desired, pressing the almonds into the
ugh just enough to make them stick. Bake in a 375° F. oven for no
nger than 18 to 20 minutes. Cool in the pan. Some people break
ese into irregular pieces, others mark the cookies, while still warm,
to bars. Store in containers with waxed paper between the layers.

SOURED CREAM BAR COOKIES

hese are best made with naturally soured heavy cream, not the com-
ercial sour cream. Let the cream stand at room temperature for at
ast 24 hours to sour naturally.

2¼ cups sifted flour
1 teaspoon cinnamon
   (optional)
½ teaspoon salt
1½ teaspoons baking soda
4 large eggs

1 pound brown sugar
1½ cups soured heavy cream
1 teaspoon vanilla extract
1½ cups chopped walnuts
1½ cups chopped pitted dates
½ to 1 cup flaked coconut

Sift the flour with the cinnamon, salt, and baking soda. Set aside. Beat
the eggs with the sugar until thick. Then add the soured cream and
vanilla. Blend in the dry ingredients and the nuts, dates, and coconut.
Spread in 2 buttered 10 by 15 by 1–inch jelly-roll pans. Bake in a
350° F. oven for 20 minutes, or until cookies test done. Cool. Frost
or not, as desired.

DOUBLE-CRUSTED PINEAPPLE BARS

PASTRY
⅓ cup butter or margarine
¾ cup light brown sugar
1 cup sifted flour
1 large egg, or 2 egg yolks
1 cup shredded coconut
FILLING
¾ cup sugar

3 tablespoons cornstarch
1 cup crushed pineapple
pinch of salt
1 teaspoon grated lemon rind
1 tablespoon lemon juice
1 tablespoon butter or
   margarine

Combine ingredients for pastry and blend thoroughly. Divide pastry in
half and press half onto the bottom of a buttered 9–inch square baking pan.
   Make the filling by stirring the sugar and cornstarch together
and then combining with the pineapple, salt, and lemon rind in a
saucepan. Cook mixture over medium heat, stirring, until clear and
thickened. Remove from heat and stir in the lemon juice and butter
or margarine. Cool filling slightly and then pour it over the pastry.
Pat out the remaining pastry on a flat surface and lay it over the filling. Brush with beaten egg yolk and sprinkle with sugar. Bake in a
350° F. oven for 25 to 30 minutes. Cool and cut into 24 bars.

REFRIGERATOR COOKIES

Refrigerator cookies are a special boon to the busy housewife because they can be made as time allows and enjoyed for weeks to come. The dough will keep in the refrigerator for 2 to 3 weeks. Any pressed cooky dough can be molded into a roll, wrapped, and refrigerated. Form the dough into rolls about 2 inches in diameter and wrap tightly in aluminum foil or waxed paper. Slice and bake as needed.

PINWHEELS. You can make these by rolling 2 different-colored doughs together.

CHECKERBOARDS. These take a little more work, but are intriguing to children. Make them as follows: Take 2 different-colored doughs, and instead of forming each into 1 roll, form each into 2 long rolls. Cut these in half to make 4 rolls. Brush each roll with milk so that they will stick together. Lay a dark roll next to a light roll, pressing so that they will stick together, and then lay the remaining rolls on top to make alternating colors. Press together, wrap, and chill thoroughly. Cut and bake.

Any refrigerator dough can be rolled in finely ground or chopped nuts before wrapping and chilling. When sliced, the cookies may be topped with half a nut or half a candied cherry, or sprinkled with colored sugar or with a mixture of sugar and cinnamon.

No business before breakfast, glum!" says the King. "Breakfast first, business next."

THACKERAY

CARDAMOM COOKIES

This is a slightly sophisticated cooky that appeals more to grownups than to children.

3¼ cups sifted flour
1 teaspoon baking powder
¾ to 1 teaspoon cardamom
1 cup butter or margarine
½ cup granulated sugar

½ cup light brown sugar
1 large egg
¾ cup heavy cream
1 cup slivered blanched
    almonds

Sift the flour with the baking powder and cardamom. Cream the butter or margarine with the sugars until light. Then beat in the egg. Stir in the sifted dry ingredients alternately with the heavy cream. Add the almonds last and knead the dough together. Form the dough into rolls 2 inches in diameter. Wrap securely in aluminum foil and refrigerate. When ready to bake, cut the dough into ⅛-inch slices and bake on ungreased cooky sheets in a 400° F. oven for 8 to 10 minutes. Makes about 3 dozen cookies.

COCONUT REFRIGERATOR COOKIES

In Hawaii they make these sweet, shortbread-type cookies with freshly grated coconut. An average-size coconut will give about 2 cups of grated meat.

2 cups sifted flour
½ teaspoon salt
1 cup butter or margarine
1 cup sugar

1 teaspoon vanilla extract
    (optional)
1½ cups freshly grated or
    shredded coconut

Sift the flour with the salt. Cream the butter or margarine and sugar until light. Add vanilla, if used. Work in the flour mixture and the grated coconut. Blend well. Shape dough into a roll about 2 inches in diameter. Wrap securely and chill at least overnight. When ready to bake, slice the dough into ¼-inch slices. Place on lightly buttered cooky sheets and bake in a 300° F. oven about 25 minutes, or until very lightly browned. Makes about 5 dozen cookies.

SPICY LAP CAKES

This fine refrigerator cooky is rich and spicy. The dough will keep in the refrigerator for several weeks.

3½ cups sifted flour
½ teaspoon cardamom
1 teaspoon baking powder
¼ teaspoon salt
½ teaspoon cinnamon
½ teaspoon cloves
½ teaspoon nutmeg
2 to 3 teaspoons anise seed
½ cup butter or margarine

½ cup sugar
½ cup light or dark molasses
2 large eggs
1 teaspoon grated lemon rind
1 tablespoon lemon juice
½ to 1 cup slivered, blanched almonds

Sift the flour with the baking powder, salt, and spices. Stir the anise seed into the sifted flour mixture. Cream the butter or margarine with the sugar and molasses until light. Add the eggs, lemon rind, and lemon juice and blend well. Then work in the sifted flour mixture and the almonds. The batter should be smooth and workable. Form the dough into 2 rolls about 2 inches in diameter. Wrap in aluminum foil and twist the ends. Chill for at least 24 hours before slicing. The flavors in this dough blend and mellow with the refrigerator storage. When ready to bake, cut the roll into slices no more than ¼ inch thick. Place on a buttered cooky sheet and bake in a 300° F. oven about 20 minutes. Recipe makes about 4 dozen.

NOTE. If desired, you may grind the almonds and roll the dough in them to form a fine coating.

ROLLED COOKIES

Christmas would hardly seem like Christmas without fancifully shaped and decorated cookies. This type of decorated cooky (in Europe the holiday cookies are often very intricately decorated) is thought to have originated in pre-Christian times as offerings to various gods.

I like to make very large cookies for Christmas giving, made as follows: Trace a design on a sturdy piece of paper. Cut it out and lay the paper over the cooky dough (the SPICED HONEY COOKIES [p. 125] are best for this) and carefully cut around it. To keep from breaking the large cookies, roll a portion of the dough out directly on the cooky sheet. After the cooky is cut, the unused portion is easily lifted off. After baking and cooling, the cookies are usually decorated with ORNAMENTAL COOKY FROSTING (p. 154). Any design appropriate to the season may be used.

Cookies that are to be rolled generally need more flour to enable the baker to roll the dough without breaking it. On the other hand, too much flour makes a dough that rolls beautifully but is virtually inedible. It is best to use as little flour as is possible and to chill the dough for at least 1 hour before rolling it. Then work with small portions at a time, keeping the rest of the dough in the refrigerator until it is used. Roll the dough out on a *very* lightly floured breadboard, or on a pastry canvas, or between sheets of waxed paper that have been sprayed with Pam (this is a clear vegetable coating which is sold in spray cans or in bottles with a brush to brush it on. It prevents sticking and is very useful). Cut the shapes as close together as possible. The excess dough can be rerolled and reused; but if much flour has been used, the dough will be less tender.

MORAVIAN WHITE CHRISTMAS COOKIES

These cookies, made by Pennsylvania Dutch housewives, are made each Christmas from recipes that have been handed down from mother to daughter for generations. This recipe, which can be rolled, chilled, and baked as ordinary refrigerator cookies, is exceptionally good.

4 to 5 cups sifted flour	3 cups sugar
1 teaspoon nutmeg	4 large eggs
1 teaspoon baking soda	1 cup heavy cream
1½ cups butter or margarine	1 tablespoon vanilla extract

Sift 3 cups of the flour with the nutmeg and baking soda and set aside. Cream the butter or margarine with the sugar until very light and fluffy. Add the eggs and beat in. Combine the heavy cream with the vanilla extract and stir into the creamed mixture alternately with the sifted flour mixture. Now add enough of the remaining flour to make a tender dough, not stiff but not too soft. Chill the dough overnight or for several days. When ready to bake, take portions of the dough and roll out on a lightly floured breadboard. The dough should be thin. Cut into shapes, hearts, stars, crescents, etc., and place on lightly buttered cooky sheets. Bake in a 350° F. oven about 10 to 12 minutes. Cool on racks. Makes approximately 5 dozen cookies, depending on size.

NEW ORLEANS ALMOND COOKIES

This rich, shortbread-type cooky shows the French influence on Louisiana cookery. It may be served plain or with a sifting of powdered sugar. The variation below has visual as well as taste appeal.

1 cup sifted flour	4 large egg yolks
pinch of salt	½ cup unblanched almonds,
1 teaspoon grated lemon rind	measured when whole and then
(optional)	grated
½ cup butter (no substitute)	½ cup very finely diced candied
½ cup sugar	fruits (optional)

Sift the flour with the salt. Using your hands, work all of the ingredients together. If the dough appears too soft to roll, chill it in the refrigerator for 45 minutes. Then roll the dough out on a very lightly floured breadboard to a thickness of about ¼ to ⅓ inch. Cut into circles or heart shapes. Place on a very lightly buttered cooky sheet and bake in a 300° F. oven for 20 to 25 minutes, or until cookies are set and are a pale golden color. Cool on racks. Makes about 18 cookies.

CINNAMON LEAF COOKIES. Make basic recipe, omitting the lemon rind and the candied fruit. Add ¾ teaspoon cinnamon. Roll the dough and chill as for refrigerator cookies. When ready to bake, cut the dough into ¼-inch slices. Pinch each circle of dough to form the shape of a leaf. Cut a center vein, and the smaller, side veins with the blunt edge of a knife spreading the cuts slightly so that they do not bake together. Bake in a 350° F. oven for about 12 minutes.

FILLED ALMOND WAFERS. Make basic recipe and roll the dough to a thickness of ¼ inch. Cut into circles, leaving enough cooky dough to form twice as many strips of dough as you have circles. Dot each circle with a small spoonful of jam or preserves. Crisscross 2 strips of dough over each circle and pinch the edges. Bake on a very lightly buttered cooky sheet in a 350° F. oven about 12 minutes, or until set and a pale golden color. Makes about 12 to 14 cookies.

BUTTERY CARAWAY CAKES

These buttery cakes are a Christmas tradition in many families and are usually cut in the shape of a star. If you don't like the flavor of caraway, the seeds can be omitted.

3 cups sifted flour	4 large eggs
½ teaspoon baking soda	¼ cup sherry, Madeira, or
½ to 1 teaspoon mace	brandy
1½ cups butter or margarine	¼ to ½ teaspoon caraway seeds
3 cups sifted powdered sugar	

Sift the flour with the baking soda and mace. Cream the butter or margarine and sugar until light. Beat in the eggs, 1 at a time, until thoroughly blended into the creamed mixture. Add the sherry or other liquor and beat for several minutes Then stir in the sifted flour mixture and the caraway seeds. Chill the dough for 2 hours or until it is firm enough to roll. Cut into desired shapes and bake on a lightly buttered cooky sheet in a 350° F. oven for 10 to 12 minutes.

NOTE. These may be brushed with cream and sprinkled with slivered or grated nuts before baking. Early recipes called for large quantities of caraway seed, but this doesn't appeal to most modern tastes.

CINNAMON STARS

One of the most popular Christmas cookies, the dough for this should be of a consistency that does not permit rolling. Using your hands, you should pat the dough to the desired thickness. The star shape is traditional, but other shapes are also appealing. The origins of this fine cooky are European, but it has been appearing on American holiday tables since early Colonial times.

¾ cup (about 6) egg whites	1 teaspoon grated lemon rind
1 pound superfine granulated sugar or sifted powdered sugar	1 pound grated, unblanched almonds
1 tablespoon cinnamon	sugar
	flour

Beat the egg whites until they form stiff peaks. Gradually beat in the sugar and then the cinnamon and lemon rind. Beat in the grated almonds last. Dust a breadboard or pastry canvas with a mixture of equal parts of sugar and flour. Working with small portions of dough at a time, pat it out to a thickness of ⅜ inch. Cut with a cooky cutter or cut into squares or oblongs. Place on lightly buttered cooky sheets and bake in a 275° F. oven about 25 to 30 minutes. Makes about 4 dozen.

VARIATIONS

1. Add 1 or 2 tablespoons cocoa to the dough. Or (and this is best) grate ¼ pound sweet cooking chocolate and add to the dough.

2. Omit cinnamon. In the blender whirl 1 vanilla bean with several tablespoons of the sugar until the bean is finely ground. Beat into the egg whites. These cookies are fragrant and delicious.

3. Finely ground hazelnuts can be used instead of the almonds.

4. Omit cinnamon and add 1 or 2 tablespoons of rose water. If you wish a stronger fragrance and flavor, these may be glazed with a thin mixture of sifted powdered sugar and rose water.

LEMONY BUTTER COOKIES

These have an especially fine, delicate, lemon flavor. Use freshly grated lemon rind and real butter for the finest flavor. This recipe may also be shaped and baked as for refrigerator cookies.

2 cups sifted flour	2 or 3 teaspoons grated lemon
1¾ cups sugar	rind
1 cup butter, softened	2 large egg yolks

Combine all ingredients and work together, using your hands, until the dough is thoroughly blended. Chill the dough for about 1½ to 2 hours. Then, using a portion at a time, roll the dough on a very lightly floured breadboard to a thickness of ¼ to ⅓ inch. Cut into any desired shape and place the cookies on a lightly buttered cooky sheet. Bake in a 325° F. oven about 15 minutes, or until set and a pale butter color. Cool on racks. Makes about 18 to 24 cookies, depending on size.

GINGERSNAPS!

Gingersnaps have been popular with children for generations, and today's children have seldom tasted a true gingersnap. This excellent recipe makes cookies that really snap.

4½ to 5 cups sifted flour	1 cup butter or margarine
¼ teaspoon cinnamon	1 cup brown sugar
¼ teaspoon cloves	1 cup molasses
1 teaspoon ginger	1 tablespoon vinegar
2 teaspoons baking soda	1 large egg

Sift the flour with the spices and baking soda. Combine the butter or margarine, sugar, molasses, and vinegar in a saucepan. Heat until the butter is melted and ingredients are thoroughly blended. Remove from heat and cool to lukewarm. Then beat in the egg and the sifted flour mixture, using enough to make a dough that can be rolled out. Roll dough on a lightly floured breadboard. Cut into desired shapes and place on buttered cooky sheets. Bake in a 350° F. oven about 10 minutes. These bear close watching as recipes using molasses will scorch easily. Cool on racks and glaze or decorate as desired.

SPICED HONEY COOKIES

This fine recipe has its origins in the spicy, fruited cookies of Germany, the *Nürnberger* and *Lebkuchen*. This is a large recipe, but as it will only make approximately 12 to 14 giant cookies, we usually double or triple the recipe so that each child can remember teachers and friends. Properly wrapped (I use plastic wrap), the cookies keep very well and, indeed, improve with age. I usually make them as the beginning of the Christmas cooky baking. If you wish to make simple, smaller cutouts, the orange peel can be omitted, or it can be ground.

6 cups sifted flour
1 teaspoon baking soda
½ teaspoon salt
1 teaspoon cinnamon
½ teaspoon ginger
½ teaspoon cloves
¼ teaspoon nutmeg
1⅓ cups (1-pound jar) mild-flavored honey such as orange or clover

1½ cups dark brown sugar
4 large eggs
1 tablespoon grated lemon rind
1¼ cups finely chopped candied orange peel
1 cup finely chopped candied lemon peel or citron
1 cup finely grated or ground unblanched almonds

Sift the flour with the baking soda, salt, and spices and set aside. Pour the honey in a saucepan and bring just to a boil. Remove from heat immediately and stir in the sugar, stirring until sugar is dissolved. Cool to room temperature. Beat the eggs with the lemon rind until light. Blend in the honey mixture. Then add the sifted flour mixture and the candied fruits and nuts. Work the dough until it is thoroughly blended. Chill the dough in the refrigerator overnight. Some cooks let the dough chill for several days to give the flavors a chance to blend. When ready to bake, work with a small portion of the dough at a time. Roll it out on a pastry canvas, or a very lightly floured breadboard, or between sheets of waxed paper that have been sprayed with Pam. Cut into shapes and place on a well-buttered cooky sheet. Bake in a 375° F.

oven about 15 minutes, or until lightly browned and done. Watch carefully.

If you wish to make giant cookies, take a portion of the dough and roll it out on a well-buttered cooky sheet. Lay the design over the dough and carefully cut around it. Remove excess dough, and bake the cooky in a 375° F. oven about 15 minutes, or until lightly browned. Cool the cooky for a few minutes on the cooky sheet so that it can then be removed to a rack without breaking. Cool thoroughly before decorating.

SHORTBREAD

Shortbread is probably the most basic of all cookies. True shortbread is made only with flour, sugar, and fine butter, and is kneaded with the hands to form a smooth dough. Baked in pans, it is broken, not cut, into pieces. We like this recipe, and the variations are almost endless—some very simple, some more difficult.

1 pound butter, softened (no substitute)

1 cup superfine granulated sugar or sifted powdered sugar

4 cups flour, preferably bread flour

1 teaspoon baking powder

Combine ingredients and, using your hands, work to form a smooth, soft dough. This will take time, but the warmth of your hands helps. Press the dough, about ½ inch thick, into ungreased pans. Or the dough may be pressed into circular shapes on an ungreased cooky sheet. Bake in a 325° F. oven about 20 minutes, or until shortbread is a pale gold. Cool. If you wish to cut the shortbread into neat wedges, cut while warm.

VARIATIONS

1. Roll dough into small balls. Press a pecan half, or a blanched almond half, or half a candied cherry in the center of each. Bake in a 350° F. oven until pale golden. Roll in powdered sugar while warm.

2. The dough may be rolled to a thickness of ¼ inch. Cut into small rounds, about 1 to 1½ inches in diameter. Decorate with candied cherry half before baking. Bake in a 350° F. oven just until golden.

3. Roll the dough to a thickness of ¼ inch. Cut with a doughnut cutter. Brush cookies with beaten egg white and sprinkle heavily with finely chopped pistachio nuts. Bake as directed above. These may be tied on a cooky tree with bright ribbon.

4. Blend 1 cup of grated pecans or other nuts into the dough. Roll dough into small balls and place on ungreased cooky sheets. Bake in 350° F. oven until a pale gold. Roll in powdered sugar while warm.

5. Blend half the dough with 1 cup finely shredded coconut and 1 tablespoon grated orange rind. Roll into small balls and bake as directed above. Roll in powdered sugar while warm.

CHOCOLATE SHORTBREAD. To half the basic recipe add 1 teaspoon vanilla extract and 2 squares unsweetened chocolate, melted. Press dough into lightly buttered pans and bake in a 325° F. oven for 20 minutes.

CHOCOLATE-CHIP SHORTBREAD. Make half the basic recipe increasing sugar to 1 cup. Add 2 large eggs, ½ teaspoon vanilla extract, and 1 cup semisweet chocolate chips. Press dough into a lightly buttered 9 by 13 by 2–inch pan. Bake in a 350° F. oven for 20 minutes. Cut into bars or squares while warm.

CHOCOLATE FROSTED SHORTBREAD. Make basic recipe, pressing it into a 10 by 15 by 1–inch jelly-roll pan. Bake as directed. Melt 1 cup semisweet chocolate chips and spread over the hot shortbread. Sprinkle generously with chopped nuts. Cut into bars while warm.

CINNAMON SHORTBREAD. Make basic recipe replacing sugar with 1½ cups light brown sugar and adding 1 or 2 teaspoons cinnamon. Press dough into two 9-inch square pans. Bake in a 325° F. oven for approximately 35 minutes. Cut into bars while warm.

RAISIN SHORTBREAD.   Make basic recipe, adding 1 cup raisins that have been plumped for 5 minutes in hot water and then drained and chopped. Roll the dough to a thickness of about ⅓ inch. Cut into shapes and place on lightly buttered cooky sheets. Bake in a 375° F. oven for 10 to 12 minutes, or until golden. Frost or decorate as desired.

RUM SHORTBREAD.   Make half the basic recipe, using butter that has been melted and browned slightly and then cooled. Add 1 tablespoon rum. Chill the dough before rolling to a thickness of ¼ inch. Cut with very small cutters and place on lightly buttered cooky sheets. Bake in a 400° F. oven for about 10 minutes.

RUM ALMOND SHORTBREAD.   To Rum Shortbread add ½ cup finely chopped, blanched almonds.

SWEDISH BRANDY SHORTBREAD.   Make basic recipe using only 1½ cups butter. Add ¼ cup brandy, rum, or lemon juice, and ½ cup chopped, blanched almonds. Roll into small balls and bake in a 350° F. oven until set, but not colored. Roll in powdered sugar while warm.

MOLDED AND DROP COOKIES

It is a thin line indeed that separates these two types of cookies. The drop cookie may be a fine wafer with the delicacy of old lace, or it may be the traditional lumpy jumble or rock cake that have been children's treats for so many generations. Other drop cooky recipes suggest chilling the dough and then molding into the balls and crescents that grace the holiday cooky tray.

Any drop cooky batter that is not lumpy can be prettily shaped by forcing through a pastry bag fitted with a large plain or serrated tube.

The cookies can be round or swirled, and are certainly more attractive than when dropped from a spoon. Even the lump cookies benefit by being chilled before baking, as this allows the baker to use a little less flour to make a more tender dough. The cooky dough can be molded into small balls instead of being dropped, to make more attractive, evenly round cookies.

BILLY GOATS

These superb date cakes evidently originated in the Western states. Many early California cookbooks list recipes for them. If desired, you may use raisins in place of any, or all, of the dates. I sometimes use a pound of each. This recipe is easily halved. But these cookies freeze well.

4 cups sifted flour	1 cup commercial sour cream
4 teaspoons baking powder	1 teaspoon vanilla extract
1 teaspoon baking soda	(optional)
½ teaspoon salt	1 or 2 teaspoons allspice or
1 cup butter or margarine	nutmeg
2 cups sugar	1 pound chopped walnuts
4 large eggs	2 pounds chopped, pitted
	dates

Sift the flour with the baking powder, baking soda, and salt. Cream the butter or margarine with the sugar until fluffy. Add the eggs and beat in, then add the sour cream and flavorings. Blend ingredients. Now add the sifted flour mixture, nuts, and dates. Work all together thoroughly. Drop from a tablespoon onto buttered cooky sheets and bake in a 350° F. oven until golden brown and done, from 12 to 15 minutes depending on the size of the cookies. Makes from 5 to 6 dozen.

HOLIDAY BONBONS

These also keep very well, and preserves other than pineapple can be used.

1½ pounds chopped pecans
¾ pound mixed candied
  fruits, chopped
½ pound dark or light raisins,
  or chopped, pitted dates
3½ cups sifted flour
1 teaspoon nutmeg
1 teaspoon cinnamon

2 teaspoons baking soda
½ cup butter or margarine
1 cup light brown sugar
4 large eggs
2 tablespoons milk
⅓ cup whisky, rum, or
  brandy
½ to 1-pound jar of pineapple
  preserves

Combine chopped pecans and fruits and blend with 1 cup of the flour. Sift the remaining flour with the spices and baking soda. Cream the butter or margarine with the sugar and eggs until light and well blended. Add the milk and liquor to the creamed mixture alternately with the sifted flour mixture. Now add the chopped fruit and nut mixture all at once and work into the batter with the hands. Work in ½ pound of the preserves, adding more if needed to make a dough that is about the consistency of a thickly fruited hermit or jumble. Bake in paper-lined muffin pans which have very small cups in a 350° F. oven about 12 minutes. Glaze with hot, clear corn syrup and cool completely before storing. Makes 6 to 8 dozen.

BREADCRUMB COOKIES

1½ cups fine, dry
  breadcrumbs
1 cup chopped nuts
1 cup chopped raisins or
  chopped, pitted dates
1¾ cups light brown sugar

1 or 2 teaspoons vanilla
  extract
pinch of salt
3 large eggs
⅓ cup evaporated milk
2 or 3 tablespoons melted
  butter

In a large mixing bowl, combine the ingredients in the order given. Using your hands, blend all ingredients thoroughly. Then drop by tablespoons onto a lightly buttered cooky sheet. Bake in a 375° F. oven about 15 minutes, or until browned. Cool on racks. Makes about 3 to 4 dozen cookies, depending on size.

CALIFORNIA PERSIMMON COOKIES

This fine fruit cooky lends itself well to variations. For example, you might use 1 cup of one of the following in place of the persimmon pulp: drained, crushed pineapple, canned, whole cranberry sauce, applesauce, or cooked, mashed prunes. And, instead of making drop cookies, you might spread the batter in 2 buttered 8-inch square pans. Bake and cut into small squares or bars while still warm.

2 cups sifted flour (you can use part whole-wheat flour)
1 teaspoon baking soda
¼ teaspoon salt
1 teaspoon cinnamon
½ teaspoon nutmeg
½ cup butter or margarine
1 to 1½ cups sugar

1 large egg
1 teaspoon vanilla extract
1 teaspoon grated lemon or orange rind (optional)
1 cup persimmon pulp
1 cup raisins or chopped, pitted dates
½ to 1 cup chopped nuts

Sift the flour with the baking soda, salt, and spices. Cream the butter or margarine with the sugar until light. Add the egg and flavorings and blend. Stir in the persimmon pulp, the sifted dry ingredients, and the fruit and nuts. Blend thoroughly. Drop by spoonfuls onto buttered cooky sheets, and bake in a 350° F. oven for 20 minutes. Cool on racks. Recipe makes 3 to 4 dozen cookies.

BUTTERMILK COOKIES

The original recipe for this old cooky called for lard or bear fat! If you don't want to roll and cut these cookies, they may be dropped from a tablespoon and baked as drop cookies. And, of course, you may add chocolate chips or chopped nuts or some raisins to the basic dough.

4 cups sifted flour
¼ teaspoon salt
1 teaspoon nutmeg
1 teaspoon baking soda
1 cup butter or margarine

2 cups sugar
1 large egg, or 2 egg yolks
1 cup buttermilk, sour milk, or thin yogurt
1 teaspoon vanilla extract

Sift 2 cups of the flour with the salt, nutmeg, and baking soda. Cream the butter or margarine with the sugar until light. Then beat in the egg or yolks, buttermilk, or other liquid and vanilla. Work in the sifted flour mixture, then add enough of the remaining flour to make a smooth dough that can be rolled, if desired. Again, do not add too much flour. Chill the dough before you roll and cut or drop and bake. Bake on buttered cooky sheets in a 400° F. oven for 10 to 12 minutes. Watch carefully. Depending on how large you cut, or drop, the cookies, this recipe will make from 3 to 5 dozen cookies.

CHERRY-NUT COOKIES

The dough for these marvelous cookies can be kept in the refrigerator for several days or frozen for a longer period. I sometimes roll the dough as for refrigerator cookies, and then slice them and bake as needed.

4 cups sifted flour
1 teaspoon baking soda
½ teaspoon salt
1⅓ cups butter or margarine, softened
2 cups brown sugar
3 large eggs

1 teaspoon vanilla extract (optional)
1 teaspoon grated lemon rind
1⅓ cups chopped pecans
1⅓ cups quartered candied cherries
1⅓ cups chopped, pitted dates

Sift the flour with the baking soda and salt. Set aside. Cream the softened butter or margarine with the brown sugar until light and fluffy. Add the eggs and beat in thoroughly. Add the flavorings and then the sifted dry ingredients. Work in the chopped nuts and fruits last. Drop by teaspoons onto buttered cooky sheets and bake in a 375° F. oven for 12 to 15 minutes, or until lightly browned and done.

CHERRY HEARTS.   Omit the dates and decrease the butter, nuts, and cherries to 1 cup *each*. Add 1 cup commercial sour cream and work the dough thoroughly. Chill the dough for several hours and then pat out on a very lightly floured breadboard to a thickness of ¼ inch. Cut with heart-shaped cutters and place on lightly buttered cooky sheets. Bake as above.

CHOCOLATE BALLS

2½ cups sifted flour
1 cup butter or margarine
½ cup sugar
1 large egg yolk
1 tablespoon brandy, rum, Kirsch, or fruit juice
1 teaspoon vanilla extract

1 cup very finely chopped or grated walnuts
3 squares unsweetened chocolate, melted and cooled, or 2 tablespoons cocoa
3 dozen walnut halves

Sift the flour again and set aside. Cream the butter or margarine until light. Add the sugar and beat until fluffy. Beat in the egg yolk, brandy or other liquid, vanilla, and chopped nuts. Stir in, just until thoroughly blended, the chocolate or cocoa. Stir in the flour last, working until the dough is well blended, but taking care not to overwork. Chill the dough for about 1 hour. Then roll the dough into small balls and roll each ball in granulated or superfine sugar. Place on buttered cooky sheets and press a walnut half into each ball, pressing slightly. Bake in a 325° F. oven about 15 minutes, or until the cookies have a crackled appearance. Cool on racks. Makes about 3 dozen cookies.

CHRISTMAS FRUITCAKE COOKIES

These are simply great! They are lovely to look at, easy to make, fabulous eating, and expensive. They keep well and can thus be made early in the Christmas baking, and of course they lend themselves easily to variety. As long as you keep the proportions in mind, you can use a variety of nuts (as I do) or all of one type of nut. The candied fruits may be varied and raisins can be substituted for all or part of the dates.

1½ pounds pitted dates, chopped
½ pound candied cherries, quartered
½ pound candied pineapple, sliced
1 cup dark or light raisins
½ pound walnuts, chopped
½ pound pecans, chopped
½ pound Brazil nuts, slivered
½ pound blanched almonds, slivered and toasted
⅓ cup brandy, rum, whisky or wine
2½ cups sifted flour
1 teaspoon baking soda
1 teaspoon salt
1 teaspoon cinnamon
1 cup butter or margarine
1½ cups sugar
2 large eggs

In a large bowl combine all the fruits and nuts. Stir in the liquor and set aside. This may be covered and left for several days, if desired. When ready to bake, sift the flour with the baking soda, salt, and cinnamon. Cream the butter or margarine with the sugar and eggs until thoroughly blended. Stir in the sifted flour mixture. Then (you will need to use your hands) add and work in thoroughly all the fruits and nut mixture. These cookies may be dropped and baked on buttered cooky sheets or the dough may be baked in muffin tins with cups that measure 1¼ inches across and less than an inch deep. You can buy tiny paper liners for these tins, and the cookies are most attractive when baked in them. Bake the cookies in a 400° F. oven for 10 minutes. Watch carefully as they must not be allowed to overbake. Cool on racks and store in airtight containers. Makes 10 dozen cookies, a large amount, but the recipe is easily halved if you think this makes too much. When you are ready to serve these, brush them lightly with clear corn syrup that has just been brought to a boil. If you wish to glaze the cookies before storing them, the glaze must be allowed to dry thoroughly before wrapping and storing the cookies.

COLONIAL POUND CAKES

This fine recipe has been in use in one family for well over a hundred years. It is a basic butter drop cookie that can be varied by using chopped nuts, candied fruit peels, or semisweet chocolate chips. I vary it further by occasionally using brandy, rum, whisky, or Kirsch in place of the lemon juice, and of course other fruit juices can be used.

3½ cups sifted flour	6 large eggs
½ teaspoon salt	3 tablespoons lemon or
1 teaspoon baking powder	orange juice
2 cups (1 pound) butter or margarine	1 tablespoon grated lemon or orange rind
2 cups (1 pound) granulated or light brown sugar	1 pound chopped walnuts or pecans

Sift the flour with the salt and baking powder. Cream the butter or margarine until very light and fluffy. Gradually add the sugar and continue beating. Add the eggs, 1 at a time, and beating after each addition. Add the flavorings with the last egg. Then work in the flour mixture and the chopped nuts. Chill the dough in the refrigerator for 1 hour. Drop by spoonfuls onto well-buttered cooky sheets. Bake in a 375° F. oven for 10 minutes, or until cookies are barely golden and set, but not brown. Cool on racks. Makes about 6 dozen.

CHESS CAKES. Bake the cakes in well-buttered muffin tins which have cups about 1¼ inches across and slightly less than an inch deep. They can also be baked in the small, fluted, tart molds that are about 1½ inches across the top. Bake at 375° F. for 12 to 15 minutes. These are very delicate and tasty.

CRESCENTS

These rich cookies are holiday favorites. Some shape the dough into upside-down U shapes, while other cooks prefer the half-moon, or crescent. They can also be shaped into various letters. Some good cooks omit any flavoring in the cooky itself, preferring that nothing detract from the delicate taste of good butter, a necessity in this cooky. But the cookies are always rolled in a flavored sugar. I have achieved good results by using grated lemon or orange rind in the cooky dough, and rolling them in LEMON SUGAR or ORANGE SUGAR.

2¼ cups sifted flour
1 cup butter (no substitute)
¾ to 1 cup superfine granulated or sifted powdered sugar
1 or 2 teaspoons vanilla extract or grated lemon or orange rind

1¼ cups grated, unblanched almonds, walnuts, pecans, or filberts
VANILLA, LEMON, or ORANGE SUGAR (p. 153)

Sift the flour again and set aside. Cream the butter with the sugar, flavoring, grated nuts, and flour. You will need to work the dough with your hands until it is smooth. If the dough appears too soft, chill it for about 45 minutes. Shape small pieces of the dough as suggested above. Place on ungreased cooky sheets and bake in a 325° F. oven about 15 to 18 minutes. They should be very lightly browned. Cool 1 minute and then roll in the flavored sugar. If desired, these may be rolled in 1 cup sifted powdered sugar which has been blended with ½ to ¾ teaspoon ground cardamom.

NOTE. The nuts may be omitted and finely chopped candied fruits may be used. The dough may be rolled, chilled, and baked as for refrigerator cookies, only bake at 325° F.

BASIC FILLED COOKY DOUGH

These cookies can be varied endlessly according to the filling used. One way of varying them is to use different shapes of cooky-cutters (filled cookies don't have to be round!). Use heart-shaped cutters, diamond shapes, bells, Santa Claus (the filling makes a fine, fat tummy), Easter bunnies, or circles with the center cut out of the top round.

3 cups flour, sifted	¾ cup butter
2 teaspoons baking powder	¼ cup milk
½ teaspoon salt	2 large eggs
1 cup sugar	1 teaspoon vanilla extract

Sift the flour with the baking powder and salt. Set aside. Cream the sugar with the softened (but not melted) butter until blended. Stir in the milk, eggs, and flavoring. Add the sifted dry ingredients gradually, stirring until thoroughly blended. Chill the dough for 45 minutes to an hour. When ready to bake, roll small portions of the dough, keeping the unused portion refrigerated, out on a lightly floured breadboard. Cut into 2- or 3-inch rounds. Place 1 teaspoon filling on half of the rounds. Top with another round and seal the edges by pressing with the tines of a fork. Place on lightly buttered cooky sheets. Bake in a 375° F. oven for 15 minutes, or until done.

FRUIT FILLINGS

APRICOT FILLING.   Combine and blend well: ¾ cup fairly stiff apricot preserves, 2 tablespoons chopped candied cherries, and 4 to 6 tablespoons chopped toasted almonds.

FIG FILLING.   Combine in a saucepan: 1½ cups chopped dried figs, ⅓ cup sugar, and ½ cup water or fruit juice. Cook over medium heat, stirring until thickened. Remove from heat and stir in 2 teaspoons lemon juice and 1 teaspoon grated lemon rind. Cool before using.

RAISIN FILLING.   Combine in a saucepan: 1½ cups chopped raisins, ⅔ cup light brown or granulated sugar, 2 tablespoons flour, an-
½ cup orange juice or water. Cook over medium heat, stirring unti-
thickened. Remove from heat and stir in 1 tablespoon grated orang-
rind if orange juice was used, or 2 teaspoons vanilla extract if wate-
was used. Cool before using.

RAISIN NUT FILLING.   Make recipe above, and when mixture ha-
cooled, stir in ½ cup chopped almonds, walnuts, or pecans.

MINCEMEAT FILLING.   Combine in a saucepan: 1½ cups mincemeat, ¼ cup sugar, 1 tablespoon cornstarch, and 1 tablespoon lemo-
juice. Cook over medium heat, stirring until thickened. Remove fro-
heat and cool before using.

MATRIMONIAL BARS

Nobody seems to remember where these cookies got their unusua-
name. They are made chiefly in the Midwest. Traditionally they ar-
always made with a date filling, but I often use the fillings that ar-
suggested for BASIC FILLED COOKY DOUGH (page 137).

1½ cups flour, sifted	½ teaspoon baking soda
½ teaspoon salt	1 cup rolled oats
1 teaspoon baking powder	¾ cup butter

Sift the flour with the salt, baking powder, and soda. Sift into a bow-
Stir in the rolled oats. Cut in the butter, as for pie pastry, until the piece-
are the size of small peas. Press half the dough into the bottom of-
buttered 9 by 13-inch baking pan. Spread with DATE FILLING or another desired filling. Cover with the second half of the dough and bakin a 325° F. oven for 1 hour. Cool. Cut into 2½ to 3 dozen squares-
or bars.

DATE FILLING.   Combine in a saucepan: 2 cups chopped pitte-
dates, 1 cup light brown sugar, ¾ cup water, and 1 tablespoon lemo-
juice. Cook over medium heat, stirring until thickened (about 10 minutes). Cool before using.

FILLED DATE DROPS

This is an easy-to-make filled cooky that is especially popular with children and men.

FILLING

2 cups chopped, pitted dates
½ cup granulated sugar or brown sugar
¾ cup pineapple juice or orange juice
¾ cup chopped nuts

COOKY DOUGH

3½ cups sifted flour
¼ teaspoon salt

1 teaspoon baking soda
1 cup butter or margarine
2 cups light or dark brown sugar
2 large eggs
½ cup buttermilk, sour milk, or yogurt
1 teaspoon vanilla extract
1 tablespoon grated orange rind (if you use orange juice)

Combine the filling ingredients in a saucepan and cook over medium heat, stirring, until thick. Set aside to cool thoroughly. Sift the flour with the salt and baking soda. Cream the butter or margarine with the sugar until fluffy. Add the eggs, buttermilk, sour milk or yogurt, and the flavorings. Blend. Then add the sifted dry ingredients and work to a smooth dough. Separate the dough into 2 parts with ⅔ of the dough in 1 part. From the larger portion of the dough, drop generous spoonfuls (not as large as a tablespoon but more than a teaspoon) of dough onto ungreased cooky sheets. Place a little more than ½ teaspoon of filling on each, and top this with about ½ teaspoon of batter from the smaller portion of dough. Bake in a 400° F. oven about 10 minutes. Recipe makes approximately 4 dozen cookies.

EGG CAKES

The use of riced, hard-cooked egg yolks intensifies the rich, eggy taste in these delicious little cookies.

3 cups sifted flour
¼ teaspoon salt
1 cup sugar
1 cup butter (no substitute)

1 or 2 teaspoons grated lemon
  rind (optional)
2 hard-cooked egg yolks
2 raw egg yolks

Sift the flour with the salt and sugar onto a breadboard or into a mixing bowl. Add the remaining ingredients and work all together with your hands until thoroughly blended. Chill the dough for about 45 minutes. Then break off pieces and roll each piece into a 5- or 6-inch roll. Shape the rolls into wreaths, or form a wreath and cross the ends. Brush the cookies with slightly beaten egg whites and sprinkle with crushed loaf sugar or with colored coarse sugar. Bake in a 375° F. oven about 12 minutes. Makes approximately 5 or 6 dozen cookies.

RICH GOLD COOKIES

These fine cookies, besides using up extra egg yolks, can be rolled into small balls as suggested, or they can be shaped into letters of the alphabet.

3¼ cups sifted flour
¼ teaspoon salt
1 cup butter or margarine
1 cup granulated or powdered
  sugar
6 large egg yolks

1 tablespoon grated lemon or
  orange rind
2 tablespoons lemon or
  orange juice
1 extra egg yolk, beaten
grated almonds

Sift the flour with the salt. Cream the butter or margarine until light and gradually beat in the sugar, creaming until mixture is fluffy. Add the egg yolks 1 at a time, and beat in after each. Then beat in the grated rind and juice. Add the sifted dry ingredients and work into the dough thoroughly. Knead the dough with your hands until it is smooth and well blended. Chill the dough for an hour. Then roll the dough into small balls, using about 2 teaspoons of dough for each ball. Dip the top of each ball in the beaten egg yolk and then in the grated almonds. Place on an ungreased cooky sheet. Bake in a 350° F. oven for 10 to 12 minutes, or until a pale gold. Makes 3 to 4 dozen cookies.

NOTE. If you wish to shape the dough into letters, first roll spoonfuls of the dough into small ropes and then shape these into the letters. Bake on a lightly buttered cookie sheet.

HERMITS

This old-fashioned cooky has been a favorite for many generations, and in the South no Christmas is complete without them.

3 cups sifted flour
1 teaspoon baking soda
½ teaspoon cloves
2 teaspoons cinnamon
¼ teaspoon mace (optional)
¼ teaspoon nutmeg
  (optional)

1 cup butter or margarine
1½ cups brown sugar
3 large eggs
1 tablespoon grated lemon
  rind
1 cup each: chopped walnuts,
  raisins, and pitted dates

Sift the flour with the baking soda and spices. Cream the butter or margarine until smooth. Add the sugar and eggs and beat in thoroughly. Then add the lemon rind and work in the sifted dry ingredients. Work in the nuts and fruits last. Drop by tablespoons onto buttered cooky sheets. Bake in a 375° F. oven until browned, 15 to 18 minutes. Cool on racks. Glaze with a simple glaze.

NOTE. For Christmas I omit the fruits and nuts mentioned in the basic recipe and use instead: 1 cup chopped filberts and 2 cups of snipped, dried apricots. The large, soft kind are best. I then use an APRICOT GLAZE (page 99).

MAPLE HERMITS. To basic recipe add 3 tablespoons maple syrup. No other substitutions necessary.

KITCHEN CUPBOARD COOKIES

A friend calls these her "take as you think" cookies. She makes the basic dough and then looks in the baking cupboard, thinking and taking from whatever happens to be there. The cookies are very good, simple, and remain moist.

3½ cups sifted flour
1 teaspoon baking soda
½ teaspoon salt
1 cup butter or margarine, softened
2 cups brown sugar
2 large eggs

⅓ to ½ cup buttermilk, sour milk, or yogurt
1 teaspoon vanilla extract
1 cup of 1 of the following: chopped walnuts; raisins; chopped, pitted dates; candied fruits; diced dried figs; shredded coconut

Sift the flour with the baking soda and salt. Set aside. Cream the butter or margarine with the sugar until light. Add the eggs and beat in. Combine the ⅓ cup of liquid used with the vanilla. Add to the creamed mixture alternately with the dry ingredients. Add a little more liquid only if necessary. Work in the nuts or fruits last. Chill the dough for at least 2 hours. Then drop by teaspoons onto lightly buttered cooky sheets and bake in a 375° F. oven about 10 to 12 minutes. Cool on racks.

NOTE. You may also add 2 cups of well-drained fruit cocktail. These will be especially moist, with a good flavor. If you use the walnuts, you might chop them very fine, add ½ teaspoon almond extract and shape the dough into small balls. Flatten the balls slightly by pressing a walnut half in the center of each.

OATMEAL COOKIES

Certainly no book with a basic theme of American baking could be complete without a recipe for oatmeal cookies. The cookies may be dropped and baked, or (I prefer this) the dough can be chilled for several hours or overnight and then shaped into balls. Place these on lightly buttered cooky sheets and, using the bottom of a glass dipped in sugar or cinnamon sugar, press the cookies to a thickness of about

¼ inch. They bake crisper and prettier. To vary the basic cooky, simply decrease the rolled oats to 1½ cups and add ½ to ¾ cup of one of the following: chopped dried apricots, chopped and pitted dates, chopped dried figs, raisins, semisweet chocolate chips, or coconut. All are good.

2 cups sifted flour	3 large eggs
½ teaspoon baking soda	1 teaspoon vanilla extract (optional)
½ teaspoon baking powder	
½ teaspoon salt	1 teaspoon cinnamon (optional)
1 cup butter or margarine	
¾ cup granulated sugar	2 cups rolled oats (not the quick-cooking kind)
¾ cup light or dark brown sugar	
	1 cup chopped walnuts

Sift the flour with the baking soda, baking powder, and salt. Set aside. Cream the butter or margarine with the sugars, eggs, and flavorings, if used. Then blend in the flour mixture, rolled oats, and walnuts. Blend well. Shape as suggested above and bake in a 350° F. oven for 12 to 15 minutes, or until lightly browned. Cool on racks. Makes about 5 dozen.

JUMBLES

In earlier cookbooks, cookies were given no space of their own but were merely listed at the end of the cake chapter. They were called by such names as "Jumbles," "Plunkets," and "Cry Babies," and the names were either self-explanatory or extremely puzzling and whimsical.

4 cups sifted flour	1 cup sugar
2 teaspoons baking soda	¼ cup butter or shortening
½ teaspoon salt	2 large eggs
½ teaspoon nutmeg	1 cup molasses
½ teaspoon ginger	1 cup buttermilk, sour milk, or yogurt
½ teaspoon cloves	
1 teaspoon cinnamon	1 cup raisins, chopped

Sift the flour with the baking soda, salt, and spices. Cream the sugar with the butter or shortening and eggs until smooth and creamy. Then add the molasses. Stir the sifted flour mixture into the creamed mixture alternately with the buttermilk, sour milk, or yogurt. Add the raisins last. Drop by spoonfuls onto buttered cooky sheets and bake in a 350° F. oven for 10 to 12 minutes, depending on size. Cool on racks. Makes about 7 dozen cookies.

KETTLE COOKIES

This is a very old recipe, given to me by a friend who swears that her family has been making these cookies for 150 years. Any dried fruits can be used, and by varying the fruits, the nuts, and the liquid, you have a basic cooky of infinite variety.

3 cups sifted flour
1 teaspoon baking powder
1 teaspoon baking soda
¼ teaspoon salt
½ teaspoon cinnamon
½ teaspoon nutmeg
2 cups any dried fruit, or a combination of dried fruits, chopped

1 cup water or fruit juice
1 cup light or dark brown sugar
1 cup granulated sugar
⅔ cup butter or margarine
3 large eggs
1 teaspoon vanilla extract
1 teaspoon grated lemon rind

Sift the flour with the baking powder, soda, salt, and spices. Set aside. Place the dried fruit and the liquid in a 3-quart saucepan. Cook over medium heat, stirring occasionally, until the liquid has evaporated. Then stir in the sugars and the butter or margarine. Stir to melt the butter and dissolve the sugar and set aside to cool. When cool, beat in the eggs and vanilla, and then add the sifted flour mixture and blend thoroughly. Drop by spoonfuls onto buttered cooky sheets. Bake in a 375° F. oven for 10 to 12 minutes, depending on the size of the cookies. Makes approximately 5 to 6 dozen cookies.

Georgie Porgie, puddin' and pie,
Kissed the girls and made them cry.
CHILDREN'S SONG

DROP RAISIN COOKIES

This is an excellent basic recipe to which you may add some chopped nuts, some chocolate chips, or even some finely chopped candied fruits.

3¾ cups sifted flour	1½ cups sugar
½ teaspoon salt	3 large eggs
1 teaspoon baking soda	1 teaspoon vanilla extract
1 cup raisins	1 teaspoon grated lemon rind
1 cup butter or margarine	(optional)

Sift 2 cups of the flour with the salt and baking soda. Put the raisins in a saucepan and add water to barely cover. Cook over low heat for 10 minutes. Cool the raisins in the liquid and then drain, reserving the liquid. Cream the butter or margarine with the sugar until light. Add the eggs, vanilla, and lemon rind, if used, and ⅓ cup of the reserved raisin liquid. Work in the sifted flour mixture, and then add enough of the remaining flour to make a smooth, workable dough. Add the raisins last, with any of the other ingredients suggested above, if desired. Drop from a tablespoon onto buttered cooky sheets and bake in a 350° F. oven for 12 to 15 minutes. Cool on racks.

NOTE. To vary the flavor, you can use pineapple juice, apple cider, or orange juice in place of the water.

PECAN BONBONS

This is a delicate cooky, easily made and very tasty. Use muffin pans with tiny cups, with paper liners.

½ cup sifted flour	2 large eggs, beaten
¼ teaspoon baking powder	1 cup light brown sugar
¼ teaspoon salt	1 cup finely chopped pecans

Sift the flour with the baking powder and salt. Beat the eggs, then add the sugar and the flour mixture and blend thoroughly. Add the nuts last. Turn the batter into muffin pans as suggested above. If desired,

you may place a pecan half on top of each. Bake in a 350° F. oven
for 8 to 12 minutes. Watch carefully. This makes 3 dozen cookies.
Store in air-tight containers. These keep well.

PEANUT BUTTER COOKIES

An old favorite with children, these rich cookies are good at any time
and, if you can hide them, keep well. This recipe is an especially fine
one.

2½ cups sifted flour	2 cups peanut butter (I use
2 teaspoons baking soda	half crunchy and half
¾ cup butter or margarine	smooth)
1 cup granulated sugar	2 large eggs
1 cup light or dark brown	¼ cup hot water
sugar	¼ cup wheat germ (optional)

Sift the flour with the baking soda. Cream the butter or margarine
gradually adding the sugars and creaming until very light and fluffy.
Blend the peanut butter into the creamed mixture and then beat in the
eggs. Stir in the flour mixture alternately with the hot water. If you
use the wheat germ, add it last. Form the dough into small balls and
place on ungreased cooky sheets. Flatten slightly with the tines of a
fork. Bake in a 350° oven about 10 to 12 minutes. Makes about
to 6 dozen cookies.

NOTE. If you wish, you may add 1 teaspoon vanilla extract for
richer flavor.

ROCKS

This very old, very favored cooky recipe has an unfortunate name that
comes, not from the taste, but from the lumpy appearance of the
cookies. The dough should be stiff. In the many, many recipes for this
basic cooky the batter seems to be consistently the same recipe; the
differences in the cooky recipes come from varying the fruits, nuts
and flavorings. Earlier, housewives liked to use rose water; today most
housewives tend to use coffee or fruit juice, or at holiday time whiskey
or some other liquor.

2½ cups sifted flour
1 teaspoon baking soda
1 teaspoon cinnamon
½ teaspoon nutmeg
½ teaspoon mace (optional)
1 cup butter or margarine
1½ cups granulated or brown sugar

3 large eggs
2 tablespoons liquid (see above)
1 teaspoon vanilla extract
1½ cups chopped, pitted dates, or raisins
1½ cups chopped walnuts, filberts, or pecans

ft the flour with the baking soda and spices. Set aside. Cream the tter or margarine with the sugar and eggs, beating until well blended. en beat in the liquid and vanilla. Stir in the sifted flour mixture to rm a smooth batter and add the fruits and nuts last. The dough ould be very stiff, so add a little extra flour if necessary. Drop dough spoonfuls onto buttered cooky sheets and bake in a 350° F. oven r 10 to 15 minutes, or until lightly browned and done. Cool on racks. akes about 4 dozen.

DTE. Candied fruit peels may replace part or all of the dates. If u use fruit juice as the liquid, add a teaspoon of grated lemon or ange rind.

SESAME SEED COOKIES

ese and the following SESAME-SEED OATMEAL COOKIES are among y most popular recipes for simple cookies. I always double or triple e recipe to make enough for my brood and their friends.

1 cup sesame seed
¾ cup shredded coconut
2 cups sifted flour
1 teaspoon baking powder
½ teaspoon baking soda
¼ teaspoon salt

¾ cup salad oil (not olive oil)
1 cup light brown sugar
1 large egg
1 teaspoon vanilla extract
1 teaspoon grated orange or lemon rind

read the sesame seed and the coconut in a shallow pan and toast ghtly in a 300° F. oven, 20 minutes. Sift the flour with the baking powder, baking soda, and salt. Beat the oil with the brown sugar, egg, and flavorings. Add the toasted sesame seed and coconut, and then blend in the sifted flour mixture. Shape dough into small balls (about a tablespoon of dough for each ball), place on a lightly buttered cooky sheet, and flatten with a fork. Bake in a 350° F. oven for 10 to 15 minutes. Cool on racks. Makes about 3 dozen.

SESAME-SEED OATMEAL COOKIES

2½ cups sifted flour
1 teaspoon baking soda
½ teaspoon salt
1 or 2 teaspoons cinnamon
1 cup raisins (optional)
1 cup salad oil (not olive oil)

2 cups light or dark brown
 sugar
2 large eggs
2½ cups rolled oats
1½ cups sesame seed
⅓ cup milk

Sift the flour with the baking soda, salt, and cinnamon. Add the raisins, if used, to the mixture. Beat the oil with the sugar and eggs. Add the rolled oats, sesame seed, and milk. Add the flour mixture last, and work it in until thoroughly blended. Drop by heaping teaspoons onto buttered cooky sheets. Flatten with a fork, if desired. Bake in a 375° F. oven for 10 to 15 minutes. Cool on racks.

RICH SOUR CREAM COOKIES

This is an old, choice recipe for a basic cooky that, again, is varied by the flavorings used. It's a drop cooky that can be rolled and cut if chilled for an hour. You can add raisins and nuts to the dough, and if these ingredients are finely chopped, the cooky dough can still be cut into shapes.

4 cups sifted flour
½ teaspoon salt
1 teaspoon baking soda
1 teaspoon nutmeg or grated
 lemon rind
1 cup butter

2 cups granulated sugar or
 light brown sugar
1 cup commerical sour cream
3 large eggs
1 teaspoon vanilla extract

ift 2 cups of the flour with the salt, baking soda, and nutmeg, if used. et aside. Cream the butter with the lemon rind (if used). the sugar, nd the sour cream. Beat in the eggs, 1 at a time, and then the vanilla. .dd the flour that has been sifted with the salt, and blend in thoroughly. .dd enough of the remaining 2 cups of flour to make a soft dough. rop onto buttered cooky sheets and bake in a 350° F. oven for bout 12 minutes, or until set and done. Cool on racks.

OLD-TIME SUGAR COOKIES

*or really good sugar cookies, quality ingredients are a must. It is specially important to use butter or a good margarine. If desired, the ough can be rolled and cut into various shapes with cooky cutters. se a lightly floured breadboard and work with small amounts of dough t a time.

3 cups sifted flour	1 tablespoon milk
2 teaspoons baking powder	1 teaspoon vanilla extract or
½ teaspoon salt	grated lemon rind
1 cup butter or margarine	2 tablespoons sugar
1½ cups sugar	1 or 2 teaspoons cinnamon
2 large eggs, or 4 egg yolks	

ft 1½ cups of the flour with the baking powder and salt. Set aside. ream the butter or margarine until light, gradually adding the 1½ ups sugar and creaming until fluffy. Beat in the eggs or egg yolks, the ilk, and the flavoring. Work in the sifted flour mixture. Add enough f the remaining 1½ cups flour to make a smooth, workable dough. ut don't add too much. Chill the dough for at least an hour. Combine e 2 tablespoons sugar with the cinnamon. When the dough is chilled, oll and cut into shapes, and sprinkle with the sugar-cinnamon mixture. lace on ungreased cooky sheets and bake in a 400° F. oven for 9 or) minutes. Watch carefully. For a delightful crackled effect, roll the ough into small balls and roll the balls in the sugar-cinnamon mixture. ake as directed. These flatten in the baking and come out with the ackled-sugar top that always used to mean "sugar cookies."

ALMOND MACAROONS

These are simple cookies, but very impressive and tasty. You can us canned almond paste, but homemade paste is preferable.

1 cup almond paste	½ to ¾ cup superfine
2 large egg whites	granulated sugar or sifted
	powdered sugar

Chop the almond paste and work it with the fingers until it is smoot Work in the egg whites and the sugar, and blend the dough until it smooth and pliable. If the dough is not soft enough, add a little mo egg white. If it is too soft, add a little almond paste. Color the doug with food coloring if desired. Pipe the dough through a pastry tub using a plain or star-shaped tip, directly onto buttered and flour cooky sheets. Cooky-sheet liners, made of silicone-treated parchme paper, help to make the baking failure-proof. Bake in a 300° F. ov about 20 minutes. If you place the liner paper on a damp tea tow for a minute, the macaroons will come off easily. Cool on racks. T nice thing about using the liners is that you can make these assembl line fashion: while one sheet of cookies is baking, you can be pipi more cookies onto another sheet; when one batch has finished bakin remove the liner with the cookies on it from the baking sheet to a dan towel and place another liner, filled with unbaked cookies, on the cool sheet. This way, even if you have only 1 cooky sheet, you don't lo much time. Store the macaroons in an airtight container with a sli of white bread to keep them from drying out. Makes 2 to 3 dozen.

CREAM CHEESE PRESS COOKIES

These have a creamy, lemony flavor that is much liked.

2½ cups sifted flour	1 cup sugar
¼ teaspoon salt	1 large egg yolk
1 cup butter or margarine	2 teaspoons grated lemon rind
4 ounces cream cheese	1 teaspoon fresh lemon juice

Sift the flour with the salt. Cream the butter or margarine with the cheese until thoroughly blended. Add the sugar, egg yolk, lemon rind and juice. Beat until light and fluffy. Blend in the flour mixture. Press through a cookie press or a canvas pastry bag into any desired shapes onto an ungreased cooky sheet. Bake in a 350° F. oven about 10 to 12 minutes, depending on the size of the cooky. Makes approximately 5 dozen cookies.

BOURBON BALLS

These evidently originated in Kentucky, and are usually made with bourbon whisky. They've become a standard Christmas cooky, and rightfully so.

1 pound vanilla wafers, finely crushed

½ cup mild-flavored honey or light corn syrup

⅓ cup brandy, Cognac, or bourbon

⅓ cup rum

1 pound walnuts and pecans, finely chopped

Combine all ingredients and work together thoroughly, using your hands. Form into small balls and roll in superfine granulated sugar or in sifted powdered sugar (the balls should have a generous coating of sugar). For best results wrap each separately in plastic wrap. Let stand for at least 24 hours before serving. Many people let them stand for a week to allow the flavors to mellow and blend. In the South they serve these mounded on a serving plate and decorated with small bunches of sugared grapes. Makes about 5 dozen cookies.

NOTE. If desired, you might add up to ⅓ cup cocoa to the ingredients. If you do not care to use liquor, substitute orange juice for the liquor and add several tablespoons of grated orange rind.

NUT SLICES OR WAFERS

This fine recipe can be varied by using different nuts or by shaping the cooky differently on the cookie sheet.

1 cup + 2 tablespoons grated
pecans, hickory nuts, or
filberts
½ cup granulated sugar or
light brown sugar
1 tablespoon flour

½ teaspoon vanilla extract
(optional)
1 large egg white
thick raspberry, strawberry, or
apricot jam or preserves (do
not use if making wafers)

Combine and work together the nuts, sugar, flour, vanilla, and egg white. If making wafers, the egg white should be beaten until stiff and folded into the other ingredients. If making slices, the egg white should be left unbeaten and worked into the mixture. To make wafers, drop the batter by teaspoons onto a buttered and floured cooky sheet, and bake in a 325° F. oven about 15 minutes, or until done. Carefully remove to racks to cool. If they harden on the pan, place in the oven for 1 or 2 minutes to loosen the wafers.

To make slices, form the dough into a long roll about 2 inches in diameter on the buttered and floured cooky sheet. Make a depression down the center of the roll, and fill it with the jam or preserves. Bake in a 350° F. oven about 15 to 18 minutes. Remove from oven and cool on the cooky sheet. Then cut into ½-inch slices and remove from cooky sheet.

COOKIE DECORATING

The simplest way to decorate cookies is to sprinkle them with colored sugar, or dragees and chocolate shot. But for holidays or special occasions the creative cook (often working with her children) experiment with numerous ways of decorating.

SUGAR TRAILING. This can be done directly on the unfrosted cooky or it can be used to decorate more intricately a lightly frosted or glazed cooky. If the cooky has first been frosted or glazed, the glaze must be allowed to dry thoroughly so that the colors do not run together. To make the sugar mixture, first sift powdered sugar; then thin it with just enough water to make a mixture that will trail from the tube but will not spread or break. Use a waxed-paper cone or canvas pastry bag which has changeable tubes. The #2 decorating tube is most useful for this, but for other effects I use #1 through #5. By using several colors and allowing each color to dry before using another, you can devise lovely and intricate designs on any size or shape of cooky.

PAINTING. The cooky is first spread, right to the edges, with a thin frosting or glaze. Set aside to dry completely. Then, using a small (size 1 through 6) camel's-hair paint brush and thinned paste food colors, you can paint anything from a multicolored peacock's tail to a child's name. Work with one color at a time, letting it dry before using another color. For this reason it is best to set aside a day just for decorating. By working assembly-line fashion you can get much done. The simple butter-type cookies such as SUGAR COOKIES (p. 149) and SHORTBREAD (p. 126) can be painted before baking by using an "egg yolk paint." As the food coloring is diluted with egg yolk, the colors won't be true; but the cookies can be lovely nonetheless. Using the small paint brushes (a separate one for each color), paint the cookies in the desired design and then bake until set but not browned. If the paint thickens too much, thin it with a few drops of water.

EGG YOLK PAINT. Beat 1 egg yolk with ¼ teaspoon water. Add a few drops of liquid food coloring or a very small amount of paste food coloring. Thin with more water if necessary.

FLAVORED SUGARS

Use these to sprinkle over the cookies either before or after baking.

CINNAMON SUGAR. 'Combine 1 tablespoon cinnamon and 1 cup granulated sugar. This will keep indefinitely if stored in a covered jar.

LEMON SUGAR. Grate the thin outer rind of 6 large lemons. Do not use the white part as it is bitter. Add the rind to 1 cup granulated sugar and stir. Store in the refrigerator. This will keep for months.

ORANGE SUGAR. Follow recipe for Lemon Sugar, using 4 large oranges. This will keep refrigerated for many months.

VANILLA SUGAR.   Sift 1 pound of powdered sugar into a canister. Take 3 vanilla beans and cut them in half lengthwise; bury the pieces in the sugar. This will keep indefinitely.

BROWNIE FROSTING

2 squares unsweetened
  chocolate, melted
2 cups sifted powdered sugar

¼ cup soft butter or
  margarine
1 teaspoon vanilla extract
coffee or light cream

Combine the melted chocolate with the sugar, butter, and vanilla extract. Beat with an electric mixer until of spreading consistency. Thin with a little coffee or cream if necessary.

ORNAMENTAL COOKY FROSTING

This frosting is excellent for decorating cookies. Spread it on the baked cookies and allow to dry. Or stiffen with more sifted powdered sugar, and pipe it through a decorating tube.

3 large egg whites
1 pound sifted powdered
  sugar

1 teaspoon vanilla extract

Beat the egg whites until they will hold soft peaks. Gradually beat in the powdered sugar and the vanilla. Use as directed above. To keep the frosting from drying out while you are using it, spread a damp cloth or paper towel over the unused portion.

4. *Fruitcakes*

At their best, fruitcakes are pretty gaudy affairs, with the rich look of a colorful mosaic or a stained-glass window. Making fruitcakes is a rewarding, creative experience, albeit one that requires time and patience. There are fruitcakes that require no baking, little if any effort, and little expense, but these are mere imitations of the real thing. Time and effort—and some expense—pay off when making fruitcakes.

One of the nicer things about the art of making fruitcakes is that tradition rules, and an impressive majority of our favorite recipes originated well before the turn of the century. It is a tribute to those fine old cooks who did everything by hand that many of these recipes are, with only minor changes, the same as those used almost two hundred years ago!

But while tradition may rule as concerns the recipe, methods have happily changed. If we candy our own fruit today, it is through choice, not necessity. The Colonial housewife broke hunks of sugar off large cone-shaped loaves and pounded it in a mortar to pulverize it. She placed her flour before an open fire to dry, pounded her own spices, and seeded her own raisins! She mixed her cake literally by hand, beating the egg whites with a hickory rod, and then baked it, as suggested by Mrs. Smith in the *Compleat Housewife,* "in a deep hoop; butter the sides, and put two papers in the bottom, and flour it, and put in your cake; it must have a quick oven, four hours will bake it."

Although it was as early as 1789 that Thomas Jefferson brought the vanilla bean to the United States, a century later the favorite flavoring for fruitcakes was still homemade rose water. Liquor was used for its preserving power as well as for its flavor, so that the busy housewife could rest assured that the rich fruitcake, a job to make, would last a long, long time.

Some good cooks still make their fruitcakes almost a year ahead of the time they will be used. However, we recognize now that such prolonged aging is not necessary, and is in fact desirable only under ideal conditions. The early cooks had spring houses, or cool, walk-in pantries. Today's houses are generally too warm for prolonged storage.

GENERAL INFORMATION

1. Fruitcakes should be made well in advance of the time that they will be used. One month of storage is a necessity. Two, three, or even four months is not too long a time if the storage facilities are cool and dry.

2. Fruitcakes freeze very well. However, they must be aged at least 4 weeks before freezing, as they do not mellow while they are frozen.

3. A high percentage of fruits and nuts to batter makes a better and more interesting cake with better keeping qualities.

4. Finely chopped fruits and nuts make a more compact cake. But fruits and nuts left in fairly large pieces give the sliced cake beauty.

5. Take several days to make your cake or cakes. Prepare the nuts and fruits, pour the liquor to be used over them, and let the mixture stand well covered for two or three days. Then make the batter and bake your cakes. The cakes will be better and the pressure in a busy household will be eased.

6. When baking powder is called for, use double-acting baking powder.

7. Always bake fruit cakes at a low temperature, no higher than 325° F., and preferably much lower. Line the pans with brown paper or waxed paper to prevent the cakes from burning during the long baking time. Always place a pan of hot water on the floor of the oven. This prevents the cakes from drying out. Test for doneness with a cake tester inserted in the center of the cake. It will come out moist, but not doughy, when the cake is done.

8. Cool fruit cakes on a rack in the pans in which they were baked. When cakes are cooled, turn them out of the pans and carefully peel off the paper. If you are not decorating the cakes before storing them, wrap them in cheesecloth. Sprinkle liberally with whatever liquor or wine was used in the recipe. Seal the cakes in plastic wrap or in plastic storage bags. Once a week brush the cakes with more liquor.

9. Perhaps most important, don't feel absolutely bound by a recipe. If the recipe calls for brandy and you don't have it (or like it), use wine or even a fruit juice of your choice. If the recipe calls for citron and you don't care for citron, substitute another candied or dried fruit. If you don't like raisins, use more chopped dates and fewer raisins. If the recipe calls for particular amounts of candied pineapple and cherries, the same weight of a fruit mix may be used. The important thing to keep in mind is that the weight of fruit and nuts should be approximately the same as in the original recipe. Within this boundary you can make substitutions of your own choice.

FRUITCAKE GLAZES. In general I brush my fruitcakes with hot clear corn syrup and decorate them just before I am ready to serve the cakes or to give them away. Some good cooks use hot apricot jam that has been puréed in the blender. Either is very good. If you wish to decorate the cakes before storing them, use a sugar glaze. This must dry thoroughly before the cakes are wrapped and stored.

SUGAR GLAZE

1 cup sugar	½ cup water
⅓ cup clear corn syrup	

Combine ingredients in saucepan. Cook, stirring constantly, until syrup reaches 300° F. on a candy thermometer, or spins a fine thread. Brush the hot syrup all over the cooled fruitcakes. Let stand just until the syrup is sticky. Now arrange the candied fruits and nuts in a design on the syrup. Brush with more glaze and let the cakes dry overnight before wrapping and storing.

LEFTOVER FRUITCAKE. If the cake is not stale, it can be cut into fingers, heated in the oven, and served hot with tea or coffee. If the cake is stale, it can be rejuvenated by steaming it in a double boiler for ½ hour. Serve the cake either hot or cold with BRANDY SAUCE (see below).

Another good way to freshen stale fruit cake is to pour a fairly liberal amount of liquor over the cake. Allow the cake a day or two to completely absorb the liquor.

BRANDY SAUCE FOR FRUITCAKE

½ cup butter	⅓ cup brandy (or rum)
1 cup granulated sugar	

Melt the butter in a saucepan. Stir in the sugar and bring mixture to a quick boil, stirring constantly to keep from burning. Remove from heat and stir in the brandy or rum. Serve immediately over slices of fruit cake.

TEXAS FRUITCAKE

A moist cake, almost black in color, this one vies with the "Graham Cracker Fruitcake" as everyone's favorite. Long aging is essential.

2 pounds candied cherries, halved
2 pounds candied pineapple, slivered
1 pound candied fruit mix
¼ pound citron, finely diced
¼ pound candied orange peel, slivered
2 pounds pitted dates, chopped
2 pounds golden raisins
2 pounds Muscat raisins

1¼ pounds shelled pecans, coarsely chopped
1 pound butter
1 pound light or dark brown sugar
1 dozen large eggs
⅓ cup lemon juice
½ cup orange juice
4 cups sifted flour
2 teaspoons baking powder
2 teaspoons baking soda
1 tablespoon cinnamon
1½ cups brandy or wine

Combine the fruits and nuts in a large bowl. Pour the wine or brandy over them, cover the bowl well, and let mixture stand at least overnight, preferably two or three days.

When ready to prepare cakes, first allow the butter and eggs to reach room temperature, about 2 hours in cool weather. Beat softened butter with an electric mixer until light and creamy. Beat in the brown sugar until mixture is light and fluffy. Now beat in the eggs, two or three at a time, and beat until well blended. Sift together the dry ingredients. Using a wooden spoon, stir in the lemon and orange juices, and the sifted dry ingredients.

If you have been mixing the ingredients in a standard-size mixing bowl, now is the time to turn the mixture into a very large bowl or pot. Now, all at once, pour in the fruit and nut mixture with any of the wine or brandy that has not been absorbed. You might try to blend this mixture with a large wooden spoon, but only elbow grease, and nice clean hands, will do a good job of it. Blend mixture thoroughly.

Grease your pans, line them with brown or waxed paper, and grease the paper. Turn batter into pans and bake in a 250° F. oven, about

4 hours for loaf pans, 6 hours for tube pans. But only careful testing will enable you to tell when the cakes are done. Recipe will make 2 9 by 5 by 3-inch loaf cakes and 2 large tube cakes.

pot. Now, all at once, pour in the fruit and nut mixture, with any of

Cool cakes in pans on racks. When cooled, carefully peel off the paper and store as directed in Number 8 in GENERAL INFORMATION (p. 157).

NOTE. If you bake these cakes at 275° F. or 300° F., be certain to place a pan of hot water on the floor of the oven, and keep the pan at least half full during the baking time.

GRAHAM CRACKER FRUITCAKE

This recipe originated in Denmark, and the use of graham cracker crumbs in a *baked* fruitcake appears to be unique. It is a delicious cake with great appeal. And now that graham cracker crumbs can be bought packaged, the preparation is no more difficult than for any other fruitcake.

1 pound seeded Muscat raisins
1 pound golden raisins
1 pound dates, pitted and chopped
½ pound candied cherries, halved
½ pound candied pineapple, slivered
¼ pound each: citron, diced; candied orange and lemon peel, slivered
½ pound each: chopped walnuts, slivered, blanched almonds, and chopped pecans
2 cups ruby port wine
2 tablespoons vanilla extract
1 pound butter
1 pound sugar
1 dozen large eggs
3 packages (13¾ ounces each) graham cracker crumbs

Combine fruits, nuts, wine, and vanilla extract in a large bowl. Cover tightly and let stand at least overnight, but preferably two or three days. When ready to prepare cakes, allow butter and eggs to reach room temperature, about two hours in cool weather. With an electric mixer, cream butter and sugar thoroughly. Beat in the eggs, two or three at a time, and blend well. Add graham cracker crumbs alternately with fruit-nut-wine mixture, including any wine that has not been absorbed. Blend thoroughly.

Grease pans, line them with brown or waxed paper, and grease the paper. Fill pans about ¾ full and bake in a 250° F. oven. Start testing cakes after 3 hours of baking time. Recipe makes 2 9 by 5 by 3-inch loaf cakes, and 1 10-inch tube cake.

Cool cakes in pans on racks. When cooled, carefully peel off the paper and store as directed in Number 8 in GENERAL INFORMATION (p. 157).

OLD-FASHIONED DARK FRUITCAKE

The following recipe is an old-fashioned one using chocolate flavor. Any cocoa will do, but Dutch cocoa is richer and better.

1 pound seeded Muscat raisins
1 pound golden raisins
1 pound pitted dates, chopped
¼ pound citron, diced
¼ pound candied orange peel, slivered
1 pound candied cherries, halved
1 pound candied pineapple, slivered

¾ pound each: chopped walnuts, chopped pecans, blanched, slivered almonds
1 cup honey or molasses
1 cup brandy, rum, or wine
½ pound butter
1½ cups light or dark brown sugar
6 large eggs
3 cups sifted flour
⅓ cup Dutch cocoa
1 teaspoon cinnamon
½ teaspoon salt

Place fruits and nuts in a large bowl. Pour the honey or molasses and the brandy, rum, or wine over them. Cover tightly and let stand for at least one night, but preferably for two or three days.

When ready to prepare the cakes, allow the butter and eggs to come to room temperature, about 2 hours in cool weather. With an electric mixer, cream the butter and sugar until light. Beat in the eggs, two or three at a time, and blend thoroughly. Sift the dry ingredients and add to the creamed mixture alternately with the fruit-nut mixture, using any liquor not absorbed by the fruit. Blend thoroughly with clean hands.

Grease pans, line with brown paper or waxed paper, and grease the paper. Fill pans ¾ full and bake in a 250° F. oven 2 hours for the loaf pan, 3½ to 4 hours for the tube pan. Start testing loaf pan at the end of 1½ hours, and the tube pan at 3 hours. Recipe makes 1 loaf cake and 1 10-inch tube cake.

Cool cakes in pans on racks. When cool, carefully peel the paper off. Wrap and store as directed in Number 8 in GENERAL INFORMATION (p. 157).

JOE PISOTT'S DARK FRUITCAKE

Mr. Pisott, the father of a friend, says that he never chops the nuts, but breaks them into pieces with his fingers. He says—and I concur—that chopping too finely results in loss of flavor when teeth bite into cake.

1 pound candied fruit mix	1¼ cups light or dark brown sugar
1 pound seeded raisins	
1 pound pitted dates, chopped	4 large eggs
¼ to ½ pound dried figs, cut into pieces	3 cups sifted flour
	¾ teaspoon salt
1 pound walnuts, broken into pieces	1 teaspoon baking soda
	1 teaspoon cinnamon
½ cup honey	½ teaspoon cloves
1 cup bourbon	½ teaspoon allspice
1 cup butter	¼ teaspoon nutmeg

Combine fruits and nuts in a large bowl. Add the honey and bourbon and stir to blend. Cover tightly and let stand overnight, or preferably for two or three days.

Cream butter and sugar in a bowl. Add eggs one at a time and blend well. Add the fruit-nut-bourbon mixture and stir to blend. Now add the sifted dry ingredients and mix by hand. Grease pans, line with brown paper or waxed paper and grease the paper. Fill pans ¾ full and bake for 2½ to 3 hours in a 275° F. oven with pan of hot water on oven floor. Begin testing cakes after 2 hours.

Cool cakes in pans on racks. When cooled, carefully peel off the paper, and wrap and store as directed in Number 8 in GENERAL INFORMATION (p. 157). Makes 2 loaf cakes.

BLACK FRUITCAKE

A very old recipe for a very dark fruitcake that will keep a year or more.

1 pound candied fruit mix	4 cups sifted flour
½ pound candied cherries, halved	4 teaspoons baking powder
½ pound candied pineapple, slivered	1 teaspoon salt
	1 teaspoon cardamom
2 pounds seeded raisins	1 teaspoon cinnamon
2 pounds golden raisins	1 teaspoon nutmeg
2 pounds currants	1 pound butter
1 pound blanched, slivered almonds	16 large eggs
	2 cups light or dark brown sugar
2 cups brandy, bourbon, or wine	2 cups orange marmalade

Combine the fruits and nuts in a large bowl. Add the liquor and stir to blend. Cover tightly and let stand at least overnight, but preferably for two or three days.

When ready to make the cakes, sift the dry ingredients and set aside. Let the butter and eggs come to room temperature, about 2 hours in cool weather. Cream the butter, adding sugar gradually. Add the eggs, two at a time, beating after each addition. Stir in the orange marmalade and blend thoroughly. Add the fruit-nut-liquor mixture alternately with the sifted dry ingredients. Blend thoroughly with clean hands.

Grease pans, line them with brown or waxed paper and grease the paper. Fill pans no more than ¾ full and bake in a 275° F. oven, with a pan of water on the oven floor. Loaf cakes will take approximately 2½ hours, and tube cakes will take approximately 3½ to 4 hours. Start testing after 2 hours. Recipe makes 2 9 by 5 by 3-inch loaf cakes and 2 10-inch tube cakes.

Cool cakes in pans on rack. When cool, carefully peel off the paper and wrap and store as directed in Number 8 in GENERAL INFORMATION (p. 157).

OLD ENGLISH FRUITCAKE

1 pound candied fruit mix
¼ pound each: citron, diced;
candied pineapple, slivered;
candied cherries, halved
¼ pound each: pitted dates,
chopped; sliced dried
apricots
½ pound Muscat raisins
½ pound seeded raisins
½ pound currants
½ pound each: chopped
walnuts and chopped pecans
1 cup brandy or wine

1 cup honey or molasses
1 ounce unsweetened
chocolate
1 cup butter
1 cup light or dark brown
sugar
½ cup granulated sugar
8 large eggs
2 cups sifted flour
1 teaspoon salt
2 teaspoons cinnamon
1 teaspoon nutmeg

In a large bowl combine the fruits and nuts. Add the liquor and the honey or molasses. Stir to blend well. Cover tightly and let stand at least overnight, but preferably for two or three days.

Let the butter and eggs come to room temperature, about 2 hours in cool weather. Melt the chocolate and cool it slightly. Cream the butter and the sugars until light and fluffy. Add the eggs 2 at a time and beat in well. Stir in the melted chocolate and blend. Add the sifted dry ingredients and blend well. Now add the fruit-nut-liquor mixture with any liquor that has not been absorbed. Blend thoroughly with clean hands.

Grease the pans, line with waxed or brown paper, and grease the paper. Fill pans not more than ¾ full. Bake in 250° F. oven for 3 to 3½ hours for tube pans, or 2 to 2½ hours for loaf pans. Start testing after 2 hours. Recipe makes 1 10-inch tube cake, or 2 9 by 5 by 3-inch loaf cakes.

Cool cakes in pans, on racks. When cooled, turn out of pans and carefully peel the paper off. Wrap and store as directed in Number 8 in GENERAL INFORMATION (p. 157).

CALIFORNIA DARK FRUITCAKE

⅓ pound each: diced citron; diced candied orange peel; diced candied lemon peel

2 pounds candied cherries, halved

2 pounds candied pineapple, slivered

1 pound pitted dates, chopped

1 pound seeded raisins

1 1-pound can pitted sour cherries, drained

1 pound chopped pecans

½ cup + 2 tablespoons brandy or wine

1 tablespoon vanilla extract

½ cup honey, corn syrup, or molasses

1 cup butter

2 cups light or dark brown sugar

7 large eggs

12-ounce jar apple or grape jelly

5 cups sifted flour

1 teaspoon baking powder

½ teaspoon baking soda

1 tablespoon cinnamon

1 teaspoon allspice

1 teaspoon cloves

1 teaspoon nutmeg

In a large bowl combine the fruits and nuts. Add the brandy or wine, vanilla extract and the honey, syrup or molasses. Stir to blend well. Cover tightly and let stand at least overnight, but preferably for two or three days.

When ready to make cakes, let the butter and eggs come to room temperature, about 2 hours in cool weather. Sift the dry ingredients and set aside. Cream butter and sugar until light and fluffy. Add eggs, 2 at a time, and beat well after each addition. Stir in the jelly and blend. Now add the fruit-nut mixture alternately with the sifted flour mixture, stirring in until thoroughly blended. You will need your hands to finish this.

Grease the pans, line them with waxed paper or brown paper and grease the paper. Fill pans no more than ¾ full. Bake in a 250° F. oven for 3½ to 4 hours. Start testing after 3 hours. Recipe makes 2 10-inch tube cakes.

Cool cakes in pans, on racks. When cooled, turn out of pans and carefully peel the paper off. Wrap and store as directed under Number 8 in GENERAL INFORMATION (p. 157).

WELSH FRUITCAKE

This is a very different kind of fruitcake, baked with an outer crust of pastry. Hard when baked, the crust softens with aging. This cake must age for 2 or 3 months.

CRUST
3 cups sifted flour
¾ teaspoon baking powder
¾ cup butter
¾ cup water

FILLING
1½ pounds seeded raisins
1 pound currants
1 pound pitted dates, chopped
2 large carrots, coarsely grated

½ to ¾ pound blanched, slivered almonds
⅔ cup brandy
1 cup buttermilk
2¼ cups sifted flour
1 cup sugar
1 teaspoon baking powder
1 tablespoon cinnamon
1 teaspoon ginger
½ teaspoon black pepper
½ teaspoon white pepper
1 egg, beaten

To make the crust, first sift the flour and baking powder into a large bowl. Cut in the butter until mixture resembles coarse crumbs. Sprinkle water, a few tablespoons at a time, over different parts of mixture, tossing quickly with fork. Form dough into a ball. Roll out on a lightly floured board until ¼ inch thick. Line bottom and sides of a buttered, 9-inch, spring-form pan. Reserve enough pastry for the top.

For the filling, combine fruits, carrots, and nuts in a large bowl. Add the brandy and buttermilk and stir to blend. Sift dry ingredients together into another bowl. Gradually add the fruit-nut mixture and blend well with the hands. Pack batter into pastry-lined pan, and cover with a top crust made with the rest of the pastry. Seal well.

Brush pastry with beaten egg and prick the top to let the steam out. Bake in a 325° F. oven for 4 hours. Cool in the pan, on a rack. When cake is cool, remove the sides and bottom of the spring-form pan. When cake is completely cold, wrap it carefully as directed in Number 8 in GENERAL INFORMATION (p. 157), and store in a cool place.

WHITE FRUIT CAKE

Many people prefer white fruitcakes. These should be made no longer than 2 or 3 weeks before serving. If they should become stale, remember that any white fruitcake is delicious toasted. Or, since white fruitcakes are less rich than dark ones, they may be sliced, heated in the oven, and served with a whipped rum butter.

1 pound golden raisins
1 pound large dried apricots, thinly sliced
½ pound candied pineapple, slivered
½ pound candied cherries, halved
¼ pound candied orange peel, slivered or diced
¼ pound candied lemon peel, slivered or diced
1 pound walnuts, chopped
1 pound pecans, chopped
1 cup brandy, bourbon, light rum, or white port wine
¾ pound butter
2½ cups sugar
3¾ cups sifted flour
4 teaspoons baking powder
3 tablespoons frozen orange juice concentrate, thawed
8 large eggs
1 teaspoon salt

Combine fruits and nuts in a large bowl. Pour the brandy, bourbon, rum, or wine over them and stir to blend. Cover tightly and let stand at least overnight, but preferably for two or three days.

When ready to prepare cakes, first allow the butter and eggs to reach room temperature, about 2 hours in cool weather. Beat softened butter with an electric mixer until light and fluffy. Beat in the sugar until mixture is creamy. Add the eggs, one at a time, and blend well. Carefully fold in the orange juice concentrate. Sift the dry ingredients together and add to the creamed mixture alternately with the fruit-nut-liquor mixture, stirring and folding in carefully.

Grease pans, line with brown paper or waxed paper, and grease the paper. Fill pans no more than ¾ full with batter. Bake in 300° F. oven. A loaf pan will require approximately 1½ hours, a tube pan approximately 3½ hours, but only careful testing will enable you to tell exactly when cakes are done.

Recipe makes 2 9 by 5 by 3-inch loaf cakes and 1 9-inch tube cake. Cool on racks, in the pans, for 15 minutes. Then turn out of pans and replace on racks until thoroughly cooled. Carefully peel off paper and store as directed in Number 8 in GENERAL INFORMATION (p. 157).

CREAM CHEESE FRUITCAKE

The following moist, deliciously light cake is one that is good throughout the year.

1 pound cream cheese	1 cup candied pineapple, slivered
1 pound butter	1 cup candied cherries, halved
3 cups sugar	1 cup chopped pecans
7 large eggs	½ cup blanched, slivered almonds
4½ cups sifted flour	
1 tablespoon baking powder	
½ cup light rum	

Allow the cream cheese, butter, and eggs to come to room temperature, about 2 hours in cool weather. Beat the cream cheese and butter together with an electric mixer until thoroughly blended. Beat in the sugar until mixture is light and fluffy. Add the eggs, one or two at a time, blending well after each addition. Sift the flour and baking powder together. Take 3½ cups of the sifted mixture and carefully fold into the creamed mixture alternately with the light rum. Stir the remaining flour mixture through the candied fruits and nuts until they are thoroughly coated. Fold into batter carefully but thoroughly.

Grease 3 loaf pans, line with waxed paper (do not use brown paper with this cake), and grease the paper. Fill pans ¾ full and bake in a 325° F. oven for 1 hour and 20 minutes. Check pans carefully before removing from oven.

Cool the cakes in the pans, on racks, for 10 to 15 minutes before removing from pans. Then turn out of pans and carefully peel off the paper. Cool thoroughly before wrapping and storing. Use these cakes within 10 days.

WATERMELON PICKLE FRUITCAKE

½ pound candied cherries, halved
½ pound candied pineapple, slivered
1 pound golden raisins
½ pound pecans, chopped
½ pound almonds, blanched and slivered

2 cups drained watermelon pickle, slivered
3 cups sifted flour
2 teaspoons baking powder
½ teaspoon salt
1 cup butter
2 cups sugar
5 large eggs
½ cup brandy or sherry

Combine fruit, nuts, and pickle in a large bowl. Sift together flour, baking powder, and salt and set aside. Take ¼ cup of the flour mixture and blend through the combined fruit-nut-pickle mixture. Cream butter until smooth. Add sugar gradually until mixture is light and fluffy. Beat in eggs one at a time until thoroughly blended. Now, preferably using a wooden spoon, stir the remainder of the flour mixture into the creamed mixture alternately with the brandy or sherry. Blend in the fruit-nut-pickle mixture last, folding in until no flour is seen.

Grease 2 loaf pans, line with brown or waxed paper, and grease the paper. Divide the batter between these 2 pans, packing the batter down. Bake in a 300° F. oven for 2 hours, or until cakes test done. Test carefully before removing from oven. Cool cakes in the pans, on racks. When cakes are cool, remove from pans and carefully peel off the paper. Wrap and store at least 1 month before using. Sprinkle several times with brandy or sherry during storage time.

LOUISIANA NUT CAKE

This marvelous cake is surely the South's most glamorous candidate for culinary honors. Very old and very Southern, it has innumerable variations and several names. Kentucky as well as Louisiana claims it and you might run across it under such names as "Pecan Bourbon Cake," "Whisky Cake," or simply "Nut Cake."

1 pound candied cherries, halved	1 cup butter
1 pound candied pineapple, slivered	2 cups sugar
1 pound pecans, left in whole halves	6 large eggs
1 cup brandy, bourbon, wine, or fruit juice	4 cups sifted flour
	1 teaspoon salt
	2 tablespoons baking powder
	1 teaspoon nutmeg or cinnamon, optional

Combine fruits and nuts in a large bowl. Pour the liquor or fruit juice over the mixture and stir to blend. Cover tightly and let stand at least overnight, but preferably for 2 or 3 days.

When ready to bake, let the butter and eggs stand at room temperature for 2 hours. For this cake it is absolutely essential that the butter *and* eggs be at room temperature. Cream the butter thoroughly. Add the sugar a little at a time and cream until light and fluffy. Add the eggs, 1 or 2 at a time, and blend thoroughly.

Sift the dry ingredients together and stir half the mixture into the fruit-nut mixture so that all is well coated. Fold the rest of the flour mixture carefully into the creamed mixture. Blend thoroughly. Now add the floured fruit-nut-liquor mixture and blend carefully but thoroughly. Turn batter into a well-buttered Bundt pan, or a 10-inch tube pan. Bake in a 300° F. oven for 2 hours. Reduce heat to 200° F. and bake ½ hour longer, or until cake tests done. Cool on rack, in pan. Turn out of pan and sprinkle top of cake with additional fruit juice or liquor. Wrap and store as directed in Number 8 in GENERAL INFORMATION (p. 157).

VARIATIONS

1. 1½ pounds raisins, plumped in liquor and drained, may replace the cherries and pineapple.

2. All of the fruit may be omitted and 4 to 6 cups whole pecan halves used.

3. You may replace some or all of the candied fruits with pitted, chopped dates.

4. The recipe is easily halved, and may be baked in the shallow 1-pound coffee cans. Bake for 1½ to 2 hours in a 275° F. oven for the coffee cans.

5. Some good cooks omit the liquor entirely and use instead a combination of: 1 tablespoon lemon juice, 1 tablespoon vanilla, and 1 teaspoon grated lemon rind.

DATE FRUITCAKE.　For this excellent cake simply add to the ingredients 1 to 1½ pounds pitted, chopped dates. No other changes are required.

KENTUCKY BOURBON CAKE

Very similar to the "Louisiana Nut Cake," this cake is just different enough to merit a page of its own.

2 cups candied cherries, halved
2 cups golden raisins
4 cups pecan halves
2 cups bourbon whisky
1 pound softened butter
2 cups granulated sugar
2 cups light or dark brown sugar
8 large eggs, separated
5 cups sifted flour
1½ teaspoons baking powder
½ teaspoon salt
1 teaspoon nutmeg
1 teaspoon cinnamon

In a large bowl combine the fruits and nuts. Pour the whisky over them and stir to blend. Cover tightly and let stand at least overnight, but preferably for 2 or 3 days.

When ready to bake, cream the butter and sugars until light and fluffy. Add the egg yolks and beat well. Sift the dry ingredients together and stir 1 cup of the flour mixture into the fruits and nuts. Add the rest of the flour mixture to the creamed mixture. Now add the fruit-nut mixture to the creamed mixture and blend well. Beat the egg whites until stiff but not dry and gently fold through the batter. You will probably have to use your hands, but it can be done.

Grease a 10-inch tube pan. line with waxed paper and grease the paper. Turn batter into pan until it is about 1 inch from the top. There will be a little bit of batter left over which can then be baked in a smaller pan. Bake in a 275° F. oven for 4½ to 5 hours, or until a cake tester inserted in the center comes out clean.

Cool cake in the pan, on a rack. When cooled, turn out of pan and carefully peel off the paper. Wrap as directed in Number 8 under GENERAL INFORMATION (p. 157) and store in the refrigerator.

GOOD 'N' EASY FRUITCAKE

This cake is in the modern tradition. You mix everything in one bowl, and there is no bother about creaming butters and sugars. Indeed, no sugar is used; the marmalade provides enough sweetness. For all its ease this is an excellent cake.

4 cups seeded raisins	4 cups sifted flour
2 cups orange juice	1 teaspoon nutmeg
1 cup butter	1 teaspoon allspice
2 cups orange marmalade	½ teaspoon salt
1 teaspoon grated lemon rind	2 teaspoons cinnamon
1 tablespoon grated orange rind	3 large eggs
	2 cups pitted, chopped dates
1 teaspoon baking soda	2 cups chopped walnuts
½ cup orange juice	1 pound candied fruit mix

In a large saucepan combine the raisins, the 2 cups orange juice and butter. Place over direct heat and bring to a boil, stirring occasionally. Reduce heat and let mixture simmer for 10 minutes. Remove from heat and cool. When mixture is cooled, stir in the marmalade and grated rind. Dissolve the baking soda in the ½ cup orange juice and add to mixture. If the saucepan is large enough, you may mix everything in the pan, if not, turn mixture into a large bowl.

Sift together the dry ingredients and stir into the fruit mixture along with the remaining ingredients. Mix well with a large wooden spoon, or with clean hands, which is much easier.

Grease a 10-inch tube pan, line it with waxed paper or brown paper, and grease the paper. Turn batter into the pan and bake in a 300° F. oven 3 to 3½ hours, or until cake tests done. Cool in the pan, on a rack. When cake is thoroughly cooled, remove pan and then carefully remove the paper. Wrap and store as directed in Number 8 under GENERAL INFORMATION (p. 157).

FRUITCAKE CONFECTIONS

If December has crept up on you and all those fabulous, traditional fruitcakes that you meant to make are still unmade, content yourself with cakes that mellow in a hurry. The following are all good, and are best if used within 2 or 3 weeks.

FRUIT CONFECTIONS

These are our favorites. I use muffin pans that have tiny cups about 1½ inches in diameter across the top. I line them with paper liners. Use the smallest-cup muffin pans you have.

1 cup chopped candied cherries
1 cup slivered candied pineapple
⅓ cup finely diced citron
2 cups chopped walnuts
2 cups chopped pecans
½ cup butter
3 tablespoons light or dark brown sugar

3 tablespoons honey
3 large eggs
½ cup sifted flour
½ teaspoon baking powder
½ teaspoon salt
¼ teaspoon nutmeg
¼ teaspoon allspice
¼ cup brandy or fruit juice

Combine candied fruits and nuts and stir to mix well. Cream the butter and sugar and add the honey. Beat well and add the eggs. Beat to blend thoroughly. Sift together the dry ingredients and stir in. Add the brandy, and then stir in all the fruits and nuts. Blend thoroughly. Fill well-buttered or paper-lined muffin pans. Fill to the top as the batter does not rise. Cover with buttered brown paper and bake in a 300° F. oven 40 to 45 minutes or until little cakes test done. The time depends on what size pans you use. Let cool in pans for 10 minutes before turning out. Glaze with hot white corn syrup. Makes 40 tiny cakes, fewer muffin-sized cakes.

CHRISTMAS BONBONS

1½ cups seeded raisins
1 cup golden raisins
½ cup currants
1½ cups candied cherries, quartered
1½ cups candied pineapple, slivered
1½ cups chopped pitted dates
½ cup finely diced citron
2 cups chopped pecans
½ cup brandy, whisky, or port wine
¾ cup softened butter

1 cup light or dark brown sugar
1 tablespoon cinnamon
1 teaspoon nutmeg
½ teaspoon allspice
3 large eggs
2¼ cups sifted flour
1 teaspoon baking powder
¼ teaspoon salt
¼ cup mild molasses
1 cup jam (strawberry, raspberry, or plum)

Combine fruits and nuts in a bowl. Add the liquor and stir to blend Cover and set aside for several hours.

Cream the butter, sugar and spices until light and fluffy. Beat in the eggs 1 at a time and blend thoroughly. Sift the flour with the baking powder and the salt. Stir into the creamed mixture. Now add the molasses and the jam and stir to blend. Add fruit mixture and blend well, either with a wooden spoon or with clean hands. Spoon the batter into well-buttered muffin pans, as for the preceding recipe. If desired part of the batter may be baked in a loaf pan. Make certain that the pan is greased, lined with waxed or brown paper, and the paper then greased.

Bake in a 300° F. oven approximately 45 minutes to 1 hour for the tiny-muffin pans, or about 2½ hours for a loaf pan. Test carefully before removing pans from oven, as the time required to bake these will depend on what size pans you use. Cool the cakes, in the pans on racks for 15 minutes. Then turn out of the pans and cool thoroughly

The tiny cakes may be stored in plastic containers with waxed paper separating the layers. The loaf cake may be wrapped and stored as directed in Number 8 under GENERAL INFORMATION (p. 157).

FRUITCAKE IN CANDIED GRAPEFRUIT OR ORANGE SHELLS

These make lovely gifts, and are an impressive addition to any Christmas buffet. Select perfect fruit, free from blemishes. Cut in half and carefully remove the pulp and membranes. The following recipe is enough for the preparation of 6 grapefruit shells or 8 orange shells.

Place shells in a large pot and cover them with boiling water. Cook 20 minutes or until shells are tender. Invert on racks and let drain overnight.

Make a syrup of 4 cups granulated sugar, 4 cups water, 1 cup corn syrup and 2 teaspoons glycerine. The glycerine keeps the shells soft. Add the fruit, making certain there is enough syrup to cover the shells. Cook the shells in the syrup until syrup becomes very thick. Cover the pot, with shells still in the syrup, and let stand overnight. In the morning reheat the syrup and shells for about 10 minutes. Remove from heat and cool shells in the syrup. Remove shells from the syrup, invert them on a rack again and let drain. Use immediately, or roll shells in sugar and let them dry thoroughly.

When ready to use, fill the shells to within ½ inch of the top with any preferred fruitcake batter. Place on a buttered cooky sheet and bake in a 250° F. oven until cake tests done, 1 to 1½ hours. Place a pan of hot water on the floor of the oven.

A big piece o' pie, and a big piece o'
puddin'—
I laid it all by fer little Billy Goodin'!
FOLK SONG

5. *Pies and Pastries*

Who invented pie? Most of us believe pie to be as truly American as the Fourth of July. Actually it is a dish of British origin. The first pies were huge pumpkins, called "pompions," emptied of seeds and strings and filled with heavily spiced raisins, apples, and chopped meat. They were baked in hot ashes for several hours, then cut into great wedges which the good folk ate without the aid of knife or fork. Later the English "pye" evolved into the very good deep-dish pie that is still popular.

Whether we Americans invented pie or not, it has certainly become the great American dessert. We consume pies in prodigious quantities and in such a variety as would have impressed and delighted our forefathers. But even with the ease of modern techniques for making them and modern freezers in which to store them, we don't come close to baking the number of pies made by our grandmothers in their Colonial kitchens.

Our grandmothers thought nothing of baking from 25 to 30 pies each week, to be eaten at breakfast, lunch, and dinner. With a spring house or cold pantry filled with fragrant pies, there was no problem of what to serve an unexpected guest.

In the dead of winter there were rich and delicious jam pies, usually made with damson-plum preserves or with various homemade berry jams. Vinegar pies, using from a tablespoon to a cup of vinegar per pie, helped to weather the lack of lemons for lemon pies. There were Bakewell tarts, and Osgood pies, lemon cheese pies that contained no cheese, and apple pies that were remarkable not only for their flavor but for the few apples used in making them. One old-time recipe calls for salt pork, apples, and sorghum molasses.

The modern cook has kept some of the great old recipes, and with typical American ingenuity has even improved upon them (for example, fluff pies, very good in themselves, have evolved into chiffon pies). Others have passed from the culinary scene, to be made only by those lucky few with access to old family "receipt" books. We think you will enjoy the sampling of the past and present contained in this chapter.

PIE SHELLS AND CRUSTS

The foundation of a good pie is undoubtedly the crust, and the old saying that a light hand makes the best pastry still holds true. The following facts, hints, and ideas will help you make good pastry every time you put your hand to it.

1. The ingredients for making pie shells and crusts should be cold. Some good cooks even chill the flour in the refrigerator overnight before making pastry.

2. Many cooks have a preference for a particular type of shortening for making pastry. I prefer margarine. But for a truly superior pastry, substitute butter for a minimum of ⅓ of the total amount of shortening used.

3. For a flaky texture, whatever type of shortening is used—whether lard, shortening, margarine or butter—it must be cut in until evenly distributed, but not *too* fine. The mixture must be light and airy, with pieces of shortening that are about the size of small peas. If the shortening is too finely blended into the flour, it will be compressed and will not result in a flaky pastry.

4. The liquid ingredient that is used *must* be very cold, preferably iced. Add *just enough* liquid when mixing. Too much will make a dough that will tear and break. A tablespoon of lemon, orange, or pineapple juice added to the liquid helps make a superior pie pastry.

5. You *must* have a clean, large work area. A slab of marble which can be placed on a kitchen table is ideal. It is always cool, and provides a superior surface for making any kind of pastry. Lacking that, a breadboard (mine is 30 inches square) is excellent. It can be as inexpensive or expensive as you wish, depending on what kind of wood you work with. Just make certain that it is well-sanded, and has beveled edges. I find it easy to keep clean and simple to store.

6. Be careful not to add too much flour when rolling pastry out. One good way of avoiding this is to roll the pastry between two sheets of waxed paper. Turn the pastry often, and keep the top sheet of waxed paper loose to prevent it from wrinkling and sticking to the pastry. To help avoid this, I spray the waxed paper with a thin coat of Pam.

7. For best results, chill the pastry before filling and baking. This may be done before or after the pastry is rolled out. Some good cooks wrap the ball of dough in plastic wrap and chill it. I prefer to roll the pastry out and fit it into a pie pan, and then chill it.

8. You may make pastry in large quantities and freeze it for future use. The pastry may first be fitted into the pie pans and stacked, with sheets of waxed paper separating the pastry from the pan on top of it. Lightweight aluminum foil pie pans are best for this. Freeze pastry as follows: Make enough pie pastry for 8 to 10 pies. Roll out rounds large enough to fit a pie pan on a lightly floured breadboard. Stack these rounds, separated by waxed paper, about 4 or 5 high. Place each stack in plastic freezer wrap, tie securely, and store in the freezer. Remove each round of pastry as needed, and let stand at room temperature

just until it thaws enough to be fitted into a pie pan. If you are making a cream or custard pie, chill the dough thoroughly before filling.

PASTRY CUT-OUTS. These add greatly to the appearance of almost any pie, and can be made by cutting the pastry dough with an appropriate cooky cutter (heart-shaped for Valentine's Day, shamrocks for St. Patrick's Day, etc.). Bake the cut-out on a cooky sheet in a 450° F. oven for approximately 10 minutes, or until browned. (Watch carefully.) Place on pie when ready to serve. For pies such as mincemeat or any pie without too moist a filling, the cut-out may be placed on top and baked with the pie.

EGG PASTRY

Makes a two-crust, 9 or 10-inch pie. Appropriate for any pie filling, and practically failure-proof.

3 cups sifted pastry or all-purpose flour (Do *not* use cake flour in *any* pastry recipe!)

1 teaspoon salt

1 cup butter or margarine (or a blend of the two)

1 large egg, slightly beaten

2 tablespoons lemon juice or vinegar

¼ to ⅓ cup ice water

Sift the flour and salt together into a large bowl. Cut in the butter or margarine just until the pieces are the size of small peas. Combine egg, lemon juice or vinegar, and water. Stir into the flour mixture just to hold the dough together, blending with a kitchen fork. Roll out on a lightly floured breadboard or between two sheets of waxed paper.

HOT WATER PASTRY

The only pastry in which you use hot water, and the water must be *very* hot! Makes a two-crust 8-inch pie, or two 8-inch pie shells. Appropriate for any filling.

¼ cup water, brought just to the boil and poured over ½ cup lard, shortening, or margarine

1½ cups sifted pastry or all-purpose flour
¼ teaspoon salt
¼ teaspoon double-acting baking powder

Stir the hot water and the fat used just until it is smooth. Sift the flour, salt, and baking powder. Combine mixtures and blend until smooth. Chill thoroughly before rolling out.

MRS. SHRIETER'S OIL PASTRY

Makes a single 9 or 10-inch pie shell. Appropriate for any filling.

1½ cups sifted pastry or all-purpose flour
1 teaspoon salt

½ cup salad oil (*not* olive oil)
2 tablespoons cold milk

Sift dry ingredients into the pie pan. Combine the oil and milk and blend with a fork. Pour, all at once, over the flour mixture. Blend with a fork until flour is dampened. Press, with the fingers, to line the bottom and sides of the pan, making certain that the dough is even.

NUT PASTRY

Makes a single 9-inch pie shell. Appropriate for chiffon pies, cream and custard pies, and some fruit pies.

11/73 good but not spectacular

1¾ cups sifted pastry or all-purpose flour
pinch of salt

½ cup ground nuts (walnuts, almonds, or Brazil nuts)
½ cup butter or margarine
3 tablespoons ice water

Sift flour and salt into a bowl. Add the nuts and stir to blend. Cut in the butter or margarine as previously directed (until the size of small peas). Add the ice water slowly. Blend with a fork and then form into a ball. Wrap in waxed paper or plastic wrap and chill thoroughly. Roll out on lightly floured board.

FAVORITE SOUR CREAM PASTRY

Makes a single 10-inch pie shell, with pastry for a few cut-outs. Halve ingredients again to make enough pastry for a double-crust 8- or 9-inch pie.

¼ pound + 2 tablespoons cold sweet butter

2 cups sifted pastry or all-purpose flour

1 cup very cold sour cream (approximately)

Cut the ¼ pound of butter into the flour until the butter is in coarse pieces. Stir in just enough sour cream to bind the mixture together. Do not use *any* water. Form the dough into a ball and roll out on a lightly floured board. Cut the remaining 2 tablespoons butter into tiny bits and sprinkle the bits over the rolled-out dough. Fold ⅓ of the dough towards the middle, and ⅓ of the dough over the folded part, to make 3 thicknesses of dough. Roll out. Fold the dough into 3 thicknesses again. Wrap in waxed paper or plastic wrap and chill for at least 2 hours before rolling out again. Cut and fit into pie pan.

CREAM CHEESE PASTRY

Makes two 10-inch pie shells, or may be used to line tart pans. An excellent pastry, appropriate with any dessert filling or main-dish filling.

2½ cups sifted pastry or all-purpose flour

pinch of salt

1 cup butter or margarine

8 ounces cream cheese

½ cup light cream

Sift the flour and salt into a bowl. Cut in the butter or margarine and the cream cheese until mixture is the size of small peas. Add enough of the light cream to bind the mixture together. Roll out on a lightly floured board.

NOTE. This pastry may be kept in the refrigerator for up to a week.

SWEET PASTRY (PATÉ SUCRÉE)

Makes one 8-inch pie shell. Appropriate for tart shells, or as a pie shell for any fruit filling. For small, fancy tarts, brush the tart pans lightly with melted butter before pressing the dough into the pans. Use your clean fingers and work quickly.

1 cup sifted pastry or all-purpose flour	slightly more than ¼ cup sugar
pinch of salt	1 egg yolk
	¼ cup softened butter

Sift flour, salt, and sugar into a bowl or onto a marble slab. Make a hole in the center and in this hole place the egg yolk and butter. Mix with a fork until the paste is smooth. No cutting in of the butter in this pastry—it must be blended until smooth. Form the dough into a ball and wrap in waxed paper or plastic wrap. Chill for at least 2 hours. Roll out on a lightly floured board. It is difficult to roll, but worth it.

ALMOND PASTRY

Makes one 8-inch pie shell. Appropriate for any fruit filling, but especially good with cherry, peach, or apricot fillings.

1½ cups sifted pastry or all-purpose flour	½ teaspoon salt
¼ cup ground almonds	½ cup butter or margarine
¼ cup sugar	1 large egg, slightly beaten
	3 tablespoons ice water

Sift the flour into a bowl. Add the ground nuts, sugar, and salt and blend well. Cut in the butter or margarine until the size of small peas. Blend in the egg and enough of the water to make a dough that will form into a ball. Wrap in waxed paper or plastic wrap and chill for at least 2 hours. Roll out on a lightly floured board.

NADINE ROE'S MILK PIE CRUST

his excellent pastry is indigenous to the Midwest. The recipe makes
two-crust, 9 or 10-inch pie and is appropriate with any pie filling.
hen pre-baked it becomes very crisp, and makes an especially fine
se for any pie requiring a prebaked pie shell.

3 cups sifted flour
1½ teaspoons salt
1 cup butter or margarine (or
    a mixture of the two)

½ cup very cold milk (you
    may need another
    tablespoon or two)
2 egg yolks

ft the flour and salt into a large bowl. Cut in the butter or margarine
st until the pieces are the size of small peas. Combine milk and egg
olks. Beat to blend. Stir into the flour mixture, using another table-
oon or two of cold milk if needed to bind mixture together. Divide
ugh into 2 parts. Roll each part out on a lightly floured breadboard
d fit into pie pans.

GRAHAM CRACKER PIE SHELL

akes one 8- or 9-inch pie shell. Appropriate for any kind of cream
e, or for lemon or orange pies, or for unbaked pie using condensed,
veetened milk.

1 cup graham cracker crumbs
3 tablespoons brown sugar

1 tablespoon honey
3 tablespoons melted butter

ombine crumbs and brown sugar in a bowl and blend well. Stir in
oney and melted butter until thoroughly blended. Press into pie pan
ith fingers. Chill for at least an hour before filling, unless shell is to
e prebaked. To prebake the shell, bake in a 375° F. oven for 8
inutes, or until edges are lightly browned. Cool before filling.

CHOCOLATE OR VANILLA WAFER SHELL

Makes one 8 or 9-inch pie shell. Appropriate for any kind of cream
pie, for lemon, orange, or chocolate pies, or for the unbaked pies using
condensed, sweetened milk.

> 1⅓ cups fine chocolate or   ¼ cup very soft butter
> vanilla wafer crumbs

Mix ingredients until crumbly. Press on bottom and sides of pie pan.
Chill for at least an hour before filling, unless shell is to be prebaked.
To prebake the shell, bake in a 375° F. oven for 8 minutes, or until
lightly browned.

COCONUT MERINGUE PIE SHELL

Appropriate for chiffon pies, or fruit and whipped cream, or for filling
with balls of ice cream and topping with an appropriate sauce.

> 2 egg whites from large eggs   ½ teaspoon vanilla extract or
> ¼ teaspoon cream of tartar   grated lemon rind
> pinch of salt   ⅔ cup flaked coconut
> ⅔ cup sugar

Combine egg whites, cream of tartar, and salt. Beat until foamy. Add
sugar, 2 tablespoons at a time, and beat until mixture holds stiff peaks.
Fold in vanilla extract and coconut. Spread on bottom and sides of a
9 or 10-inch pie pan. Bake in a 325° F. oven for 30 minutes, or until
meringue is dry and firm. Cool on rack.

CHOCOLATE COCONUT PIE SHELL

Appropriate for chiffon pies, for cream pies made with a pre-cooked
filling, or for condensed milk pies.

2 ounces sweet chocolate   2 tablespoons water
2 tablespoons butter   1⅓ cup flaked coconut

Combine chocolate, butter, and water in a saucepan. Place over low heat and stir until chocolate melts. Remove from heat and blend in the coconut. Spread over bottom and sides of a buttered 9-inch pan. Chill until firm.

TO PREBAKE PIE SHELLS. These instructions are for all of the pastry recipes that do not include prebaking instructions with the recipe. Line pie pan with pastry desired. Chill thoroughly. Prick the pie shell all over with a fork. Bake in a 450° F. oven for 10 to 15 minutes, or until browned to your liking. If sides do droop a little, you can press them back into shape while pastry is still baking. Cool on rack before filling so that pie shell will remain crisp.

MERINGUES

The most successful and glamorous of all pie toppings is a meringue. But to obtain a tender, fluffy meringue takes more than just adding sugar and beating the egg whites. The following suggestions will be helpful.

1. Egg whites must be at room temperature.

2. Use a small, deep bowl, rather than a wide, shallow bowl. The volume will be considerably greater.

3. Beat egg whites with the electric mixer at medium speed just until whites are foamy; then start adding the sugar, a few tablespoons at a time, increasing the speed of the mixer.

4. The egg whites must be beaten thoroughly after each addition of sugar to thoroughly dissolve the sugar. If not, moisture will form on the meringue after it is baked.

5. Spread meringue on a hot or slightly cooled filling, not on a cold or chilled filling.

6. When spreading meringue on pie, make certain that the meringue touches the pie shell all the way around.

7. Brown the meringue in a 350° F. oven for 15 to 20 minutes, or until done to your taste. Remember that overbaking makes a tough meringue.

8. Cool meringue-topped pies away from a draft. Meringue-topped pies *must* be completely cooled before refrigerating, otherwise the meringue will weep.

9. Most cookbooks recommend a 2 egg white meringue for an 8-inch pie; a 3 egg white meringue for a 9-inch pie and so on. However, this amount will not make those gorgeous, cloud-like meringues that you see on magazine covers. Those meringues are invariably made with 4 or 5 egg whites.

MERINGUE FOR 8-INCH PIE

2 egg whites
¼ teaspoon cream of tartar
dash of salt

¼ teaspoon vanilla extract, or almond extract or other flavoring
4 tablespoons sugar

MERINGUE FOR 9-INCH PIE

3 egg whites
¼ teaspoon cream of tartar
¼ teaspoon salt

½ teaspoon vanilla extract, or ¼ teaspoon almond extract or other flavoring
6 tablespoons sugar

MERINGUE FOR 10-INCH PIE

4 or 5 egg whites
¼ teaspoon cream of tartar
¼ teaspoon salt

1 teaspoon vanilla extract
8 to 10 tablespoons sugar

Allow egg whites to come to room temperature. Place whites in a deep bowl with the cream of tartar, salt and flavoring. Beat, with an electric mixer, at medium speed until mixture is foamy and frothy. Increase mixing speed and add the sugar, 2 tablespoons at a time, beating well after each addition. Beat until sugar dissolves, and then continue beating until meringue is smooth and glossy.

LEMON MERINGUE. Make any meringue above, omitting the cream of tartar and using 1 teaspoon fresh lemon juice. Many cooks prefer this meringue.

BROWN SUGAR MERINGUE. Make any basic meringue using brown sugar in place of white sugar.

MERINGUE TOPPINGS. To add to visual appeal as well as taste, sprinkle the unbaked meringue with flaky coconut, chopped nuts, or crumbled pralines. A baked meringue can be sprinkled with shaved chocolate or grated orange or tangerine rind.

AMERICAN HERITAGE PIES

Most housewives of today make modern pies using recipes from blessedly modern cookbooks. The easy-to-make pies using condensed milk, the chiffon pies that were virtually unknown a mere 30 years ago, and the marvelous cheese pies using cream cheese and sour cream are all modern. But the pioneer recipes, those that were popular 100 or more years ago, hold a particular fascination for the discriminating cook of today. And a peek into the early-day cookbooks arouse feelings that are part historic interest, part nostalgia, and part gratitude. The authors wasted no time on minute instructions. In the 1884 edition of the *Virginia Cookery Book* Mrs. Smith tells us to make Apple Pies Without Apples thus, *"Put ten large square soda crackers in a bowl; pour over them a quart of boiling water; let soak for an hour; then mash them up very fine; add to them the grated peel and juice of four lemons, and five teacupfuls of brown sugar; put it in a pastry, and bake like any other pie."*

And even earlier Colonial cooks, braver than we, were undaunted by recipes that began, "To a peck of flour, you must have three-quarters the weight in butter;"

But it is a rare cook who isn't proud of at least one up-dated heirloom recipe for a pie, cake, or cooky. The following are all delicious, and in the main, easy to make.

JAM PIE

Deliciously rich and buttery! One other excellent version of this old-time pie, called "Caramel Pie," uses Damson plum preserves in place of a berry jam. One half teaspoon of vanilla is added and the eggs are separated. The yolks are creamed with the butter and sugar, and the stiffly beaten egg whites are folded in last. Both versions are so old that they could well be considered brand new.

8 or 9-inch pie shell, unbaked	½ cup any berry jam
½ cup butter	(boysenberry jam is very
½ cup sugar	good)
3 large eggs	½ cup heavy cream

Cream the butter and the sugar. Add the eggs and beat thoroughly. Add the jam and the cream and blend very well. Pour into the pie shell and bake in a 450° F. oven for 10 minutes. Reduce heat to 350° F. and bake another 30 minutes. Cool. Serve slightly warm.

OSGOOD PIE

It is impossible to check back far enough to find out where some of the early-day pies got their names. One old book had a recipe for a "Bob Andy" pie!

8 or 9-inch pie shell, unbaked	1 tablespoon vinegar
½ cup butter	1 teaspoon nutmeg
1 cup sugar	½ teaspoon cinnamon
2 eggs, separated	½ cup chopped pecans
1 tablespoon flour	½ cup raisins

Cream the butter and sugar. Add the egg yolks and beat well. Add flour, vinegar, and spices and blend thoroughly. Fold in the nuts and the raisins. Beat the egg whites until stiff, and fold into the mixture. Pour into the pie shell and bake in a 375° F. oven until set, approximately 30 to 35 minutes. Cool on a rack. When ready to serve, top each slice with a dollop of whipped cream.

BUTTERSCOTCH PIE

8-inch pie shell, unbaked	2 tablespoons melted butter
1 cup commercial sour cream	1 tablespoon flour
2 egg yolks	1 teaspoon vanilla extract
1 cup brown sugar	MERINGUE

Combine sour cream, egg yolks, sugar, butter, flour, and vanilla. Beat until light. Pour into the pie shell and bake in a 450° F. oven for 10 minutes. Reduce heat to 350° F. and bake another 35 to 45 minutes. Spread with MERINGUE (see pp. 185–7) desired and brown as directed.

VINEGAR PIE

Old and unusual, the recipes for this pie vary with the cook. Some recipes call for a pre-cooked filling, as for lemon pie, others just mix the ingredients and allow them to thicken while baking. Some old recipes call for a tablespoon of vinegar and appear to be little more than chess pies flavored with vinegar when the lemons ran out. Other recipes call for as much as a cup of what was hopefully a mild-flavored vinegar. Some recipes call for spices, usually cloves and cinnamon. This one has a creamy filling, the consistency of a pecan pie without the nuts.

9-inch pie shell, unbaked	3 egg yolks
¼ cup flour	1¾ cups water
1½ cups sugar	½ cup mild vinegar
1 teaspoon grated lemon rind	1 tablespoon melted butter

Combine flour, sugar, and lemon rind. Stir to blend thoroughly. Combine egg yolks, water, vinegar, and melted butter. Blend thoroughly. Combine mixtures, blending until smooth. I give it a quick whirl in the blender. Pour into the pie shell. Bake in 450° F. oven for 10 minutes. Reduce heat to 350° F. and bake another 20 to 30 minutes. Cool on a rack.

SHOOFLY PIE

Although there are several theories as to how Shoofly Pie acquired its name, including the one that says that it is a corruption of the French *chou-fleur* (cauliflower), no one knows for sure. All that we do know is that this pie originated with the Pennsylvania Dutch. There are three versions: a very dry pie used mainly for dunking; a moist type, termed "wet" by the practical Pennsylvania Dutch; and the cake type which is often called Shoofly Cake in spite of the fact that it is baked in a pie shell. Within these versions there are variations. Some versions of the "wet" type called for the crumbs to be placed in the pie crust first and the molasses mixture poured over the crumbs. Other recipes for the same "wet" type called for the molasses mixture first and then the crumbs. Some called for the two mixtures to be stirred together, and others said that the crumbs should be very carefully placed on top of the molasses so as not to disturb it.

In an effort to discover if there were some earth-shaking significance to all this, I spent one entire afternoon baking Shoofly Pies and all I can tell you is that, no matter how you stir it, if you like gingerbread you will like these pies.

9-inch pie shell, unbaked
¾ cup flour
½ cup brown sugar
½ teaspoon cinnamon
2 tablespoons butter

½ cup light molasses
¾ cup very hot water
1 egg yolk, beaten
½ teaspoon baking soda.

Combine the flour, brown sugar, and cinnamon. Cut in the butter until mixture is like crumbs. In another bowl combine the molasses and hot water. Beat in the egg yolk very quickly so that it does not begin to harden. Stir in the baking soda. Now you must work quickly so that you do not lose the leavening power of the baking soda. Either put the crumb mixture in the bottom of the pie shell and pour the molasses mixture over the crumbs or vice versa. My sons preferred it with the crumbs on top as it makes a slightly moister pie. I didn't find that it really made that much difference. Bake in a 375° F. oven 40 to 45 minutes.

NOTE. Some recipes omit any spice at all and use instead a teaspoon of vanilla extract. Good either way.

CAKE-TYPE SHOOFLY PIE

9-inch pie shell, unbaked
1½ cups flour
½ cup brown sugar
1 teaspoon baking powder
2 tablespoons butter

½ cup light molasses
½ cup very hot water
¾ teaspoon baking soda
½ teaspoon cinnamon

Combine the flour, brown sugar, and baking powder. Stir to blend. Cut in the butter to make crumbs. Combine molasses, water, baking soda, and cinnamon. Pour ⅓ of the molasses mixture into the pie shell. Add about ⅓ of the crumb mixture. Continue, alternating the two mixtures, ending with the crumb mixture. Bake in a 350° F. oven for 30 to 40 minutes.

ANGEL PIES

These marvelous pies combine the crisp meringue shell with a rich, creamy filling. The most important thing about them is the shell. Make them on a cool, dry day. Humid weather makes soft meringues. Separate the eggs while cold, but let the egg whites warm to room temperature before beating.

MERINGUE PIE SHELL

4 egg whites	1 teaspoon vinegar
¼ teaspoon salt	1 cup sugar

Beat the egg whites with the salt and vinegar until soft peaks form. Gradually add the sugar, beating until all the sugar is dissolved (a tiny bit rubbed between two fingers should not feel grainy), and mixture holds stiff peaks. The meringue will be shiny and moist. Spread over bottom and sides of a well-buttered 10-inch pie pan. Build up the sides, making fancy edges if desired. Bake in a 275° oven for 1 hour. Turn off heat and let dry in the oven for another hour. The center of the shell will crack and may fall, but this is all right.

NUT MERINGUE SHELL.   Fold ½ cup of finely chopped nuts into the meringue.

CHOCOLATE RUM ANGEL PIE

1 6-ounce package semisweet chocolate pieces	1 cup heavy cream
2 egg yolks	¼ cup sugar
2 tablespoons water	MERINGUE PIE SHELL
2 tablespoons rum	(see above)

Melt the chocolate over hot water. Cool just slightly, and spread 2 tablespoons of the melted chocolate over the bottom of the cooled meringue pie shell. To the remaining chocolate add the egg yolks, rum, and water. Blend. Chill until mixture thickens. Combine heavy cream and sugar and whip. Fold whipped cream into the chocolate mixture. Pour into shell and chill for at least 4 hours, preferably overnight.

LEMON ANGEL PIE

4 egg yolks
½ cup sugar
⅓ cup lemon juice

1 teaspoon grated lemon rind
1 cup heavy cream
MERINGUE PIE SHELL (p. 192)

Beat the yolks until light. Gradually beat in the sugar, lemon juice, and rind. Place in the top of a double boiler and cook over hot water, stirring, until mixture thickens, about 6 minutes. Cool. Whip the cream until it forms soft peaks. Spread cooled lemon mixture in the meringue pie shell, and top with whipped cream. Some good cooks spread half of the lemon mixture in the shell, fold the rest into the whipped cream, and spoon this over the lemon mixture. Chill overnight.

ORANGE ANGEL PIE

4 egg yolks
1 large egg
⅔ cup sugar
¼ cup frozen orange juice
  concentrate, thawed

1 teaspoon grated orange rind
1 tablespoon lemon juice
1 cup heavy cream
MERINGUE PIE SHELL (p. 192)

Combine egg yolks and whole egg and beat until thick and light. Add sugar, orange juice and rind and lemon juice. Stir well and cook over hot water, stirring constantly, until thickened. Chill. Whip the heavy cream and fold into the chilled orange mixture. Turn into the meringue pie shell and chill overnight.

FRUITED ANGEL PIE

Some good cooks fold diced or crushed fresh fruit, berries, or well-drained canned fruit into sweetened and flavored whipped cream, and pour into the MERINGUE PIE SHELL (p. 192). Others place the fruit in the bottom of the shell and top with whipped cream. Both are very good. Chill these well before serving.

APPLE PIES

Apple Pie must surely reign as the king of American desserts. And, like so many other great dishes, there are as many versions as there are creative, imaginative cooks. One creative cook, whose apple pie I dearly love, spreads the pie shell with several tablespoons of orange marmalade before pouring in the apple filling. Another always sprinkles the filling with the juice of half a lemon, or with 2 tablespoons of pineapple juice, before arranging the top crust. Another excellent idea is the one used in the recipe immediately following.

JUICY APPLE PIE

pastry for a 2-crust, 9 or 10-inch pie	1½ cups sugar (part may be brown sugar)
8 to 10 medium apples, or enough to make 6 to 7 cups apple slices	1 teaspoon cinnamon
	1 teaspoon nutmeg
	2 tablespoons butter

The night before the pie is to be made, peel, core, and slice the apples. Turn into a bowl and add the sugar, cinnamon, and nutmeg. Stir to blend. Cover the bowl and let stand overnight. When ready to make the pie, pour off all the juices from the apples and reserve. Line the pie pan with pastry and arrange the apples in the shell. Dot with butter and arrange the top crust. Flute the edges and cut vents into the top crust, and make a hole in the center. Bake in a 425° F. oven until the crust is a golden brown and the apples are done, about 40 minutes. Remove the pie from the oven and insert a funnel into the hole in the crust. Carefully pour all the reserved juices into the funnel. The hot apples will absorb the juice and expand to fill the entire crust. Delectable and juicy.

COUNTRY APPLE PIE

This marvelous pie originated in farm country, where the good cooks have cream to spare.

pastry for a 2-crust, 9-inch pie

6 cups peeled and cored apples, thinly sliced	1 cup sugar (part may be brown)
¾ cup heavy cream	¼ teaspoon salt
2 tablespoons flour	1 teaspoon cinnamon
2 tablespoons melted butter	2 teaspoons lemon juice or vanilla extract
1 large egg	

Line pie pan with pastry. Arrange the apples in the pie shell. Combine all the remaining ingredients and blend thoroughly. Pour over the apples. Arrange top crust over filling. Flute edges and cut vents in the top crust. Brush the crust with milk or half and half. Bake in a 400° F. oven for 45 minutes to 1 hour, or until apples test done.

OPEN-FACE APPLE PIE

An unusual and very tasty pie.

9-inch pie shell, unbaked	3 tablespoons flour
6 cups peeled, cored, thinly sliced apples	¼ cup butter
	½ teaspoon salt
1 cup sugar (part may be brown)	¼ teaspoon cinnamon
	⅓ cup light cream or milk

Arrange sliced apples in the pie shell. Combine the sugar, flour, butter, salt, and cinnamon to make a crumbly mixture. Pour half the mixture over the apples and stir lightly to blend into the apples, but be careful not to puncture the bottom crust. Pour the cream or milk over the apples and top with the rest of the crumbs. Bake in a 350° F. oven for 1 hour, or until apples are tender and pie is bubbly. A piece of foil should be placed over the pie for the first half hour to keep the crust from burning.

APPLE CHEESE PIE

Some people prefer an apple pie with cheese. My husband vouches for the tastiness of this pie.

9-inch pie shell, unbaked
6 cups peeled, cored, thinly
   sliced apples
½ cup sugar
1 teaspoon cinnamon

⅓ cup brown sugar
⅓ cup flour
¼ cup butter
1 cup shredded Cheddar
   cheese

Combine apples, sugar and cinnamon. Toss to blend and turn into the pie shell. Combine brown sugar, flour, and butter, mixing until crumbly. Sprinkle mixture over the apples. Bake in a 400° F. oven for 35 minutes or until apples are tender. Sprinkle with the cheese, and return to the oven just until the cheese melts. Serve warm.

APPLE NUT PIE

10-inch pie shell, unbaked
8 to 10 medium-sized apples,
   peeled, cored, and thinly
   sliced.
½ teaspoon grated lemon rind

juice of ½ lemon
1¼ cups brown sugar
½ cup flour
⅓ cup butter
½ cup chopped nuts

Fill pie shell with the apples. Sprinkle with the grated lemon rind and lemon juice. Combine brown sugar, flour, and butter to make a crumbly mixture. Blend in the chopped nuts. Sprinkle sugar mixture over the apples. Bake in a 425° F. oven for 10 minutes. Reduce heat to 350° F. and continue baking for 50 minutes or until apples are tender.

DEEP-DISH APPLE PIE.   Decrease sugar to ¾ cup. Alternate the apples and sugar mixture in a buttered baking dish. Dot the top with 3 tablespoons butter. Cover top with pie pastry. Cut vents in the crust and brush the crust with milk or half and half. Bake in a 450° F. oven for 15 minutes. Reduce heat to 350° F. and bake 30 minutes longer. Serve hot with cheese or cream.

FAVORITE MARLBOROUGH PIE

Regional America has always had its favorite pies. In the South it's the rich pecan and chess pies, and in the region called "Down East" mince, cranberry, and pumpkin vie with a glorified apple pie called "Marlborough." In earlier times the housewife had to cook and mash the apples before making this pie. The modern housewife can open a can of applesauce.

10-inch pie shell, unbaked	½ teaspoon salt
2 cups tart applesauce	3 tablespoons lemon juice
¼ cup melted butter	1 teaspoon grated lemon rind
1 cup sugar	4 large eggs

Combine ingredients in order listed and blend thoroughly. Pour into the unbaked pie shell. Bake in a 450° F. oven for 15 minutes to set the crust. Then reduce heat to 350° F. and continue baking for approximately 30 minutes, or until a silver knife inserted in the center comes out clean. The pie will have a golden color and will cut like a custard pie.

APPLE PIE WITH YOGURT

A delicious, modern pie. In this, as in the other pies in this book using yogurt or sour cream, the two may be used interchangeably. The recipe for HOMEMADE YOGURT is on pages 346–7.

9-inch pie shell, unbaked
¾ cup sugar
2 tablespoons flour
1 cup yogurt or sour cream
1 large egg

½ teaspoon vanilla extract
pinch of salt
2 cups peeled and chopped
  apples

Blend sugar and flour. Combine with rest of ingredients and blend thoroughly. Pour into pastry shell and bake in a 375° F. oven for 45 to 50 minutes or until apples are tender. Cool on rack. To serve, top each slice with a dollop of yogurt or sour cream, and sprinkle with chopped, toasted nuts.

HONEY AND SOUR CREAM APPLE PIE

pastry for a 2-crust, 9-inch pie
6 to 8 tart apples, peeled,
  cored, and sliced
½ cup sour cream or yogurt
½ cup mild-flavored honey

¼ cup light brown sugar
pinch of salt
1 teaspoon cinnamon
½ teaspoon nutmeg

Line a 9-inch pie pan with pastry and fill with the cored and sliced apples. Combine the rest of the ingredients and blend thoroughly. Pour over the apples. Cover with the top crust and slash decoratively. If desired, the top crust may be brushed lightly with cream or half and half and sprinkled with sugar. Bake in a 425°F. oven 20 minutes, then reduce heat to 350° F. and continue baking another 20 minutes.

COTTAGE CHEESE AND SOUR CREAM PIES

One and all, these are delectable taste delights. Some are made with sour cream, some with cottage cheese, and others with cream cheese.

The latter are variations of the luxurious cheesecake, and while several pies are included here, there is a section on CHEESECAKES in the Cakes chapter (pp. 45–50).

COTTAGE CHEESE PIE

My family loves this light, delicious pie. For an added taste treat I take slivered, blanched almonds, toast them lightly and fold through the batter before baking.

9 or 10-inch pie shell,
  unbaked
1 pound cottage cheese
½ cup sugar
¼ cup heavy cream

4 large eggs, separated
¼ teaspoon salt
1 teaspoon grated lemon rind
¼ cup lemon juice

Combine the cheese, sugar, cream, egg yolks, and salt. Mix well and force through a sieve, or whirl in a blender until smooth. Add the grated rind and juice and blend well. Beat the egg whites until stiff and fold them into the cheese mixture. Pour filling into the pie shell. Bake in a 450° F. oven for 10 minutes. Reduce heat to 350° F. and bake another 35 minutes or until firm. Chill before serving.

NOTE.   You might sprinkle a buttered 8-inch square pan with graham cracker crumbs, or press with the mixture for GRAHAM CRACKER CRUMB PIE SHELL (p. 183), pour in the above filling, and bake in a 325° F. oven for 45 to 50 minutes, or until firm.

COTTAGE CHEESE CUSTARD PIE.   Follow the recipe for Cottage Cheese pie, omitting the heavy cream and using instead 1 cup milk or half and half. Bake as directed until a knife inserted in the center comes out clean.

NOTE.   To either recipe given above you might add a cup of flaked coconut for a "Coconut Cottage Cheese Pie," or a ½ cup of well-drained, crushed pineapple for a "Pineapple Cottage Cheese Pie." Both are delicious.

COTTAGE CHEESE APPLE PIE

For this delectable pie I sometimes use a can of apple slices. NOT the
apple pie filling, as that is too sweet.

9-inch pie shell, unbaked	2 large eggs
2 cups peeled, cored, thinly sliced apples	½ cup sugar
	¼ teaspoon salt
¼ cup brown sugar	1 cup milk or half and half
½ teaspoon cinnamon	1 teaspoon vanilla extract
¼ teaspoon nutmeg	1 cup cottage cheese

Combine sliced apples, brown sugar, cinnamon, and nutmeg and stir
to blend. Pour into bottom of pie shell. Bake in a 425° F. oven for
15 minutes. Remove from oven. Combine the eggs, sugar, salt, milk
or half and half, vanilla, and cottage cheese. Beat until smooth. If
desired, mixture may be whirled in a blender. Pour cheese mixture
over the prebaked apples. Bake in a 325° F. oven for 40 minutes, or
until a knife inserted in the center comes out clean.

COTTAGE CHEESE JAM PIE

A delicious pie that changes character with the jam used. We prefer
raspberry or blackberry jam, but any kind may be used.

9-inch pie shell, unbaked	1 cup heavy cream
⅓ to ½ cup any preferred jam	⅔ cup sugar
	3 large eggs, separated
1½ cups cottage cheese	1 teaspoon grated lemon rind
1 tablespoon flour	2 tablespoons lemon juice
pinch of salt	

Spread the jam over the bottom of the pie shell. Combine cheese, flour,
salt, cream, sugar, egg yolks, lemon rind and juice. Blend well and
whirl in a blender until smooth. Beat the egg whites until stiff and

fold into the cheese mixture. Pour over the jam. Bake in a 450° F. oven for 10 minutes. Reduce heat to 350° F. and continue baking for another 45 minutes, or until firm.

SOUR CREAM DATE PIE I

Very good and very simple, especially with pre-chopped dates. The brandy may be omitted if desired, and a teaspoon of vanilla extract used instead.

8 or 9-inch pie shell, unbaked	2 large eggs
1 cup commercial sour cream	1 tablespoon brandy
¾ cup brown sugar	1 cup pitted dates, chopped
pinch of salt	½ to ¾ cup chopped nuts
½ teaspoon nutmeg	

Combine sour cream, sugar, salt, nutmeg, eggs, and brandy. Beat until smooth. Add the dates and nuts and blend well. Pour into pie shell. Bake in a 425° F. oven for 10 minutes, then reduce heat to 325° F. and continue baking for 25 minutes, or until firm.

SOUR CREAM DATE PIE II

This one is just a little different, but very tasty. You might substitute 1 to 1½ cups raisins or cooked, well-drained dried apricots for the dates.

10-inch pie shell, unbaked	¼ cup water or fruit juice
1 cup sugar	1 cup commercial sour cream
3 large eggs	1 teaspoon vanilla extract
¼ cup mild vinegar	1 cup pitted dates, chopped

Combine sugar, eggs, vinegar, liquid, sour cream, and vanilla. Whirl in a blender or beat with hand or electric mixer until perfectly smooth. Add dates and stir to mix well. Pour into pie shell. Bake in 400° F. oven for 10 minutes, reduce heat to 325° F. and bake another 45 to 50 minutes, or until custard is firm.

SOUR CREAM RAISIN PIE

A great pie recipe, and a very old one. In some parts of the country it is called, for some unknown reason, "Funeral Pie." Don't let that keep you from enjoying it!

10-inch pie shell, unbaked
2 cups commercial sour cream
2 tablespoons cornstarch
1½ cups light brown sugar
1 tablespoon lemon juice
pinch of salt

pinch of nutmeg
¼ teaspoon cinnamon
¼ teaspoon cloves
2 large eggs
½ cup raisins

Blend sour cream and cornstarch until smooth. Add the sugar, lemon juice, salt, spices, and eggs. Beat until smooth and blended. Stir in the raisins. Pour into pie shell. Bake in a 375° F. oven until firm, approximately 45 minutes.

NOTE. You might omit the raisins and spices. Use 1½ cups cooked well-drained dried apricots and 2 or 3 drops of almond extract.

SOUR CREAM FRUIT PIE I

We like this pie almost as much as cheesecake, which it somewhat resembles. Its well-chilled smoothness is just great on a hot summer day.

9-inch graham cracker pie
    shell, baked in a 350° F.
    oven for 5 to 7 minutes
2 cups commercial sour cream
2 teaspoons cornstarch

2 large eggs
½ cup + 2 tablespoons sugar
1 #2½ can fruit cocktail; or
    fruits for salad; or tropical
    fruits, well-drained

Combine sour cream and cornstarch and mix until smooth. Add the eggs and sugar and blend thoroughly. Stir into the well-drained canned fruits. Pour into graham cracker pie shell and bake in a 350° F. oven for 20 minutes. Cool and then chill thoroughly.

SOUR CREAM FRUIT PIE II

Like twins, these two pies are similar yet different. Each has its avid fans.

9-inch pie shell, unbaked, with lattice strips for the top
1 #2½ can peaches or pears, well-drained; or enough fresh peaches, peeled and sliced, to make 4 cups; or a package of frozen blackberries, barely thawed;

or a mixture of well-drained canned mandarin oranges and fresh, sliced, firm-ripe bananas
1 cup sugar
⅓ cup flour
pinch of salt
1 cup commercial sour cream

Turn fruit into the pie shell. Combine sugar and flour and blend thoroughly, so there will be no lumps. Add salt and sour cream and blend well. Pour over the fruit. Arrange lattice strips over sour cream mixture. Sprinkle lightly with sugar, and, depending on what fruit is used, a bare sprinkling of cinnamon. Bake in a 425° F. oven for 10 minutes. Reduce heat to 350° F. and bake 40 minutes longer. Cool and chill.

EASY YOGURT PIE

This is a delicious, very simple pie that requires no baking. I sometimes line the pie shell with very well-drained fruit, and pour the cheese mixture over it. Still no baking.

8-inch graham cracker pie shell, baked
1 cup thick yogurt
8 ounces cream cheese

½ cup sugar
½ teaspoon vanilla extract
½ teaspoon grated lemon rind

Combine yogurt, cream cheese, sugar, vanilla, and lemon rind in a bowl. Beat with an electric mixer until smooth and blended. Pour into baked and cooled pie shell. Chill overnight.

YOGURT PIE

This pie is more of a production, but looks and tastes lovely.

9-inch graham cracker pie
 shell, baked
1 tablespoon unflavored
 gelatin
¼ cup cold water
2 egg yolks

¼ cup milk
1 pound cream cheese
1 teaspoon vanilla extract
3 tablespoons honey
2 cups yogurt

Soften the gelatin in the cold water and dissolve over hot water. Beat
the egg yolks lightly with the milk and stir into the gelatin. Cook over
hot water until mixture thickens enough to coat a spoon. Cool. Cream
the cheese with the vanilla and honey. Stir in 1 cup of the yogurt.
Pour the cooled custard mixture into the cheese mixture, stirring to
blend well, and then add the remaining cup of yogurt. Blend mixture
well and pour into the baked graham cracker pie shell. Chill until firm
and then sprinkle lightly with a mixture of graham cracker crumbs
and finely chopped nuts.

CREAM CHEESE PIES

These fabulous pies, all made with cream cheese and sour cream, are
variations of the classic cheesecake. Each variation, although seemingly
slight, has its advocates, staunchly proclaiming it to be the best.

*"If I eat one of these cakes it's sure
to make some change in my size."*
ALICE
FROM ALICE IN WONDERLAND

BASIC CREAM CHEESE PIE

9-inch graham cracker pie
    shell, baked in a 350° F.
    oven for 5 to 7 minutes,
    and cooled
9 ounces cream cheese
½ cup sugar

2 large eggs
½ teaspoon vanilla extract
2 cups sour cream
¼ cup sugar
½ to 1 teaspoon vanilla
    extract

Combine cream cheese, ½ cup sugar, eggs, and ½ teaspoon vanilla.
Beat until thoroughly creamed. Pour into pie shell. Bake in a 325° F.
oven for 20 minutes. Combine sour cream, ¼ cup sugar, and ½ to 1
teaspoon vanilla. Beat well and pour over the cream cheese mixture.
Return to oven for 5 minutes. Cool pie on rack, and chill before serving.

JOAN'S CHEESE PIE

9-inch unbaked graham
    cracker pie shell,
    well-chilled
1 pound cream cheese
⅔ cup sugar

1 tablespoon vanilla extract
3 large eggs
2 cups sour cream
⅓ cup sugar
2 teaspoons vanilla extract

Combine cream cheese, ⅔ cup sugar, 1 tablespoon vanilla, and eggs.
Beat until thoroughly blended. Pour into well-chilled pie shell and bake
in a 350° F. oven for 25 to 30 minutes. Combine sour cream, sugar,
and vanilla. Pour over cream cheese mixture and return to oven. Bake
5 minutes longer. Cool pie on rack, and chill before serving.

LEMON CHEESE PIE. Add ¼ to ⅓ cup of lemon juice to the
filling and omit the vanilla. To the topping add 1 tablespoon grated
lemon rind and omit the vanilla.

SOUR CREAM CHEESE PIE

9 or 10-inch graham cracker
   pie shell, unbaked and
   well-chilled
1 pound cream cheese
⅔ cup sugar

1 tablespoon flour
½ cup sour cream
1 teaspoon vanilla extract
1 tablespoon lemon juice
4 large eggs, separated

Combine cream cheese, sugar, flour, sour cream, flavorings and egg
yolks. Beat until thoroughly blended. Beat the egg whites until stiff
and fold into cheese mixture. Pour into pie shell and bake at 325° F
for approximately 45 minutes. This pie requires no topping.

FRUITED CHEESE PIE

9-inch pie shell, unbaked
1½ cups fresh or frozen
   berries; peeled and sliced
   fresh peaches; or any
   well-drained, canned fruit

12 ounces cream cheese
1 tablespoon flour
3 large eggs
⅓ cup sugar
¾ to 1 cup sour cream

Pour fruit into pie shell. Cream the remaining ingredients thoroughly
and pour over the fruit. Bake in a 350° F. oven for 30 to 35 minutes.
Cool on rack. Chill before serving.

CHOCOLATE CHEESE PIE

In this heavenly pie I fold the whipped cream through the chocolate
cheese mixture to make a high, fluffy, beautiful pie. But some good
cooks prefer to sweeten the whipped cream slightly and spread it over
the chocolate-cheese mixture.

9-inch graham cracker pie
   shell, baked
8 ounces cream cheese
¾ cup brown sugar
pinch of salt

1 teaspoon vanilla extract
2 large eggs, separated
6-ounce package semisweet
   chocolate bits, melted
1 cup heavy cream

Combine the cream cheese, sugar, pinch of salt, vanilla, and egg yolks and beat until smooth. Beat in the melted chocolate. Beat the egg whites until stiff. Whip the cream. Fold the beaten egg whites into the whipped cream. Fold mixture carefully but thoroughly through the cream cheese mixture. Turn into the pie shell. Chill at least overnight.

FARMER'S CHEESE PIE

This is certainly one of the best of all cheese pies.

9-inch graham cracker pie
   shell, baked at 350° F. for
   5 to 7 minutes and cooled
¾ cup cottage cheese
8 ounces cream cheese
¾ cup sugar
2 large eggs

1 teaspoon vanilla extract
1 teaspoon grated lemon rind
3 tablespoons lemon juice
½ cup heavy cream
1 cup commercial sour cream
2 tablespoons sugar

Whirl the cottage cheese in a blender until perfectly smooth or else press through a sieve. Combine cottage cheese, cream cheese, sugar, eggs, vanilla, lemon rind, and juice. Beat until smooth and blended. Pour into pie shell and bake in a 350° F. oven for 30 minutes. Cool on rack. Whip the heavy cream until stiff. Add the sour cream and sugar and blend well. Spread over cooled filling. Chill thoroughly before serving.

CHESS PIES

The term refers to the old-fashioned lemon-cheese pie, minus any cheese, of course. The pie is descended from the old English cheese

cakes which were made with warm milk and rennett. The early-da
cooks were careless about terms, and the words pie and cake wer
often used interchangeably. And in the handwritten cookbooks of a
earlier time, uneducated cooks wrote chess for cheese, much as th
word 'receipt' was used instead of 'recipe.'

Some of the very old recipes were unbelievably rich. One, from Mrs
Smith's *The Compleat Housewife,* is written thus: "Take two larg
Lemons, grate off the Peel of both and squeeze out the Juice of one
Add to it half a Pound of fine Sugar; twelve Yolks of Eggs, eigh
Whites well beaten; then melt half a Pound of Butter in four or fiv
Spoonfuls of Cream; then stir it all together, and set it over the Fire
stirring it 'till it begins to be pretty thick; then take it off, and whe
'tis cold, fill your Patty-pans little more than half full."

The modern day chess pies are still very popular in the South. Th
first one was supposed to have been the preferred dessert of the famou
statesman and president of the Confederate States.

JEFFERSON DAVIS PIE

8- or 9-inch shell, unbaked
½ cup butter
1½ cups granulated or brown
    sugar
2 large eggs

½ cup heavy cream
2 teaspoons cornmeal
pinch of salt
1 teaspoon vanilla extract

Cream the butter and sugar. Add the eggs and cream and, in the word
of one old cookbook, "beat like the very devil." Stir in the cornmea
salt, and vanilla and blend well. Pour into the pie shell and bake in
450° F. oven for 10 minutes, then reduce heat to 350° F. and bak
another 30 to 35 minutes.

LEMON CHEESE PIE

9-inch pie shell, unbaked
½ cup butter
1½ cups sugar

3 large eggs
juice and grated rind of 2
    large lemons

Cream butter and sugar. Add eggs and beat thoroughly. Add lemon juice and rind and blend well. Pour into the pie shell. Bake in a 350° F. oven for 35 to 40 minutes.

NOTE. You may separate the eggs, if desired. Add the yolks as directed for the whole eggs, and beat in the beaten egg whites separately. Or you may use 6 egg yolks instead of 3 whole eggs.

DATE CHESS PIE. Follow the recipe for Lemon Cheese Pie, decreasing sugar to 1 cup, and adding 1 teaspoon vanilla extract, 1 cup chopped dates, and ½ cup chopped walnuts.

BLACKBERRY CHESS PIE

This is very good. I used to make it often when we grew our own blackberries. You might use blackberries, raspberries, loganberries or boysenberries. All are good.

10-inch pie shell, unbaked	½ teaspoon nutmeg
¼ cup melted butter	pinch of salt
½ cup sugar	3 large eggs
⅓ cup honey	1 quart berries
2 tablespoons flour	

Cream butter, sugar, and honey. Blend in the flour. Add the nutmeg, salt, and eggs and blend thoroughly. Now add the berries and stir through the butter mixture carefully to prevent breaking the berries. Pour into the pie shell and bake in a 450° F. oven for 12 minutes, then reduce heat to 350° F. and bake 20 to 25 minutes longer.

MOLASSES PIE

I include this recipe for its historical value. The lady who gave me the recipe said that it had been invented by a Southern cook long before the Civil War. It's rich, and typical of the period.

9-inch pie shell, unbaked	3 tablespoons melted butter
4 large eggs	2 tablespoons flour
1 cup sugar	¼ cup water
1 teaspoon nutmeg	1½ cups light molasses

Combine the ingredients in the order named. Blend thoroughly. Pour into the pie shell and bake in a 450° F. oven for 10 minutes, reduce heat to 350° F., and continue baking another 25 minutes, or until firm.

CHIFFON PIES

Elegant, memorable, light as a cloud, these are strictly modern pies. Chiffon pies give the imaginative housewife an opportunity to use her ingenuity. For example, I like to make two-tone pies. One very tasty pie has a layer of lemon chiffon and a layer of orange chiffon. And a pie that never fails to receive raves has layers of lemon chiffon, lime chiffon, and raspberry chiffon.

1. To achieve fluffy chiffon pies, do not let the gelatin mixture get too firm before folding in the beaten egg whites, and (if used) the whipped cream.

2. To freeze chiffon pies, place them unwrapped in the freezer and freeze until firm. Then place in a freezer bag, tie firmly to seal, and return to freezer. When ready to serve, unwrap pies and place in the refrigerator for 1 to 1½ hours before serving.

3. Some chiffon pies are topped with whipped cream. If you are going to freeze the pie, do not add the whipped cream until ready to serve

APRICOT-ALMOND CHIFFON PIE

9-inch pie shell, baked
11 or 12-ounce package dried
   apricots
3 large eggs, separated

½ cup sugar
1 cup heavy cream
2 tablespoons powdered sugar
toasted, slivered almonds

Rinse the apricots and place in a saucepan. Cover with water and simmer until soft. When soft, mash to a smooth pulp or whirl in the blender. You should have 2 cups of pulp without lumps or excess juice. Combine apricot pulp with the egg yolks and sugar. Stir to blend and then cook over low heat for 2 to 3 minutes, stirring constantly. Cool mixture. Beat egg whites until they hold stiff peaks and then fold into the cooled apricot mixture. Turn into the baked pie shell and chill thoroughly. When ready to serve, whip the heavy cream with the powdered sugar until stiff. Spread over the pie and sprinkle with toasted, slivered almonds.

LEMON OR LIME CHIFFON PIE

9-inch pie shell, baked, or a
   graham cracker pie shell,
   baked
1 envelope unflavored gelatin
1 cup sugar
⅛ teaspoon salt

4 large eggs, separated
1 teaspoon grated lemon or
   lime rind
½ cup lemon or lime juice
⅓ cup water

Combine gelatin, ½ cup of the sugar, and the salt in the top of a double boiler. Beat the egg yolks, grated rind, lemon juice, and water together. Stir into the gelatin mixture. Cook, stirring constantly, over very hot water until gelatin is dissolved, about 5 minutes. Remove from heat and chill until mixture is partially set. Stir mixture occasionally while it is cooling. When ready, mixture will mound slightly when dropped from a spoon. Now beat the egg whites until soft peaks

form, add the remaining ½ cup sugar a tablespoon or two at a time
and beat until mixture will stand in stiff peaks. Fold beaten whites into
the lemon or lime mixture very gently. Turn into the baked pie shell
and chill until firm. Garnish with whipped cream if desired.

FRESH BERRY CHIFFON PIE

9-inch pie shell, baked
1½ envelopes unflavored
  gelatin
¼ cup cold water
4 large eggs, separated
1 tablespoon lemon juice
1 teaspoon grated lemon rind
¾ cup sugar

1½ pints fresh raspberries,
  blackberries or
  boysenberries; or a
  10-ounce package of frozen
  berries
⅛ teaspoon salt
½ cup heavy cream

Soften the gelatin in the cold water. In a small saucepan combine the
egg yolks, lemon juice and rind, and ½ cup of the sugar. Cook over
medium heat, stirring constantly, until mixture thickens and coats the
back of a metal spoon. Remove from heat and add the softened gelatin.
Stir to blend and dissolve the gelatin. Whirl the berries in a blender
until puréed. You should have 1 cup of purée. Stir into the gelatin mixture gently but thoroughly. Chill until mixture just mounds slightly.
Beat the egg whites with the salt until soft peaks form. Add the remaining ¼ cup of sugar gradually and beat until stiff peaks form. Whip
the cream. Fold the egg whites into the gelatin mixture, and then the
whipped cream. Turn into the baked pie shell and chill until firm. Top
with more whipped cream and some extra berries, if desired.

RUM CHIFFON PIE I

9-inch pie shell, baked
3 large eggs, separated
1 cup sugar
½ cup dark rum

1 envelope unflavored gelatin
½ cup cold water
1 cup heavy cream
2 tablespoons powdered sugar

at the egg yolks just until mixed. Stir in ½ cup of the sugar and the
m and blend. Turn into the top of a double boiler and cook over hot
ter, stirring constantly, just until the consistency of custard. Cool,
rring occasionally. Soften the gelatin in the cold water and dissolve
by placing mixture in a small saucepan and placing over hot water.
at the egg whites until they hold soft peaks, and then beat in the
her ½ cup sugar. Fold the dissolved gelatin into the egg white mix-
re. Then fold the cooled egg yolk mixture into the egg whites, care-
lly but thoroughly. Turn into the baked pie shell. Whip the cream and
eeten with the powdered sugar. Spread over pie and chill thoroughly.

RUM CHIFFON PIE II

is marvelous company pie freezes well and makes a dramatic and
pressive dessert.

10-inch graham cracker crumb crust, baked	½ cup cold water
	½ cup dark rum
6 egg yolks from large eggs	1 pint (2 cups) heavy cream
1 cup sugar	chocolate curls
1 envelope unflavored gelatin	

at the egg yolks until thoroughly mixed and then gradually beat in
e sugar until mixture is light and fluffy. Soak the gelatin in the cold
ter in a small saucepan. Place over low heat and bring just to a boil,
rring constantly. As soon as the mixture comes to a boil, remove
cepan from heat. Add the gelatin mixture to the egg-sugar mixture,
rring constantly. Add the rum and blend well. Now whip the cream
til stiff and carefully fold into the rum-egg mixture. Chill in the
frigerator just until it begins to set and then turn into the baked
mb crust. Chill until firm, or freeze if desired. Just before serving,
rinkle top with chocolate curls shaved from a bar of semisweet choco-
e or sweet chocolate, as desired.

ORANGE CHIFFON PIE

excellent company pie with the sweet flavor of an orange liqueur.

9-inch pie shell, baked
1 envelope unflavored gelatin
¼ cup cold water
4 large eggs, separated
⅓ cup orange juice
1 cup sugar

pinch salt
2 teaspoons grated orange rind
2 tablespoons Cointreau or Triple Sec

Soften the gelatin in the cold water. Beat the egg yolks until thick and fluffy and then beat in the orange juice and ½ cup of the sugar. Stir in salt and gelatin. Turn into a double boiler and cook over hot water stirring constantly, until thickened. Add the orange rind and the liqueur and stir in well. Remove from heat and cool. When filling is cooled, beat the egg whites until soft peaks form. Add the remaining ½ cup sugar gradually and beat until mixture stands in stiff peaks. Fold into the gelatin mixture and turn into the baked pie shell. Chill until firm.

WHISKEY-CREAM CHIFFON PIE

9-inch pie shell, baked
1½ envelopes unflavored gelatin
¼ cup cold water
7 egg yolks
1 cup sugar

1½ teaspoons grated lemon rind
2 tablespoons lemon juice
½ cup Irish whiskey
2 egg whites
2 tablespoons sugar
1 cup heavy cream

Put the cold water in the top of a double boiler. Sprinkle the gelatin over the water. Place over hot water and heat, stirring constantly, until gelatin is completely dissolved. Beat the egg yolks until light and then beat in the sugar, the lemon rind and juice. Continue beating until smooth. Now add the whiskey and the dissolved gelatin and blend thoroughly. Beat the egg whites until they hold soft peaks, add the tablespoons sugar, and beat until whites hold stiff peaks. Whip the cream. Fold the meringue and the cream into the gelatin mixture. Pour into the pie shell, and chill until filling is firm. Top with more whipped cream, if desired, when ready to serve.

CHOCOLATE PIES

OUR FAVORITE CHOCOLATE PIE

10-inch pie shell, unbaked
1 4-ounce package sweet
  chocolate
¼ cup butter
1 can (14½ ounces)
  evaporated milk
1½ cups sugar

3 tablespoons cornstarch
pinch of salt
2 large eggs
1 teaspoon vanilla extract
1 cup flaked coconut
½ to ¾ cup finely chopped
  pecans

mbine chocolate and butter in a saucepan and place over low heat
melt. Stir to blend. Remove from heat and blend in evaporated
lk. Combine sugar, cornstarch, and salt. Blend thoroughly to prevent
nping. Stir eggs and vanilla into sugar mixture. Gradually add the
ocolate mixture. Pour into the pie shell. Combine coconut and
:ans. Sprinkle over filling. Bake in a 375° F. oven 45 to 50 minutes,
until top puffs and cracks. Cool on rack for 3 to 4 hours before
ving. This is necessary to allow the filling to finish setting. If cut too
on after baking the filling will be runny.

CHOCOLATE CANDY PIE

9-inch pie shell, baked and
  cooled (VANILLA WAFER
  or CHOCOLATE CRUMB
  CRUST, p. 184)
½ cup milk

6 1¼-ounce chocolate bars
  with almonds
18 large marshmallows
¼ teaspoon vanilla extract
1 cup heavy cream

mbine milk, chocolate bars, and marshmallows in the top of a double
iler. Cook over hot water, stirring occasionally, until melted. Cool.
d vanilla. Whip the cream until stiff and fold into chocolate mixture.
ur the filling into the cooled crust. Chill overnight before serving.

CHOCOLATE COCONUT PIE

A mixture of two favorite flavors, topped with meringue.

9-inch pie shell, baked
3 squares unsweetened
   chocolate
2 cups milk
¾ cup sugar

¼ cup flour
¼ teaspoon salt
3 egg yolks
1 cup shredded coconut
1 teaspoon vanilla extract

Break the chocolate into bits and put into the top of a double bc
with the milk. Heat over hot water until chocolate is melted. Bl
thoroughly, using an egg beater if necessary. Combine sugar, flour,
salt, blending well so that mixture will not be lumpy. Stir into
chocolate mixture. Cook, stirring constantly, until mixture thick
When mixture is thickened continue cooking, stirring occasionally,
another 10 minutes. Beat the egg yolks and pour a small amount
hot chocolate mixture over them, stirring quickly to prevent yolks fi
cooking. Now add yolks to hot chocolate mixture and stir and c
for another 2 minutes. Remove from heat and add the coconut
vanilla. Cool. When completely cooled, turn into baked pie sh
Spread with desired meringue (see MERINGUES, pp. 185–7) and bro
as directed.

MOCHA PIE

This marvelous pie is a visual as well as a taste delight.

9-inch baked pie shell
   (preferably a nut pastry)
½ cup butter
¾ cup sugar
1 square unsweetened
   chocolate, melted

1 teaspoon instant coffee
2 large eggs
2 cups heavy cream
1 tablespoon instant coffee
½ cup powdered sugar

Cream the butter and the sugar and beat until light and fluffy. Bl
in the melted and slightly cooled chocolate and the 1 teaspoon inst

ffee. Stir to blend well. Add the eggs and beat 2 or 3 minutes with
electric mixer. Turn the filling into baked and cooled pie shell.
over with plastic wrap, or put in a large plastic envelope, and chill
ernight. Early the next day, combine the heavy cream, 1 tablespoon
stant coffee and the powdered sugar. Cover and refrigerate for several
ours. When thoroughly chilled, beat the mixture until stiff. Pipe cream
ixture onto the pie with a large decorating tube, or spoon the mixture
to the pie, making swirls with the back of the spoon. Refrigerate for
veral hours before serving. If desired, pie may be garnished with
ocolate curls.

CONDENSED MILK PIES

aking pies with the modern condensed (NOT evaporated) milk is so
mple that these pies are staples in many homes. No cooking or baking
required and a prebaked crumb crust is always used. The pie fillings
ill to the required firmness. Use a good brand of condensed milk for
nsistent results. One large can holds 1⅓ cups of condensed milk. The
lings suggested are enough for an 8-inch crumb shell or a shallow
inch crumb shell.

FRUIT MERINGUE PIE

8 or 9-inch crumb crust shell,
   baked
1 can sweetened condensed
   milk
2 tablespoons lemon juice

1 teaspoon grated lemon rind
2 egg yolks
1 cup of any fresh fruit or
   berries
MERINGUE (pp. 185–7)

ombine the milk, lemon juice and rind, and egg yolks. Beat well. Stir
the fruit. Pour into cooled pie shell. Top with meringue and brown.
ill thoroughly.

LEMON MERINGUE PIE

8 or 9-inch crumb crust shell,
baked
1 can sweetened condensed
milk

½ cup lemon juice
1 teaspoon grated lemon rind
2 egg yolks
MERINGUE (pp. 185–7)

Combine ingredients and beat thoroughly. Pour into baked crumb crust and top with meringue. Brown. Chill.

AVOCADO PIE FILLING

The delicate green color and cool tart flavor will fool you into thinking this is a lime pie.

8 or 9-inch crumb crust shell,
baked
1 can sweetened condensed
milk
1 cup mashed avocado

½ cup lemon juice
1 or 2 teaspoons grated lemon
rind
2 egg yolks

Combine ingredients and beat thoroughly. Mixture should start to thicken. Turn into baked and cooled crumb crust. Chill.

CHOCOLATE PIE FILLING

I sometimes make this in a coconut crust and sprinkle the top with more coconut.

8 or 9-inch crumb crust shell,
baked
2 squares unsweetened
chocolate

1 can sweetened condensed
milk
⅓ cup water
½ teaspoon vanilla extract

elt the chocolate in the top of a double boiler. Add the condensed
ilk and stir and cook over hot water until mixture thickens, about
minutes. Remove from heat and stir in the water and vanilla. Cool.
ur into pie shell and top with whipped cream, coconut, or MERINGUE
p. 185–7). If meringue is used, brown slightly before chilling the
e.

REAM AND CUSTARD PIES

e ideal combination of a crisp, flaky crust and a creamy, smooth
ling is not easy to come by. Some good cooks achieve this by baking
e pie shell and the filling separately, in two pie pans of the same size.
e filling is then slipped into the shell just before serving. If it works,
s beautiful. But sometimes it just doesn't work and you end up with
lumpy mass of custard in a flaky pie shell. If you are serving the pie
th a whipped cream topping this won't make any difference, and the
ethod might work very well. To insure flakiness one authority recom-
ends rolling the pie crust in graham cracker crumbs, being careful
keep the crumbs only on the side of the pastry next to the pie pan.
ried this and no matter how carefully I rolled the pastry, or how thin
made it, the finished pie shell still resembled cardboard. It was crisp,
it with an artificial crispness that was not desirable. Still others recom-
end pre-baking the crust for 5 minutes. But in practice, the hot pie
ell simply absorbs the moist filling more readily. The method that
find works best (it is not a perfect solution but is better than most)
as follows:

Fit the pastry into the pie pan and flute the edges. EGG PASTRY
age 179) seems to work best for cream and custard pies. Brush the
e shell with a very thin coating of melted butter or slightly beaten
g white. Chill the pie shell thoroughly. When ready to bake, place
e filled pie shell on the lower shelf of the oven. Always cool pies
a rack.

DOWN EAST CREAM PIE

9-inch pie shell, unbaked and
   prepared as directed above
4 egg whites
1 tablespoon flour
½ cup brown or maple sugar

2 cups scalded cream or half
   and half
1 teaspoon vanilla extract or
   rose water

Beat the egg whites until they hold soft peaks. Combine the flour and
sugar and mix well. Fold into beaten egg whites. Add the cream and
flavoring used. Pour into a well-chilled pie shell. Bake in a 450° F
oven 10 minutes. Reduce heat to 325° F. and continue baking another
30 to 35 minutes.

FRENCH CRÉME BRÛLÉ PIE

A fabulous production, as luscious to eat as to look at. The bottom
of the pie shell may be spread with a coating of any desired jam, preserve, or marmalade, or sprinkled with chopped nuts.

9 or 10-inch pie shell, baked
2 cups heavy cream
⅓ cup brown sugar
6 egg yolks

¼ teaspoon almond extract,
   or 1 teaspoon vanilla
   extract, or 1 tablespoon rum
⅛ teaspoon salt

Combine the cream and 3 tablespoons of the brown sugar in the top
of a double boiler and heat to scalding. Combine egg yolks, flavoring
and salt. Beat to blend. Stir some of the scalded cream mixture into the
egg yolk mixture. Add egg yolk mixture to double boiler and blend
thoroughly. Continue cooking over hot water until mixture thickens.
Stir constantly. When mixture coats a metal spoon remove at once from
heat so that it does not curdle. Cool. When mixture is cooled turn into
the baked, cooled pie shell. Chill thoroughly. When chilled, and just
before serving, sprinkle with the remaining 3 tablespoons of sugar.
Place pie under a broiler to caramelize the sugar, being careful not to
let the pie burn. Serve immediately or refrigerate until serving time.

COUNTRY CREAM PIE

A rich, creamy old-timer.

9-inch pie shell, unbaked but
well-chilled
½ cup light brown sugar
½ cup granulated sugar
2 tablespoons flour
2 cups "half-and-half"
1 teaspoon vanilla extract

Combine the sugars and the flour, blending well so that mixture will not be lumpy. Stir in the "half-and-half" and vanilla. If desired, you might give the whole mixture a whirl in the blender to assure a smooth consistency. Pour into the well-chilled pie shell. Bake in a 400° F. oven for 30 to 40 minutes, or until a silver knife inserted halfway between the center and edge of pie comes out clean. Cool on a rack and chill before serving.

GOLDEN BUTTERMILK CUSTARD PIE

A delicious pie that will be liked even by those who profess to dislike buttermilk.

10-inch pie shell, unbaked
1 cup sugar
pinch of salt
3 tablespoons flour
3 large eggs, separated
2 cups buttermilk
½ cup melted butter
2 teaspoons vanilla extract
1 teaspoon grated lemon rind

Combine sugar, salt, and flour and stir to blend. Beat egg yolks slightly and add to sugar mixture with the buttermilk, melted butter, vanilla, and grated lemon rind. Blend thoroughly. Beat the egg whites until stiff and fold into the custard mixture. Turn into the prepared pie shell and bake in a 425° F. oven 5 minutes. Then reduce heat to 325° F. and bake 45 to 50 minutes, or until a knife inserted in the center of the pie comes out clean.

FRENCH CUSTARD PIE

The *crème de la crème* of custard pies. Extravagant and fabulously delicious! Since I make this pie only for special occasions, I go all the way and make it with FAVORITE SOUR CREAM PASTRY (p. 181), but EGG PASTRY (p. 179) is also good.

10-inch pie shell, unbaked,
   brushed with melted butter
   and thoroughly chilled
2 cups half and half
1 cup heavy cream

⅓ cup sugar
6 egg yolks, from large eggs
1 teaspoon vanilla extract
½ cup brown sugar

Combine the half and half, heavy cream, ⅓ cup sugar, egg yolks, and vanilla. Beat until thoroughly blended. Sprinkle the brown sugar over the bottom of the pie shell. Pour in the custard mixture and bake in a 350° F. oven for 45 to 50 minutes, or until almost set in the center. Cool on a rack before chilling. Serve plain, with a fruit sauce, or with fresh fruit that has been slightly sweetened.

LAYERED CUSTARD PIE

When baked, there will be a glossy brown topping, a layer of yellow custard beneath, and a thin layer of white custard on the bottom. Delicious!

9- or 10-inch pie shell, unbaked
½ cup butter or margarine
1½ cups light brown sugar
4 large eggs, beaten

1 teaspoon cinnamon
2 tablespoons flour
2 cups sour milk

Cream butter and sugar until light and fluffy. Blend in the eggs. Combine cinnamon, flour, and 2 tablespoons of the sour milk to make a smooth paste. Add, with remaining sour milk, to first mixture. Blend horoughly and pour into prepared pie shell. Bake in 450° F. oven for 10 minutes, then reduce heat to 350° F. and bake 40 minutes longer, or until custard is firm.

MARIAN'S LEMON CUSTARD PIE

A delicious old-timer.

10-inch pie shell, unbaked
1⅓ cups sugar
2 tablespoons flour
1½ to 2 teaspoons grated lemon rind

juice of 2 large lemons
¼ cup melted butter
4 large eggs, separated
1 cup milk

Combine sugar, flour, and grated lemon rind. Blend well so that flour will not lump. Now stir in the lemon juice, melted butter, egg yolks, and milk. Beat thoroughly. Beat the egg whites until they hold stiff peaks. Fold the beaten egg whites into the milk mixture. Pour into pie shell. Bake in a 450° F. oven for 10 minutes, then reduce heat to 350° F. and bake another 30 to 35 minutes.

PERSIMMON PIE

This is very similar to a pumpkin pie.

9 or 10-inch pie shell, unbaked
1¼ cups persimmon pulp (I whirl the pulp in a blender to get it perfectly smooth.)
2 large eggs

½ cup sugar
½ teaspoon cinnamon
2 cups half and half
2 tablespoons butter
1 teaspoon lemon juice

Combine all ingredients and beat until smooth. Again, I whirl this in a blender for perfect smoothness. Pour into well-chilled, prepared pie shell. Bake in a 450° F. oven for 10 minutes. Reduce heat to 350° F. and bake another 30 to 35 minutes.

PEANUT BUTTER PIE

10-inch pie shell, baked
⅓ cup smooth or crunchy
   peanut butter
½ cup sugar

4 egg yolks
5 tablespoons cornstarch
3 cups milk
1 teaspoon vanilla extract

Cream the peanut butter and the sugar. Add the egg yolks and beat thoroughly. Combine cornstarch and milk and mix until smooth. I whirl it in the blender. Add to creamed mixture and cook over low heat, stirring constantly, until thick. Add vanilla and cool. When cooled, turn mixture into pie shell, top with desired MERINGUE (pp. 185–7) and brown as directed. If desired, the meringue might be sprinkled with the following mixture before browning: combine 1 tablespoon melted butter, 1 tablespoon chopped peanuts, and 2 tablespoons sugar.

COCONUT PIE

This lovely pie has a macaroon-crunchy flavor, and the ingredients are always available.

9 or 10-inch pie shell,
   unbaked
¼ cup finely chopped nuts
   (slivered almonds are best)
3 large eggs
½ cup water, milk, coconut
   milk, or orange juice

1½ cups sugar
¼ cup flour
1⅓ cups flaked coconut
½ cup melted butter
½ teaspoon vanilla extract, or
   grated lemon rind

Sprinkle nuts over bottom of unbaked pie shell. Combine eggs, liquid used, sugar, and flour. Beat until smooth. Stir in the remaining ingredients and pour into the pie shell. Bake in a 450° F. oven for 10 minutes. Reduce heat to 350° F. and bake for another 25 to 35 minutes, or until pie is almost set. Cool on rack.

FRUIT PIES

BERRY PIE

In the eyes of some—and I am one—berry pies are the most luscious of all pies. And now that large packages of a variety of freshly frozen berries are available, they become a year-round pleasure. In general, I bake all of my berry pies with a top crust, but some good cooks prefer a lattice top. Very tasty pies can be made by combining several types of berries. Blackberries and red raspberries make a good combination, as do cranberries and blueberries. Most good pie makers add a tablespoon or more of lemon juice to almost any fruit pie, to enhance the flavor. But some good cooks omit the lemon juice and use ½ teaspoon cinnamon in berry pies. In general, all berry pies are basically the same as the one given below. Some may use a combination of berries as suggested, some may use an extra cup of berries, or a tablespoon of butter. The amount of sugar depends both on the tartness of the berries and on how sweet you prefer your pie. The amount of flour depends on how juicy the berries are.

pastry for a 2-crust, 9-inch pie

1 to 1¼ cups sugar
2½ tablespoons quick-
   cooking tapioca, *or*
¼ to ⅓ cup flour
1 tablespoon lemon juice, *or*
½ teaspoon cinnamon

4 cups ripe berries
   (blackberries, boysenberries,
   blueberries, raspberries,
   huckleberries, strawberries,
   or gooseberries)
2 tablespoons butter

Combine sugar and tapioca or flour. Stir well. Add lemon juice or cinnamon and the berries. Stir gently but well. Pour into pastry-lined pie pan. Dot with butter. Arrange top crust over filling. Flute and seal the edges. Cut vents in top crust. Brush top crust lightly with milk and sprinkle with a tablespoon of sugar. Bake in a 450° F. oven for 10 minutes. Reduce heat to 350° F. and bake 40 to 45 minutes longer.

CRANBERRY PIE

A Thanksgiving special, very popular in the New England states. Add a few drops of almond extract, and this rates the label of "Mock Cherry Pie."

9-inch pie shell, unbaked, with
    pastry for lattice topping
¾ cup sugar
1 tablespoon cornstarch
¾ cup clear corn syrup
⅓ to ½ cup water

2 teaspoons grated lemon
    rind or orange rind
½ cup raisins
½ cup chopped walnuts
2 tablespoons butter
3 cups cranberries

Combine sugar and cornstarch and mix well. Turn into a saucepan and add the corn syrup, water, and grated lemon or orange rind. Bring to boil. Stir in the raisins, nuts, and cranberries. Cover and cook just until the cranberry skins pop. Remove from heat and add butter. Cool, but do not stir while cooling. When cooled, turn into the pie shell. Arrange pastry strips on top. Brush them slightly with milk and sprinkle with sugar. Bake in a 425° F. oven for 40 to 50 minutes.

FRESH STRAWBERRY PIE

The sun-drenched warmth of summer is in this pie. It is at its very best when made with absolutely fresh berries, rather than the frozen ones.

pastry for a 2-crust, 9-inch pie,
    or 1 9-inch pie shell,
    unbaked, with pastry for a
    lattice top
1 cup sugar

3 tablespoons flour
¼ cup lemon juice
4 to 5 cups whole or sliced
    strawberries
3 tablespoons butter

Combine sugar and flour. Blend well. Sprinkle the lemon juice over the berries and then add the sugar-flour mixture. Turn into pie shell.

and dot with butter. Arrange top crust or lattice strips over the pie. Flute and seal the edges. Bake in a 400° F. oven for 15 minutes. Reduce heat to 350° F. and bake another 30 minutes. Serve warm, with heavy cream or vanilla ice cream.

GREEN GRAPE PIE

9-inch pie shell, unbaked, with pastry for a lattice top
1 cup sugar
¼ cup flour
1 tablespoon quick-cooking tapioca
½ teaspoon cinnamon
5 cups seedless grapes
2 tablespoons butter

Combine sugar, flour, and tapioca. Stir to blend. Add cinnamon and grapes. Stir. Turn into pastry-lined pie pan. Dot with butter. Arrange lattice strips. Bake in 450° F. oven for 10 minutes. Reduce heat to 350° F. and bake 30 minutes longer.

CHERRY PIE

We sometimes add some chopped walnuts to this basic—and to my mind, best—cherry pie recipe.

pastry for a 2-crust, 9-inch pie
1¼ to 1⅓ cups sugar
2½ tablespoons quick-cooking tapioca, or ⅓ cup flour
⅛ teaspoon salt
⅛ to ¼ teaspoon almond extract
1 teaspoon lemon juice
4 cups pitted, fresh, pie cherries, or 2 (1 pound) cans unsweetened pie cherries, drained
2 tablespoons butter

Combine sugar, quick-cooking tapioca or flour, and salt and stir to blend. Add the rest of the ingredients except the butter and blend. Pour into pastry-lined pie pan and dot with the butter. Arrange crust over filling. Seal and flute the edges. Cut vents in the top. Bake in a 425° F. oven for 40 to 45 minutes. Pie will be a golden brown.

DATE PIE

Once a year we make the long trip from our home in a valley near the ocean to the hot, bright desert floor of the Coachella Valley, and its exotic "date gardens." We try to make the trip during the month of February for the annual Date Festival in the town of Indio. Indio proudly considers itself the date capital of the world, and the Date Festival is the most important yearly event. We always come home with pounds and pounds of all kinds of dates. The chopped *Deglet Noor* and *Zahidi* freeze well, and are used year-round in all kinds of baking. The soft, juicy *Barhia* and the large, soft *Iteema* dates are for immediate, luxurious eating, as they do not ship or keep well. We buy containers of date butter for various baking projects, as well as to spread on bread.

The shop owners and residents are more than willing to share their recipes, and following are some that we consider special. I often substitute a tablespoon of brandy for the vanilla extract. At serving time, cut the pie into thin wedges and top with whipped cream to which you have added another tablespoon brandy.

9-inch pie shell, unbaked	½ cup pecans or walnuts
1 cup sugar	¼ cup butter
1 cup chopped dates	1 teaspoon vanilla extract
1 cup boiling water or orange juice	3 large eggs

Combine the sugar and dates in a bowl. Pour the boiling water or orange juice over them and stir until dates are soft. Add the remaining ingredients and mix well. Pour into the pie shell and bake in a 350° F. oven for 30 to 40 minutes, or until filling is firm.

OLD-FASHIONED DATE PIE

An old California taste delight, this rich pie is best served in small pieces after a light meal.

9 or 10-inch pie shell,
  unbaked
1 pound chopped dates
2 cups half and half
1 large egg

2 large eggs, separated
¼ cup sugar
½ teaspoon grated orange
  rind

Soak the dates in the half and half for several hours, or overnight. When ready to bake, beat in the whole egg and 2 egg yolks. Pour into the pie shell and bake in a 450° F. oven for 10 minutes, then reduce heat to 350° F. and bake until an inserted knife comes out clean, approximately 30 to 35 minutes longer. Make a meringue with the reserved egg whites, sugar, and orange rind. Spread on the pie and brown in a 350° F. oven.

DATE PECAN PIE

A crustless pie, very easy to make. The vinegar provides a good, elusive flavor. Serve with a dollop of whipped cream on each wedge.

1 cup chopped dates
1 cup chopped pecans
½ cup sugar

1 teaspoon mild vinegar
⅓ to ½ cup sugar
4 egg whites

Combine the dates, pecans, the ½ cup sugar, and vinegar. Stir to blend well. Add the rest of the sugar to the egg whites, beaten stiff. Fold into the date-nut mixture and blend lightly, but well. Pour into a buttered 9-inch glass pie pan. Bake in a 300° F. oven for 30 to 35 minutes.

FRESH APRICOT, PEACH, OR MANGO PIE

Use the exotic mango as you use fresh peaches, only make certain that it is not under-ripe. Ripe nectarines could also be used in this pie.

9-inch pie shell, unbaked, with pastry for a lattice top
⅓ cup water
½ to ¾ cup sugar
1 tablespoon lemon juice
1 teaspoon grated lemon rind
1 tablespoon cornstarch

3 tablespoons water or fruit juice
3 to 4 cups fresh fruit, peeled, pitted, and sliced
2 teaspoons flour mixed with 2 teaspoons sugar

Combine water, sugar, lemon juice, and rind in a saucepan. Bring to a boil. Reduce heat. Combine cornstarch and water and blend until smooth (I whirl it in the blender), then stir into the hot mixture. Simmer, stirring, until it thickens slightly. Remove from heat and add the fruit. Stir so that all of the fruit is in the hot syrup. Let stand for 20 to 30 minutes. Sprinkle the unbaked pie shell with the flour-sugar mixture. Turn in the fruit mixture and dot with butter. Arrange the lattice strips over the filling. Sprinkle lightly with sugar. Bake in a 400° F. oven for 10 minutes. Reduce heat to 350° F. and bake 20 minutes longer.

FRENCH PEAR PIE

Delicious and delicate, this is my favorite way with pears.

9-inch pie pan lined with SWEET PASTRY (p. 182)
6 large Bartlett pears
½ cup + 2 tablespoons sugar

1½ cups milk
2 egg yolks
2 tablespoons flour

Peel, core, and cut pears in half. Place in a saucepan or a small skillet and add water to not quite cover the pears. Cook over medium-low heat. After 20 minutes, sprinkle pears with ¼ cup of the sugar. Cook until pears are soft and then carefully, with a wide spatula, remove them from the pan. Let the juice continue to cook until syrupy. Cool. In another pan, combine the milk and the remaining sugar. Heat. Blend the egg yolks with the flour until smooth. Add a little of the hot milk mixture to the egg yolk mixture, stirring so that mixture does not coagulate. Now stir the remaining yolk mixture into milk mixture. Stir well, but do not cook. Arrange the pears in the pastry-lined pie pan. Cover with the custard mixture. Bake in a 400° F. oven for 40 minutes. Remove pie to a rack and pour the syrup over the custard. For a decorative touch, heat a fork and sear a pattern on the round part of each pear.

PEAR CRUMB PIE

9-inch pie shell, unbaked
4 firm-ripe pears
3 tablespoons cornstarch
⅛ teaspoon salt
½ cup water
½ cup clear corn syrup

1 teaspoon grated lemon rind
1 tablespoon lemon juice
1 tablespoon butter
1 cup flour
½ cup brown sugar
½ cup butter

Peel and core the pears. Cut into lengthwise slices. Combine cornstarch, salt, water, and corn syrup and stir until smooth. I give this a whirl in the blender. Add the lemon rind, lemon juice, the tablespoon butter, and pears. Cook over low heat, stirring constantly, until mixture comes to a boil. Remove from heat and turn into pastry-lined pie pan. Cover with topping made by combining the flour, brown sugar and the ½ cup butter until mixture is like coarse crumbs. Bake in a 450° F. oven for 20 to 30 minutes. Cool on a rack and serve warm.

PINEAPPLE PIE

A very good pie. This amount of filling will also fill 2 ready-made, 8-inch, frozen pie shells.

9-inch pie shell, unbaked
⅓ cup butter
⅔ cup sugar
3 egg yolks

1½ cups crushed pineapple
1 tablespoon flour
⅔ cup heavy cream
3 egg whites, stiffly beaten

Cream the butter and the sugar. Add the egg yolks and beat until creamy. Drain the pineapple just a little and add pineapple to the creamed mixture. Stir the flour into 2 tablespoons of the cream to form a smooth paste, and then stir this into the rest of the cream. Add to pineapple mixture and blend. Beat the egg whites until stiff and fold into cream mixture. Pour into the pie shell. Bake in a 450° F. oven for 10 minutes. Reduce heat to 325° F. and continue baking until top is browned and filling is firm, about 45 to 50 minutes.

FRESH PINEAPPLE PIE

pastry for 2-crust, 9-inch pie
3 cups fresh pineapple, shredded or cut into small pieces
2 large eggs
1½ cups sugar

2 tablespoons flour
2 teaspoons grated lemon rind
1 tablespoon lemon juice
1 tablespoon butter

Combine eggs, sugar, flour, lemon rind, and lemon juice and beat thoroughly. Add the pineapple and blend mixture gently but thoroughly. Turn into pastry-lined pie pan and dot with butter. Arrange top crust and seal and flute the edges. Cut vents in the top and sprinkle lightly with sugar. Bake in a 450° F. oven for 10 minutes. Reduce heat to 350° F. and bake for another 30 minutes.

GUAVA PIE

Guavas are familiar to many of us only in the form of jams and jellies. But did you know that they make an excellent fruit *kuchen?* And you will enjoy this pie. The variation, using cubed melon, is very good and allows the use of melons that are slightly overripe.

9-inch pie shell, unbaked, with pastry for a lattice top
12 ripe pineapple or strawberry guavas, washed and peeled
2 tablespoons lime or lemon juice

½ cup light brown sugar
1 teaspoon grated lime or lemon rind
¼ teaspoon cinnamon or nutmeg
2 to 3 tablespoons flour
2 to 3 tablespoons butter

Cut the guavas into quarters and scoop out the pulp. Press through a sieve to remove the seeds. If you whirl the pulp in a blender, you will still need to strain it. Cut the shells into slices. Combine the pulp with the juice, sugar, rind, spice and flour. Add the sliced shells. Turn into the unbaked pie shell. Dot with the butter and arrange lattice strips over the filling. Sprinkle with sugar and bake in a 400° F. oven for 15 minutes. Reduce heat to 350° F. and bake another 20 minutes.

CANTALOUPE PIE. Follow above recipe, using 2½ to 3 cups cantaloupe or honeydew melon, cut into cubes or small balls.

PURPLE PLUM PIE

9-inch pie shell, unbaked, with leftover pastry for a lattice top, or for pastry cut-outs.
1 can (1 pound, 13 ounces) purple plums

½ to ¾ cup plum juice
½ cup sugar
2 to 3 tablespoons flour
¼ teaspoon cinnamon
2 tablespoons butter

Drain the plums, reserving ½ to ¾ cup of the juice. Pit the plums and halve them. Lay halved plums in the bottom of the pie shell. Pour the reserved juice over plums. Combine the sugar, flour, and cinnamon and cut the butter into the flour mixture until it resembles coarse meal. Sprinkle this evenly over the plums. Cover with lattice topping, or with pastry cut-outs. Bake in a 425° F. oven 35 to 40 minutes.

PUNAHALE PIE
(HAWAIIAN BANANA PIE)

A delicious, two-crust pie, rich with the flavor of Hawaiian pineapple and bananas.

pastry for a 2-crust, 10-inch pie

4 or 5 cups sliced, firm-ripe bananas (about 6 bananas)

⅓ cup pineapple juice

2 tablespoons fresh lemon juice

½ cup sugar

1 teaspoon cinnamon

2 tablespoons butter

Slice bananas into a bowl. Pour pineapple juice and lemon juice over the bananas and stir so that they are mixed. Let stand 20 to 30 minutes, stirring occasionally. Drain, reserving the juice. Turn the bananas into the pastry-lined pan. Sprinkle with the sugar and cinnamon. Pour 2 tablespoons of the reserved juice over the bananas and dot with the butter. Arrange top crust over bananas. Slash crust decoratively. Seal and flute the edges. If desired, the top crust may be brushed lightly with cream and sprinkled lightly with sugar. Bake in a 425° F. oven for 30 to 40 minutes or until crust is beautifully browned. Serve warm.

EUROPEAN RAISIN PIE

In this old European recipe, beer is used for zest.

pastry for a 2-crust, 9-inch pie

2 cups raisins

1 cup water

1 cup beer

1 teaspoon grated lemon rind

2 tablespoons lemon juice

⅔ cup sugar

2 tablespoons cornstarch

½ teaspoon cinnamon

2 tablespoons butter

Combine raisins, water, beer, and the lemon rind and juice in a saucepan. Heat until mixture is hot, and simmer for 5 minutes. Combine sugar, cornstarch, and cinnamon and blend well. Stir into the raisin mixture and simmer, stirring constantly, until mixture is smooth and thickened, about 5 minutes. Add the butter. Remove from heat and cool. Pour the cooled filling into the pastry-lined pie pan. Arrange the top crust and seal and flute the edges. Cut vents in the top crust and sprinkle lightly with sugar. Bake in a 425° F. oven for 30 to 40 minutes, or until crust is a lovely golden brown.

ORANGE RAISIN PIE

pastry for a 2-crust, 9-inch pie

2 cups raisins	¾ cup mild honey
1 tablespoon grated orange rind	pinch salt
1 cup fresh orange juice	¼ cup cornstarch
¼ cup lemon juice	¾ cup cold water
	2 tablespoons butter

Place the raisins, orange rind and juice, lemon juice, honey, and salt in a saucepan. Stir the cornstarch into the water until smooth. Add to the raisin mixture. Bring to a boil, reduce heat, and simmer, stirring, until smooth and thickened. This will take about 4 or 5 minutes. Remove from heat and stir in the butter. Cool. When cooled, pour into the pastry-lined pie pan. Arrange top crust and seal and flute the edges. Cut vents in the top crust and sprinkle lightly with sugar. Bake in a 425° F. oven for 30 to 40 minutes. Crust will be a golden brown.

LEMON OR LIME PIES

LEMON OR LIME WHEY PIE

Our grandmothers made their own cottage cheese. And being careful cooks who made good use of the ingredients at hand, everything, even the whey, was used. If you make your own cottage cheese (complete instructions are given in the cheesecake section of this book) often or just occasionally, you will enjoy this delicious pie. NADINE ROE'S MILK PIE CRUST (p. 183) makes a crisp base for this or any other lemon pie.

9-inch pie shell, baked and
  cooled
1½ cups whey
1 cup sugar
3 tablespoons cornstarch
3 large eggs, separated

2 tablespoons butter
½ teaspoon salt
¼ cup lemon or lime juice
2 teaspoons grated lemon or
  lime rind
MERINGUE (pp. 185–7)

Put 1 cup of the whey in a 1½-quart saucepan. Bring to a boil. Combine sugar and cornstarch, blend into the remaining ½ cup whey, and mix to a smooth paste. Turn into the hot whey (turn the heat down first so that mixture does not boil over) and cook over medium heat, stirring constantly, until mixture thickens. Put the egg yolks into a small bowl. Add a tablespoon or two of the hot whey mixture and blend thoroughly. Now stir this into the large quantity of whey, along with the butter, salt, lemon or lime juice, and the grated rind. Cook 2 minutes longer, stirring constantly. Remove from heat and cool. When cooled turn filling into baked and cooled pie shell. Cover with desired meringue and brown as directed.

NOTE: Recipe for the filling is easily doubled with no loss of quality. Whenever I make this pie, I make one as directed above and one as directed in the following recipe.

LEMON OR LIME SNOW PIE

This is one of my favorite lemon/lime pies.

8 or 9-inch pie shell, baked
  and cooled
1 recipe for filling as in above
  recipe

MERINGUE using 3, 4, or 5 egg
  whites (see pp. 185–7)

Make the meringue using 3, 4, or 5 egg whites. Fold meringue into *hot* pie filling. Cool for several minutes before turning into baked and cooled pie shell. Chill thoroughly.

LEMON OR LIME COCONUT PIE.   To either recipe above, or to the LEMON MERINGUE PIE (p. 238) or the BUTTERMILK LEMON MERINGUE PIE (p. 238), add ½ cup coconut to the filling. If a meringue is used, sprinkle the meringue with another ¼ cup coconut before browning.

DOUBLE CRUST LEMON PIE

A delicious old-time lemon pie, tart with slices of fresh lemons.

pastry for 2-crust 8 or 9-inch
   pie
1¼ cups sugar
2 tablespoons flour
pinch of salt
¼ cup butter or margarine

3 large eggs
1 teaspoon grated lemon rind
1 large lemon, peeled and
   thinly sliced (there should
   be ½ cup lemon slices)
⅓ cup water

Combine sugar, flour, and salt. Blend well. Add the butter or margarine, eggs, and lemon rind. Blend thoroughly. Now add the lemon slices that have been carefully peeled to remove all the white membrane. Stir in the water so that all ingredients are lightly but thoroughly mixed. Pour into pastry-lined pie pan. Arrange the top crust over the pie, flute the edges, and slash the top decoratively. Sprinkle top crust with sugar and bake in a 400° F. oven for 30 to 35 minutes, or until crust is a golden brown.

LEMON FLUFF PIE

My favorite of all lemon pies, this is an extravagant but worthwhile taste delight. Make it when eggs are inexpensive.

10-inch pie shell, baked
9 large eggs, separated
¾ cup + 2 tablespoons sugar

juice of 4 large lemons
1 tablespoon grated lemon
rind

Beat the egg yolks until well mixed. Place yolks in the top of a double boiler. Add the sugar, lemon juice, and lemon rind. Stir to blend well and then cook over boiling water until thick, stirring constantly. Cool slightly. Beat the egg whites until stiff and then carefully fold into the egg-yolk mixture until blended. Pour into the baked pie shell and bake in a 350° F. oven until set, about 20 minutes. Cool on a rack and then dust the top with sifted powdered sugar and sprinkle with slivered, toasted almonds.

LIME FLUFF PIE. Make as above, substituting the juice of 5 limes for the lemons and the rind of 4 limes for the lemon rind. If desired a drop of green food color may be added.

LEMON MERINGUE PIE

9-inch pie shell, baked
2 cups sugar
½ cup + 1 tablespoon flour
pinch salt
2½ cups hot water
6 egg yolks, beaten

¼ cup butter or margarine
½ cup lemon juice
1 tablespoon grated lemon
  rind
MERINGUE (pp. 185–7)

Combine sugar, flour, and salt in the top of a double boiler and stir to blend thoroughly. If the flour is not thoroughly mixed with the sugar it tends to lump in the cooking. Gradually stir in the water and then the beaten egg yolks. Cook over boiling water, stirring constantly, until thickened and smooth. Cover and cook 7 to 10 minutes longer. Add butter, lemon juice, and rind. Cool, taking time occasionally to beat the filling with a wooden spoon as it cools. This makes for a more tender texture. When filling is cooled, pour into a baked pie shell. Cover with meringue and brown as directed.

BUTTERMILK LEMON MERINGUE PIE

This is an old-timer, not too widely known, and very good.

9-inch pie shell, baked
2 cups buttermilk
1 cup white sugar
1 tablespoon grated lemon
  rind
½ cup light brown sugar

3 tablespoons cornstarch
pinch salt
3 egg yolks
⅓ cup lemon juice
MERINGUE (pp. 185–7)

In the top of a double boiler combine the buttermilk, white sugar, and grated lemon rind. Over direct heat, bring to a boil. In a bowl combine the brown sugar, cornstarch, salt, egg yolks, and lemon juice. Sti to blend well. Now, gradually add the boiling buttermilk to the corn-starch mixture, stirring to prevent the mixture from curdling. Return blended mixtures to top of double boiler and place over hot water. Cook, stirring constantly, until thickened and clear. Remove from heat and beat rapidly for a minute, preferably with a wooden spoon. Cool slightly and then turn into a baked pie shell. Cover with meringue desired and brown as directed.

FRESH LIME PIE

11/73 w/Key Limes Tart – good – not really enough for 9"

My family prefers this lime pie, which is thickened only with egg yolks, to the Key West type of lime pie.

8-inch pie shell, baked
6 egg yolks
½ cup lime juice
pinch salt

1 teaspoon grated lime rind
1 cup sugar
MERINGUE (pp. 185–7)

Beat the egg yolks until thick. Add the lime juice, salt, and grated rind. Stir in the sugar and cook over direct heat, stirring constantly, until thickened. Remove from heat and cool, stirring occasionally with a wooden spoon. When cool, pour into the baked pie shell, top with meringue desired and brown as directed.

MINCEMEAT
(AND SEVERAL PIES)

Mincemeat is, very simply, a mixture of fruits and spices cooked with or without minced meat and generally doused with brandy, rum, or whiskey. It evolved some 500 years ago in England and mince pies are still considered as essential an accompaniment to holiday dinners as the traditional plum pudding.

NOTES ON USING MINCEMEAT

1. Homemade mincemeat freezes well, but recommended storage time is no longer than 3 months.

2. Dress up commercial bottled mincemeat by adding to each 2 cups of mincemeat ½ cup finely chopped apple, ½ teaspoon cinnamon, ⅓ cup candied fruit peels, 1 tablespoon orange juice, and ¼ cup whiskey, brandy, or rum. Stir well and refrigerate overnight or for several days, before using.

3. Mincemeat pies are best served faintly warm. Serve with coffee or wine.

4. Mincemeat makes an excellent filling for cakes, cookies, coffee-cakes, and cake rolls.

APPLE MINCEMEAT (MEATLESS)

1 large orange
1 large lemon
2 cups seeded raisins
2 cups golden raisins
1 cup pitted dates, chopped
9 or 10 medium-sized green apples
1½ cups apple cider

3 cups firmly packed brown sugar
1½ teaspoons salt
1 teaspoon cinnamon
1 teaspoon nutmeg
1 teaspoon cloves
1 tablespoon vanilla extract

Cut the orange and lemon into halves and remove the seeds. Cut them into pieces, unpeeled, and put through a food chopper or into a blender. I use a blender and it works beautifully. Put into a large pan and add the raisins and dates. Chop the unpeeled apples into fine pieces and add to the pan. Add the apple cider, stir, and bring to a boil. Reduce heat and simmer, uncovered, for 15 to 20 minutes. Stir in the remaining ingredients and simmer for another 20 minutes, or until mixture is thick. Pour into containers and add 2 tablespoons to ¼ cup of brandy, rum, or whiskey per pint of mincemeat. This will keep, refrigerated, for 4 to 6 weeks, or frozen for up to 3 months. Makes enough filling for 3 9- or 10-inch pies.

FAVORITE MINCEMEAT (WITH MEAT)

In this excellent mincemeat the marmalade provides the necessary sweetening. You may replace 1 to 2 cups of the orange marmalade with another, such as tangerine or kumquat marmalade.

2 pounds lean beef, any cut
1 pound beef heart
1 pound pitted dates, chopped
1 cup chopped or ground suet
3½ pounds firm, ripe apples, chopped
12-ounce box seedless raisins
12-ounce box golden raisins
½ pound currants
4 cups orange marmalade
2 quarts apple cider
1 tablespoon cinnamon
2 teaspoons nutmeg
1 teaspoon cloves
2 teaspoons salt

Simmer the beef and the beef heart in water to cover until tender. Cut away any fat or gristle. Put through a food chopper, using the coarse blade. Turn into a large pan and add the rest of the ingredients. Stir to blend, and bring to a boil. Reduce heat and simmer, stirring occasionally, for 1½ to 2 hours. Remove from heat and turn into containers. Add, if desired, 2 tablespoons to ¼ cup of brandy, rum, or whiskey to each pint of mincemeat. Refrigerate for 4 to 6 weeks, or freeze for up to 3 months. Makes approximately 10 pints.

He went forth, and brought some food, and put it before him, saying, Eat, oh my master, that the bond of bread and salt may be established between us; and may God (whose name be exalted) execute vengeance upon him who is unfaithful to the bond of bread and salt.'"
THE ARABIAN NIGHTS

GREEN TOMATO MINCEMEAT (WITH MEAT)

1½ pounds green tomatoes
1½ pounds corned beef
1½ pounds green apples
1 pound brown sugar
½ pound seeded raisins
½ pound golden raisins
1 or 2 teaspoons salt
½ cup suet
½ cup + 1 tablespoon cider vinegar

1 tablespoon cinnamon
1 teaspoon cloves
1 teaspoon nutmeg
1 tablespoon grated lemon rind
1 tablespoon grated orange rind
¼ cup citron, diced
¼ cup cream sherry, brandy, rum, or whisky (optional)

Wash the tomatoes, chop fine, and drain. Place in a saucepan, cover with cold water, and bring to a boil. Reduce heat and simmer for 5 minutes. Turn into a large pan. Grind the corned beef with a coarse blade and add to the chopped tomatoes. Wash and dry the apples. Do not peel them. Dice them fine, or put them through a food chopper. Turn into the pan with the rest of the ingredients. Add the broth from the corned beef and simmer, stirring occasionally, for at least 1½ hours. Remove from heat and pour into containers adding, if desired, 2 tablespoons to ¼ cup brandy, rum, or whisky per pint of mincemeat. Will keep in the refrigerator for 4 to 6 weeks, or up to 3 months in the freezer. Makes enough mincemeat for 5 pies.

PEAR MINCEMEAT (MEATLESS)

If desired you may replace up to 3 pounds of the pears with firm ripe apples.

7 pounds ripe Bartlett pears
2 large lemons
1 pound seeded Muscat raisins
1 pound chopped, pitted dates
½ pound dried figs, diced
6½ cups sugar
1 cup vinegar (pear vinegar is a superb choice)

1 tablespoon cloves
1 tablespoon nutmeg
1 tablespoon allspice
1 tablespoon cinnamon
1 teaspoon ginger
brandy, rum, or whiskey

Core and quarter the pears. Chop them finely. Cut the lemons into halves and remove seeds. Chop the lemons into small pieces and add to the pears. Add the raisins, dates, and dried figs, and stir to blend ingredients. Put this mixture into a large pot and add the sugar, vinegar, and spices, stirring well. Cook over medium heat until the mixture comes to a boil. Simmer, stirring occasionally, for 45 minutes to an hour. Pour into containers and add 2 tablespoons to ¼ cup of brandy, rum, or whiskey to each pint of mincemeat. Refrigerate or freeze. Will keep in the refrigerator 4 to 6 weeks, or in the freezer for up to 3 months. Makes approximately 9 pints.

UNCOOKED MINCEMEAT (MEATLESS)

12-ounce box seedless raisins
12-ounce box golden raisins
12-ounce box currants
¼ pound citron, diced
¼ pound mixed candied fruits
1½ pounds apples, chopped
12 ounces beef suet
juice and grated rind of 1 lemon
juice and grated rind of 1 orange
½ teaspoon salt
2 teaspoons nutmeg
1 teaspoon cinnamon
1 teaspoon mace
½ teaspoon cloves
1½ cups firmly packed brown sugar
1½ cups cream sherry
1½ cups brandy

Combine all ingredients in a large bowl. Stir to blend well. Turn into containers and refrigerate for a week, to allow the flavors to blend and mellow. This may be kept frozen for up to 3 months. Makes 6 or 7 pints.

MINCEMEAT PIE

pastry for a 2-crust 9- or 10-inch pie
4 cups homemade mincemeat
1 tablespoon melted butter
half and half, if desired

Line pie pan with pastry. Pour in the mincemeat and brush the filling with the melted butter. Adjust top crust and flute the edges. Cut vents in the top crust and brush the crust with half and half, if desired. Bake in a 450° F. oven for 10 minutes. Reduce heat to 350° F. and continue baking 25 to 30 minutes longer. If you have not added any liquor to the mincemeat, you might add it now. When you remove the pie from the oven, insert a small funnel into one of the vents. Into this pour 3 tablespoons brandy, or equal parts brandy and sherry. Return to a warm oven for 5 minutes. Serve warm.

NOTE: You might substitute 1 cup crushed, drained pineapple or 1 cup drained, canned peaches or pears for 1 cup of the mincemeat.

MRS. SHRIETER'S SOUR CREAM MINCEMEAT PIE

9 or 10-inch pie shell,
  unbaked
2½ cups homemade or
  bottled mincemeat

¼ cup brown sugar
2 tablespoons flour
1 cup heavy sweet cream or
  sour cream

Spread the mincemeat evenly over the bottom of the pie shell. Combine the brown sugar and flour and blend well so that the flour does not lump. Stir in the cream and blend. Pour over the mincemeat and, if desired, arrange pecan or walnut halves over the cream. Bake in a 425° F. oven for 25 to 30 minutes.

NOTE.   Mrs. Shrieter sometimes makes this with a top crust. Brush the top crust with half and half before baking. All other directions are the same.

CHERRY MINCEMEAT PIE

I sometimes use commercial mincemeat, but homemade is best

pastry for a 2-crust 9- or 10-inch pie
1 1-pound can unsweetened
  pie cherries, drained
½ cup sugar

2 cups mincemeat
¼ cup flour
1 large egg

Combine drained cherries and sugar. Combine the remaining ingredients and stir the two mixtures together. Pour into pastry-lined pie pan. Arrange crust over the top. Seal and flute the edges. Cut vents in the top crust. Bake in a 425° F. oven for 35 to 40 minutes.

NUT PIES

MRS. DE ATLEY'S CRACKER PIE

This simple recipe also goes by the names of "Macaroon Pie" and "Soda Cracker Pie." Some cooks use a cup of graham cracker crumbs in place of the soda cracker crumbs. Top it with scoops of ice cream or a dollop of whipped cream. It makes a good dessert either way. When serving the pie to adults, I sometimes add a tablespoon or 2 of rum to the recipe and top it with rum-flavored whipped cream.

¾ to 1 cup soda cracker
    crumbs or graham cracker
    crumbs
1 cup sugar
2 teaspoons baking powder

1 cup chopped nuts
1 teaspoon vanilla extract or
    ½ teaspoon almond extract
3 large egg whites

Blend the cracker crumbs, sugar, baking powder, and chopped nuts. Stir in the flavoring. Beat the egg whites until stiff and fold into the crumb mixture, blending well. Turn into a well-buttered 8 or 9-inch pie pan. Bake in a 350° F. oven for 35 to 40 minutes. Cool on a rack, and chill for several hours. Spread with whipped cream or ice cream before serving.

NOTE. You may double the recipe and bake in a 9 by 13 by 2-inch pan.

OUR FAVORITE PECAN PIE

Pecan pies, as opulent and rich as any pastry anywhere in the world, are the cream of Southern baking. Cut any pecan pie into small pieces.

2 10-inch pie shells, unbaked
1 pound light brown sugar
1 cup light corn syrup
6 large eggs (if desired you
  may use only 4 eggs)
1 cup melted butter or
  margarine
2 teaspoons vanilla
½ teaspoon salt
3 to 4 cups pecan halves

Combine ingredients in order given except for the pecans. Blend ingredients thoroughly and then fold the pecans into the blended mixture. Pour into the 2 pie shells. Bake in a 350° F. oven for approximately 45 to 50 minutes.

PECAN CREAM PIE

9-inch pie shell, unbaked
1 cup broken pecans
2 large eggs
1 cup sugar
1 cup sweet cream or
  commercial sour cream
1 teaspoon flour
¼ teaspoon salt
½ teaspoon grated lemon rind
⅛ teaspoon cinnamon
1 teaspoon lemon juice

Sprinkle broken pecans over the bottom of a pastry-lined pie pan. Set in the refrigerator while you make the filling. Beat the eggs until mixed. Beat in the sugar and the cream. Add the remaining ingredients and stir until well blended. Pour into the pie shell over the pecans. Bake in a 450° F. oven for 10 minutes, reduce heat to 350° F. and bake 25 to 35 minutes longer, or until filling is firm. Serve with whipped cream.

CHOCOLATE PECAN PIE

This is a rich, pastry-less pie. Perfect for company.

1 tablespoon soft butter
1 cup minced pecans
6 ounces package semisweet
  chocolate bits
2 large eggs
pinch of salt
1 teaspoon vanilla extract
½ cup dark corn syrup
⅓ to ½ cup pecan halves

pread butter on bottom and sides of an 8-inch pie pan. Sprinkle with
ie minced pecans and spread evenly. Melt the chocolate bits over hot
not boiling) water. Combine the eggs, salt, vanilla, and corn syrup
nd beat until well blended. Stir in the melted chocolate and blend
ipidly but thoroughly. Pour into the prepared pie pan. Arrange pecan
alves over the top. Bake in a 350° F. oven for 25 to 30 minutes.
erve warm or cold with whipped cream on top.

WHITE HOUSE PECAN PIE

9-inch pie shell, unbaked
1 cup soft butter
1 cup sugar
1 cup dark corn syrup

¼ teaspoon salt
1½ teaspoons vanilla extract
3 large eggs
2 cups chopped pecans

'ombine the butter, sugar, corn syrup, salt, and vanilla and beat until
nooth. Add the eggs and beat until thoroughly blended. Fold in the
iopped pecans and pour into the pie shell. Bake in a 375° F. oven
ntil the top is a toasty brown and the filling is set, about 40 to 45
iinutes.

MOCK PECAN PIE

his makes a rich, delicious pie. The oatmeal becomes toasted and
iewy, with a decidedly nutlike flavor.

8 or 9-inch pie shell, unbaked
3 large eggs
⅔ cup sugar
⅔ cup dark corn syrup
¼ teaspoon salt

1 teaspoon vanilla extract
½ cup butter or margarine,
melted
⅔ cup quick-cooking oatmeal

'ombine the eggs, sugar, corn syrup, salt, vanilla, and melted butter
r margarine and blend thoroughly. Fold in the quick-cooking oats
id pour the mixture into the pie shell. Bake in a 350° F. oven for
pproximately 50 minutes to an hour, or until filling is firm.

VARIATIONS

Because Pecan Pies are relatively simple to make, they lend them selves to variations. All of the following are good and may be used with any of the preceding recipes.

1. Add to mixture, before baking, ¾ cup shredded coconut.

2. Add to mixture, before baking, ¾ cup chopped, pitted dates.

3. Add to mixture, before baking, 1 tablespoon grated orange rind or 1 teaspoon grated lemon rind. This may be combined with #2.

4. Add to mixture, before baking, ¾ cup soft, dried apricots, coarsely chopped.

5. Add to mixture, before baking, 5 tablespoons golden rum.

MACADAMIA NUT PIE.   The first commercial planting of the macadamia tree was in Hawaii in 1922. Today close ot 4000 acres of the trees grow on the island of Hawaii alone. The tasty nuts are delicious in this pie. Make any of the preceding recipes for Pecan Pie as directed, but omit the pecans and use unsalted, chopped macadamia nuts.

WALNUT PIE.   Make any of the preceding recipes for Pecan Pie as directed, but omit the pecans and use chopped walnuts or walnut halves.

TARTS, TURNOVERS, DUMPLINGS, AND DEEP-DISH PIES

Tarts make ideal party desserts, because they can be as simple or as complicated as you wish and because, however simple or complicated, they are delicious and impressive. I have dozens of small molds that I use for making tarts, and whenever the spirit moves me, I make tart shells by the dozen and freeze them. I fill the tart shells the day they are to be served, unless a particular recipe recommends filling them the day before, as for mincemeat tarts. In general, you can use any desired pastry recipe. You can bake the shell over inverted muffin pans. Prick the pastry well with a fork to prevent the shells from puffing and getting out of shape and bake the shells in a 450° F. oven for 8 to 10 minutes. Cool and remove from pans carefully. These are best not frozen. My favorite tart pastry is given below, and freezes very well.

SWEET TART PASTRY

This dough is ideal, as you don't have to roll it out. Simply press the sweet dough into molds or small muffin pans. Butter the pans lightly, so that the baked tart shells slip out more easily. The tarts may be any size, from tiny to quite large, and the pastry holds up beautifully. It is appropriate for any filling.

2 cups sifted flour
¼ cup sugar
¼ teaspoon salt

¾ cup softened butter
2 egg yolks

Combine the flour, sugar and salt. Add the butter and egg yolks, and work the mixture with the fingers. The heat of the hands helps to soften the butter further and bind the mixture together. When thoroughly blended, press the pastry into molds or muffin pans, making an even layer of pastry. This pastry may also be used to line regular pie pans. Bake shells in a 300° F. oven for 20 minutes or until shells are lightly browned. Cool on racks, in the molds. When cool, tap molds lightly on the bottom to free the shells. You may need the tip of a knife to free the edges of some. Turn the shells out carefully. To freeze the shells, allow them to cool completely, wrap in plastic envelopes, and seal tightly.

TART FILLINGS.   The list of tart fillings is virtually endless. Filling for almost any pie may be used. Chiffon pie fillings are lovely and impressive, as is lemon meringue. Spoon the filling into the tart shells, top with meringue, and brown as usual. Your guests will love them! Any pre-cooked cream or custard-pie filling, topped with either a meringue or whipped cream, may be used. The simplest fillings consist of whipped cream and fruit. Canned pie fillings may be used if time is very short. Topped with whipped cream these can be tasty.

LEMON CHEESE FILLING

An old English recipe, sometimes called "Lemon Curd." Use on toast, biscuits, muffins, or to fill layer cakes, pies and tart shells. This will keep, refrigerated, for at least a month.

1 cup butter (for best flavor, do not substitute)	3 cups sugar
	¼ teaspoon salt
¾ to 1 cup lemon juice	6 large eggs
2 teaspoons grated lemon rind	6 egg yolks

Melt butter in the top of a double boiler. Stir in lemon juice, lemon rind, sugar, and salt. Beat the eggs and yolks, and stir into the butter mixture, blending thoroughly. Cook over hot water, stirring constantly, until smooth and thickened. Cool. Pour into clean containers and store in the refrigerator. When used to fill tart shells, the tarts may be left plain, or topped with whipped cream or MERINGUE (pp. 185–7). If you use meringue, place the tarts on a cookie sheet and brown the meringue as directed.

MODERN LEMON CHEESE FILLING

3 large eggs
⅔ cup sugar
⅓ cup lemon juice

2 teaspoons grated lemon
rind
8 or 9 ounces cream cheese

Combine the eggs, sugar, lemon juice and lemon rind in the top of a double boiler. Stir to blend. Cook over very hot water until mixture thickens, stirring constantly. Remove from heat. Cream the cheese. Combine the two mixtures and beat thoroughly. Cool. Use to fill baked tart shells. Top with whipped cream. Mixture will keep, refrigerated, for up to a week.

ORANGE CHEESE FILLING

3 large eggs
2 egg yolks
1 cup sugar
1 tablespoon grated orange
rind

¾ cup orange juice
½ cup butter
1 tablespoon lemon juice

Combine eggs, egg yolks, sugar, orange rind, and orange juice in the top of a double boiler. Stir to blend. Add butter. Cook over very hot water, stirring often, until smooth and thick. Add lemon juice. Remove from heat and cool. Use to fill baked tart shells. Top with whipped cream or meringue. If you top the tarts with MERINGUE (pp. 185–7), place tarts on cooky sheet and brown the meringue as directed. Mixture may be stored in refrigerator, in a tightly covered container, for several weeks. It can be used in any of the ways suggested with either of the Lemon Cheese Filling recipes.

ALMOND TARTLETS

⅔ cup ground almonds
1 cup sugar
¼ cup sifted flour
2 egg yolks
2 large eggs
⅓ cup very soft butter

¼ cup brandy
½ cup chopped candied fruits
⅔ cup heavy cream
½ cup apricot jam, heated
    slivered almonds

Combine the ground almonds, sugar, and flour. Mix well. Beat the egg yolks and whole eggs, and stir into the nut mixture. Add the butter, brandy, and candied fruits. Whip the cream to a custard-like consistency and stir into the blended mixture. Line 24 small tart shells with SWEET PASTRY (p. 249). Spoon filling into the unbaked shells. Bake in a 450° F. oven for 10 to 12 minutes. While tartlets are still very hot, top each with 1 teaspoon hot apricot jam, and sprinkle with slivered almonds. Slip tarts out of molds while still warm. These tartlets are very delicious and impressive.

CHEESE TARTS

8 or 9 ounces cream cheese,
    softened
⅓ cup sugar
1 teaspoon grated lemond rind

1 egg
1 egg yolk
2 tablespoons lemon juice

Combine all ingredients and beat thoroughly. Line small tart shells with SWEET PASTRY (p. 249). Spoon filling into the unbaked shells. Bake in a 400° F oven for 18 to 22 minutes. Cool on a rack for 15 to 20 minutes before slipping tarts out of molds. Top with whipped cream and a whole berry, or with chopped nuts.

MERINGUE TARTS

3 egg whites
pinch of salt
1 teaspoon lemon juice

½ cup sugar
⅓ cup chopped pecans
⅓ cup chocolate chips

In a deep bowl, combine the egg whites, salt, and lemon juice. Beat until soft peaks form. Gradually add the sugar, beating constantly. Beat until mixture will hold stiff peaks. Fold in the nuts and chocolate chips. Line small tart shells with SWEET PASTRY (p. 249). Spoon mixture into the unbaked tart shells and bake in a 400° F. oven for 18 to 22 minutes. Cool on rack for 15 to 20 minutes before slipping tarts out of molds.

COCONUT TARTS

½ cup butter
1½ cups sugar
3 large eggs
3 egg yolks
1 teaspoon vanilla extract

1 teaspoon grated lemon, orange, or tangerine rind
2 cups unsweetened grated coconut

Cream the butter and sugar until light. Add the eggs and egg yolks. Beat thoroughly. Stir in the flavorings and the coconut. Line small tart shells with SWEET PASTRY (p. 249). Spoon mixture into the unbaked shells. Bake in a 350° F. oven for 25 to 35 minutes, or until golden brown.

APPLE TURNOVERS

This is my own recipe, developed to satisfy my family's love for apple turnovers.

½ cup brown sugar
½ cup granulated sugar
½ teaspoon cinnamon
¼ teaspoon nutmeg
3 cardamom seeds, crushed
1 teaspoon grated lemon rind

1 recipe for EGG PASTRY
   (p. 179)
5 large apples, peeled and
   sliced
butter

Combine the sugars, seasonings, and lemon rind. Roll out pastry and cut into 16 squares. Place a portion of the sliced apples on each square of pastry. Sprinkle the apples with a heaping tablespoon of the sugar mixture. Dot with butter. Fold squares into turnover shapes. Seal the edges. Brush turnovers with milk or cream, and cut a vent in the top of each with a knife. Bake on a cookie sheet at 350° F. until well browned. Cool on racks. While still warm, glaze with a powdered-sugar glaze.

OTHER TURNOVER FILLINGS. Make turnovers as above, either smaller or larger, always being careful to seal the edges so that the juices do not run out. You might use mincemeat, either homemade or commercial, mixed with some extra chopped apples, if desired. Jams or preserves may be used to fill small turnovers. Sliced canned fruit, well-drained and sweetened and seasoned to taste, may be used. Peach turnovers are especially good.

FRIED PIES

These are especially good served with a sauce such as lemon or custard, or with a scoop of ice cream.

pastry for a 2-crust pie, rolled and cut into 5-inch circles
canned apple or other pie filling

Place about 2 tablespoons of filling on each round of pastry. Fold pastry over to make a half moon. Seal edges with moistened fingers, and then press with the tines of a fork. Cut small vents in the tops. Fry in deep, hot fat, 375° F., until a golden brown, 3 to 5 minutes. Drain on racks and dust with powdered sugar.

APPLE DUMPLINGS

A delicious old-time dessert. My children consider these an extra special treat. We like them best served with a custard sauce.

biscuit recipe using 2 cups
  flour
4 apples, peeled, cored, and
  halved

sugar
cinnamon

Roll the biscuit dough to a thickness of about ¼ inch. Cut into 4-inch squares. On each square place half an apple, 2 teaspoons sugar, and a pinch of cinnamon. Some good cooks use a tablespoon of orange marmalade instead of sugar. Pull the corners of the dough up around the apples, moisten slightly, and press to seal. Tie each dumpling in a square of cheesecloth and drop into a pan of boiling water. Cook for 20 minutes, or until the dumplings test done. You will have to remove one and cut it open to see. Serve hot.

BAKED DUMPLINGS. Prepare dumplings as above, pressing edges to seal well. Place them in a buttered baking pan with sides. Bake in a 375° F. oven for 30 minutes. While they are baking make a sauce using 2 cups boiling water, 1 cup sugar, and ½ cup butter. Simmer until sugar is dissolved. Pour this over the apples and bake for another 10 to 20 minutes, basting frequently. Serve warm.

DEEP-DISH PIE

⅔ cup sugar
¼ cup cornstarch
pinch of salt
2 cups fresh berries or sliced
  rhubarb
1 teaspoon lemon juice

2 tablespoons butter
4 cups pitted pie cherries or 2
  cans (1 pound each)
  drained, unsweetened pie
  cherries
pastry for an 8 or 9-inch pie

Combine sugar, cornstarch, and salt. Blend well. Turn into a saucepan with the berries or rhubarb and lemon juice. Bring to a boil, stirring constantly. Reduce heat and simmer 5 minutes. Strain the sauce to remove berry seeds. Add the butter and cherries and mix well. Turn into a buttered 1½ or 2-quart baking dish. Cover with pie pastry, sealing the edges of the pastry to the dish. Cut a decorative vent in the top and brush pastry with milk, cream, or melted butter. Sprinkle with sugar and bake in a 425° F. oven until pastry is golden brown, about 30 to 40 minutes. Serve hot or cold.

NOTE. Any fruit fillings for pies may be used in deep-dish pies. Some good cooks like a mixture of homemade mincemeat and large quantities of sliced fresh fruit, such as apples, pears, peaches, or cherries. Deep-dish pies always have a pie-pastry topping. Cobblers, as tasty and easier to make, usually have a soft, sweet, biscuit topping, or a pour-on dough, and are usually served with a sauce or with cream.

APPLE COBBLER

5 cups peeled, cored, sliced apples
½ cup brown sugar
1 tablespoon quick-cooking tapioca
1 tablespoon lemon juice
2 or 3 tablespoons butter

TOPPING

1 large egg
½ cup granulated sugar
½ cup brown sugar
¾ cup buttermilk
⅓ cup molasses
2 cups sifted flour
½ teaspoon baking soda
1½ teaspoons double-acting powder
½ teaspoon salt
½ teaspoon ginger
1 teaspoon cinnamon
2 tablespoons melted butter

Combine apples, ½ cup brown sugar, tapioca, and lemon juice. Stir to blend and pour into a well-buttered baking dish. Dot with 2 or 3 tablespoons butter. Bake in a 350° F. oven for 20 to 25 minutes.

To prepare the topping, beat the egg with the sugars, buttermilk, and molasses. Sift the dry ingredients together and stir into the liquid ingredients. Stir in the melted butter. Pour the batter over the baked apple mixture. Bake another 30 to 40 minutes, or until topping is done.

CRISPY COBBLER

We can't decide which we like better, this luscious dessert or the deep-dish pie.

½ cup butter
1 cup sifted flour
1 cup sugar
2 teaspoons double-acting
  baking powder
⅛ teaspoon salt

¾ cup milk
4 cups fresh or frozen berries
  or rhubarb, or canned or
  fresh sliced peaches or
  apricots

Place butter in an 8 by 10 by 2-inch baking pan. Place in a warm oven to melt the butter. In a bowl, sift together the· flour, sugar, baking powder, and salt. Stir in the milk and blend until smooth. Turn into the baking pan, over the melted butter. Spread with the fruit. Bake in a 375° F. oven for 40 minutes or until topping is browned and crisp. Serve with cream or half and half.

NOTE. If desired, the fruit can be placed in the pan over the melted butter, and the topping poured over the fruit.

VEGETABLE PIES

MASHED POTATO PUDDING PIE

This is a very old recipe and makes a surprisingly good pie. Surprising because we don't expect to find a sweet pie made with mashed potatoes. My family enjoyed this pie and I think yours will also.

9-inch pie shell, unbaked
1 cup hot mashed potatoes
¼ cup butter
½ cup half and half
3 large eggs, separated

1 to 1½ cups sugar
1 tablespoon grated lemon
rind
⅓ cup lemon juice

Combine hot mashed potatoes and butter. Stir until butter is melted.
Add the half and half and blend in. Now add the egg yolks, sugar,
lemon rind, and lemon juice. Beat the egg whites until stiff and fold
into the potato mixture. Pour into the pie shell. Bake in 450° F. oven
for 10 minutes. Reduce heat to 350° F. and continue baking 35 to 40
minutes, or until custardlike mixture tests done. Sprinkle the pie with
powdered sugar while it is still hot. Cool on a rack.

HOLIDAY PUMPKIN PIE

If you insist on gilding the lily, you might top this marvelous pie with
whipped cream. But it doesn't need it.

10-inch pie shell, unbaked
2 cups cooked, mashed,
winter squash or pumpkin,
or 2 cups canned pumpkin
1 to 1½ cups heavy cream
1 cup brown sugar

6 medium eggs
1 to 2 teaspoons cinnamon
¼ teaspoon cloves
1 teaspoon ginger (optional)
¼ teaspoon salt
¼ cup brandy or Cognac

Combine ingredients in the order given, beating until thoroughly
blended. Pour into the unbaked pie shell. Place in a 450° F. oven for
10 minutes then reduce heat to 325° F. and continue baking until firm,
about 40 minutes longer.

NOTE. If desired, you may omit the brandy or Cognac, and add a
tablespoon of vanilla extract.

SOUR CREAM PUMPKIN PIE

11/73 Delicious & pretty!

This makes a very special holiday pie. You may, if desired, omit the sour cream topping, and garnish the chilled pie with sweetened whipped cream instead.

9 or 10-inch baked pie shell
  (a nut pastry is preferable)

FILLING

1 cup commercial sour cream
2 cups canned pumpkin
¼ teaspoon salt
¼ teaspoon nutmeg
½ teaspoon ginger
1 teaspoon cinnamon
1 cup brown sugar, firmly packed
4 large eggs, separated

TOPPING

1 cup commercial sour cream
2 tablespoons sugar
1 teaspoon vanilla extract

To make the filling, combine in the top of a double boiler the sour cream, pumpkin, salt, spices, and sugar. Stir to blend ingredients. Add the egg yolks, and beat with a fork until blended. Cook over hot (not boiling) water, stirring occasionally, until thickened, about 20 minutes. Remove from heat and cool. Beat the egg whites until stiff and fold into the pumpkin mixture. Pour into the baked pie shell. For the topping, combine the sour cream, sugar, and vanilla. Beat lightly and then spread the mixture over the filling. Bake in a 325° F. oven about 15 minutes. Cool on rack before chilling.

RHUBARB PIE

Rhubarb is actually a vegetable; but sweeten it a little, place it between layers of flaky pastry, and it rivals any fruit pie for flavor. It also blends marvelously with strawberries (2 cups each of rhubarb and strawberries) or with pineapple (3 cups rhubarb to 1 cup drained, crushed or chunk pineapple) or with mandarin orange slices (3 cups rhubarb to 1 11-ounce can mandarin orange slices, drained). No other changes in the following recipe are needed. Old-time cooks followed basically the same recipe except that they used only 2 tablespoons flour and added 3 large eggs, beaten and blended into the filling, to make what they called "Rhubarb Custard Pie."

pastry for a 2-crust, 9-inch pie
1 to 1½ cups sugar
¼ cup flour
1 teaspoon grated orange rind

4 cups rhubarb, cut into
    ½-inch pieces
2 tablespoons butter

Combine sugar, flour, and orange rind. Stir through the rhubarb. Turn into a pastry-lined pie pan. Dot with butter. Arrange top crust over filling. Flute and seal the edges. Cut vents in the top. Sprinkle lightly with sugar if desired. Bake in a 425° F. oven for 40 to 50 minutes, or until juice is bubbly and crust is golden brown.

SLICED SWEET-POTATO PIE

Old-time pie recipes were, as often as not, puddings baked in pie shells. And the sweet ancestor of this luscious pie was a pudding that called for more eggs and butter than sweet potatoes, and brandy was always added. You can substitute mashed, cooked, sweet potatoes for the pumpkin, in any pumpkin pie recipe.

pastry for a 2-crust, 9-inch pie
1½ pounds sweet potatoes,
    cooked until tender
1 cup brown sugar
½ teaspoon cinnamon

½ teaspoon ginger or mace
1 teaspoon grated orange rind
⅓ cup butter
¼ cup sherry or brandy
¼ cup water

Peel and slice the potatoes. In a pastry-lined pie pan, layer the potatoes, sugar and spices and orange rind and dot each layer with butter. When all ingredients are used, combine the liquor and water and pour over the top. If desired, omit these two and use instead ½ cup heavy cream. Arrange top crust over filling and seal and flute the edges. Cut vents in the top crust and sprinkle very lightly with sugar. Bake in a 450° F. oven for 10 minutes. Reduce heat to 350° F. and bake another 25 to 30 minutes.

CREAM CHEESE SWEET-POTATO PIE

We think that this one is the best. I sometimes add ¼ cup of brandy, for a heady pie.

10-inch pie shell, unbaked
2 3-ounce packages cream
  cheese
2½ cups mashed, cooked,
  sweet potatoes

¼ cup heavy cream
½ cup brown sugar
2 large eggs
2 teaspoons vanilla extract

Cream the cream cheese. Add the potatoes, cream, brown sugar, eggs, and vanilla. Beat thoroughly with an electric mixer. Turn into the pie shell. Bake in a 450° F. oven for 10 minutes. Reduce heat to 350° F. and continue baking another 30 to 40 minutes, or until a silver knife inserted halfway between the center of the pie and the edge comes out clean. Cool on rack. When ready to serve, top with whipped cream and sprinkle with chopped nuts.

GREEN TOMATO PIE WITH APPLES

One of the pleasures of living in California is that one can, if inclined (and I am), have a year-round vegetable garden. I have experimented with growing everything from avocado (trees) to zucchini (vines). A staple in my garden is the tomato and I always pick some of them green—for mincemeat, dinner pies, and for this dessert pie. Make a plain "Green Tomato Pie" the same as this one, only omit the apples and use another ⅓ cup sugar.

pastry for a 2-crust, 9-inch pie
2½ cups peeled and sliced
  green tomatoes
2½ cups peeled and sliced
  apples
½ cup brown sugar

½ cup granulated sugar
2 tablespoons flour
½ teaspoon cinnamon
¼ teaspoon nutmeg
1 teaspoon grated lemon rind
2 tablespoons butter

To peel the tomatoes, let them stand in boiling water 2 or 3 minutes. The skins will then slip off easily. Combine tomatoes, apples, sugars, flour, spices, and lemon rind. Stir to blend. Turn into pastry-lined pie pan. Dot with the butter and then arrange the top crust over the filling. Flute the edges and cut decorative vents in the top crust. Bake in a 450° F. oven for 10 minutes. Reduce heat to 350° F. and bake another 45 to 50 minutes.

6. *Baking-Powder Breads and Coffeecakes*

The Colonial housewife used a variety of ingredients to achieve lightness in her breads and cakes. She made yeast out of the things at hand—hops, grated potatoes, the leaves of some trees, beer. Lacking these, she developed salt-rising bread (use of true sourdough appears to have been limited to the western United States—the gold and silver prospectors and the cowboy cooks). She also made quick breads, but they weren't often light. And if they were, this was achieved—with varying results—by the addition of spirits or by laboriously beating air into the eggs, which were then very carefully incorporated into the dough. Some cooks achieved lightness in their cakes and quick breads by using water in which hardwood ashes had been soaked. This was undoubtedly the forerunner of pearlash, a refined form of potash, which was obtained from wood ashes or from the residue of some other burned plant such as kelp. This water produced the carbon dioxide which leavened the dough.

By the nineteenth century, the housewife was combining soda (called saleratus) with cream of tartar to raise her quick breads and cakes. Because the mixture quickly absorbed moisture from the air, it had to be freshly made each time it was used, and often it was haphazardly made with unreliable results.

It wasn't until the 1850's that a more reliable formula for baking powder was developed and baking powder was commercially produced. This revolutionized home baking, and was certainly the direct cause of the fact that today no nation in the world comes even close to making the variety of quick breads and biscuits that are proudly served up by the American housewife.

GENERAL INFORMATION

1. In all recipes in this section the baking powder used is a double-acting baking powder.

2. If you should find yourself out of baking powder at the last minute, use 2 teaspoons cream of tartar, 1 teaspoon baking soda, and ¼ teaspoon salt for each cup of flour called for.

3. Many old-time recipes calling for baking soda suggest that it first be dissolved in a liquid before being added to the dough. It has since been discovered that the leavening power of baking soda is greater if it is sifted with the dry ingredients. You can make this change yourself in any recipe.

4. Remember that no recipe can specify *exactly* how much flour will be required. It depends on the brand and type of flour used and the weather. So always start with a slightly lesser amount of flour and then add as needed. You can always *add* more flour if needed, but you cannot remove it if too much has been used. This will not vary as much in baking-powder doughs as it can in yeast doughs, but it is still a point that must be kept in mind.

5. All fruit and nut breads should be mixed as for muffins. In other words, *do not* beat the batter! Blend liquid and dry ingredients just until the dry ingredients are thoroughly moistened.

6. All fruit and nut breads are improved by resting the dough for 15 to 20 minutes before placing it in the oven to bake. This allows the bread to rise just a little, but this little is enough to keep the top of the bread from cracking during the baking period. Do this, however, *only* if you use a double-acting baking powder. Other baking powders release their leavening properties immediately, and breads made with them should be placed in a hot oven as soon as they are mixed and turned into a pan.

7. All fruit and nut breads can be frozen successfully.

8. Since fruit and nut breads are so easily made and can be kept frozen, they are ideal for company serving. Slice the breads thinly, and serve with whipped cream cheese and/or whipped butter. The butter might be flavored with the grated rind of orange or tangerine if desired. The following is also very good:

ROSE BUTTER

This is very simple and very appealing. Simply layer fresh, very clean rose petals in a jar with softened butter. Cap and store for several days before using. The delicate scent and flavor of the rose permeates the butter.

LEMON BREAKFAST MUFFINS

The glossy green leaves of the lemon tree can do more than just perfume the air around them. They can also be used to flavor custards. And the delicate blossoms are delicious, as well as lovely and novel, when sprinkled over fresh fruit salad.

½ cup butter or margarine
½ cup sugar
2 large eggs, separated
1 cup sifted flour
1 teaspoon baking powder

⅛ teaspoon salt
¼ cup fresh lemon juice
1½ teaspoons grated lemon rind

Cream butter or margarine and sugar until light and fluffy. Add egg yolks and beat well. Sift flour with baking powder and salt. Add to creamed mixture alternately with the combined lemon juice and rind. Blend ingredients thoroughly. Beat egg whites until stiff but not dry, and fold into the batter. Fill buttered muffin tins ⅔ full and bake in a 400° F. oven 12 to 15 minutes, or until lightly browned and done. Makes approximately 18 medium muffins.

CRANBERRY MUFFINS

The cranberry that we buy in the markets is indigenous to North America. The Indians, for obvious reasons, called them "bitter berries", but the early settlers called them "crane berries," because the cranes feasted on them. While cranberries are in season only during October, November, and December, they are easily kept for year-round use in the freezer. These are delicious with holiday breakfasts. If desired, ¼ cup chopped pecans or walnuts may be added. Tangerine rind makes a fine substitute for the grated orange rind.

1 cup cranberries, chopped
½ cup sugar
2 cups sifted flour
1 tablespoon baking powder
½ teaspoon salt
2 tablespoons sugar

1 tablespoon grated orange rind
1 large egg
1 cup milk
¼ cup melted butter

Combine the cranberries and the ½ cup sugar. Stir to blend. Sift together the flour, baking powder, salt, and 2 tablespoons sugar. Combine grated orange rind, egg, milk, and melted butter. Add liquid ingredients all at once to the sifted dry ingredients, blending only until dry ingredients are thoroughly dampened. Stir in chopped cranberries. Fill buttered muffin tins ⅔ full and bake in a 400° F. oven 20 to 25 minutes. Makes 12 large muffins.

EASY BREAKFAST FRITTERS

Very simple. Use a refrigerator bread or roll dough, a hot roll mix, or frozen bread dough. Take spoonfuls of the dough, shape into balls and let rise until light. Lift the light balls of dough very carefully and drop into hot fat. Fry until browned and serve with butter and jam, preserves, applesauce, apricot purée, or syrup.

MY BISCUITS

This is the way biscuits are made at my house, and everyone loves them. For my family I always, but always, triple the recipe. I cut them large for dinner, and very small to serve hot with a chef's salad luncheon for the ladies. The leftover biscuits are sometimes dipped into a French Toast mixture and fried, and sometimes toasted to use in Milk Toast. My husband, a Texas man, likes them with gravy. The single most important thing to remember about biscuits is to work them very, very lightly.

2 cups sifted flour
1 tablespoon baking powder
½ teaspoon salt

⅓ cup butter
2 large eggs
about ½ cup milk

Sift flour, baking powder, and salt. Cut in the butter with a pastry blender or fork. Add the eggs and enough of the milk to make a dough that holds together and can be kneaded. Turn dough out onto a very lightly floured breadboard (I often spread the board with oil), and knead very, very lightly, no more than 10 times, although I often knead them less than that. Pat the dough (I never, or almost never, roll dough out) out to a thickness of approximately ½ inch. Cut into rounds (1, 2, or 3-inch) and bake on an unbuttered cooky sheet in a 450° F. oven for 12 to 15 minutes.

VARIATIONS

1. Add ½ teaspoon cinnamon and ½ cup finely diced apple to the dough. Sprinkle tops with a cinnamon-sugar mixture.

2. Add ½ cup crisp pieces fried bacon to dough.

3. Add ½ cup finely diced Cheddar cheese to dough.

4. Add 2 or 3 tablespoons sugar to dough, or sprinkle tops with any flavored sugar.

ROLLED BISCUITS. For all rolled biscuits the dough is rolled (or patted) out and spread with any desired filling, usually fruit or jam. Then the dough is rolled as for a jelly roll, cut into slices and baked, either in muffin tins or in a baking pan with sides, although sometimes a cooky sheet can be used.

CINNAMON ROLLS. Roll or pat dough to a thickness of ½ inch. Spread with ¼ cup soft or melted butter and sprinkle with ½ cup brown or maple sugar mixed with 1 or 2 teaspoons cinnamon. Roll and cut into ¾-inch slices. Bake on a cooky sheet in a 450° F. oven for 12 to 15 minutes.

BASIC MUFFINS

Fresh, hot muffins go well with meals, or as between-meal or late-night snacks. They are more quickly and easily made than are biscuits, and the variations, as with biscuits, are almost limitless.

The liquid ingredients are stirred into the dry ingredients all at once. The batter is then stirred until all ingredients are moistened but still lumpy. The batter should never be beaten. Fill buttered or Teflon-lined muffin pans no more than ⅔ full to allow for expansion. The average muffin recipe, using 2 cups of flour, will make 20 to 24 medium-sized muffins.

2 cups sifted flour	2 large eggs
2 teaspoons baking powder	¾ cup cold milk
½ teaspoon salt	¼ cup melted butter
2 to 4 tablespoons sugar	

Sift the dry ingredients into a bowl. Add the liquid ingredients all at once. Stir just until the dry ingredients are thoroughly moistened but the batter is still lumpy and rough. Fill buttered muffin pans ⅔ full. Bake in a 400° F. oven for 20 to 25 minutes. Serve hot with plenty of butter and/or jam.

VARIATIONS

1. To the dry ingredients add ½ to ¾ cup sharp Cheddar cheese, grated.

2. Omit the sugar and add ½ cup of crumbled, cooked bacon, finely chopped dried beef, or cooked ham to the dry ingredients.

3. One cup of any other flour, such as whole wheat, graham, or buckwheat, may replace an equal amount of white flour. Use brown sugar in place of granulated sugar.

APPLE MUFFINS. Add ¾ to 1 cup of finely chopped apple, and ¼ to ½ teaspoon cinnamon to batter.

BARBECUE MUFFINS.   Replace ½ cup of flour with ½ cup coarse-grind cornmeal. Add 1 tablespoon each: finely minced green pepper and onion, and ⅓ cup grated sharp Cheddar cheese.

DRIED FRUIT MUFFINS.   Use brown sugar in place of granulated. Snip into small pieces and add to dry ingredients ½ to ¾ cup of dried dates, currants, raisins, figs, or soft dried apricots.

HONEY MUFFINS.   Replace ½ cup of flour with ½ cup whole wheat or graham flour. Omit sugar. Substitute ½ cup mild-flavored honey for ½ cup milk, and add ½ cup chopped walnuts or pecans. Very good.

MACADAMIA NUT MUFFINS.   Add ½ to ¾ cup chopped macadamia nuts to the dry ingredients. Spoon batter into muffin pans. Carefully drop 1 teaspoon pineapple, poha, papaya, or guava jam into the center of each. Bake as usual.

OATMEAL MUFFINS.   Replace 1 cup flour with 1 cup uncooked, quick-cooking oatmeal.

SOUR CREAM MUFFINS.   Use 1 to 1¼ cups commercial sour cream in place of milk and melted butter. Decrease baking powder to ½ teaspoon, and add ½ teaspoon baking soda.

SWEET POTATO PUMPKIN MUFFINS.   Use brown sugar in place of granulated. Add ½ cup mashed, cooked sweet potato, pumpkin, or winter squash to batter. You may also use ½ teaspoon cinnamon and ⅓ to ½ cup Grapenuts breakfast cereal, or chopped walnuts, or pecans.

SPOONBREAD

As American as apple pie with cheese—and probably much older—this fine bread is best when served with fried chicken or at outdoor barbecues. Spoonbread also serves as a fine base for creamed dishes. A fine cold weather dish is made with spoonbread, cut into squares and then halved, with creamed chicken or turkey spooned between the layers as well as on top.

2 large eggs
2 cups sour milk or buttermilk
1 cup medium or coarse-grind cornmeal
½ teaspoon baking soda
½ teaspoon baking powder
½ teaspoon salt
3 tablespoons melted butter, chicken fat or salad oil

Combine the eggs and buttermilk and beat just until thoroughly blended. Combine in a bowl the cornmeal, soda, baking powder, and salt. Stir to blend. Stir the dry ingredients into the liquid mixture and blend, adding the melted butter last. Pour into a buttered, 9-inch square pan, and bake in a 400° F. oven for 35 to 45 minutes.

ORANGE ROLLS

1 recipe MY BISCUITS (p. 266)
¼ cup butter or margarine
½ cup orange juice
½ cup sugar
2 teaspoons grated orange rind
1 teaspoon cinnamon
¼ cup sugar

Combine butter or margarine, orange juice, sugar, and orange rind in a saucepan. Bring to a boil, reduce heat, and simmer for 2 minutes. Divide syrup among 12 buttered, medium-sized muffin tins. Roll or pat the biscuit dough into a rectangle. Combine cinnamon and the ¼ cup sugar and sprinkle over the dough. Roll up as for jelly roll. Cut in 12 slices. Place, cut side down, in muffin tins. Bake in 450° F. oven for 20 to 25 minutes. Turn out onto a heated platter.

RHUBARB ROLLS

Delicious! These are favorites at our house.

1 recipe MY BISCUITS (p. 266)
2 cups diced rhubarb
1 to 1½ cups sugar
6 tablespoons butter or margarine, melted
½ teaspoon cinnamon
½ teaspoon grated orange rind
¼ cup butter, melted
1 cup brown or maple sugar

'ombine diced rhubarb and sugar to taste. Set aside. Roll or pat out
1e biscuit dough. Brush with 6 tablespoons melted butter or margarine
nd spread with rhubarb mixture. Sprinkle with cinnamon and orange
ind. Beginning with the wide edge, roll up, very carefully, as for a
·lly roll. Pinch edges to seal. Cut into ½-inch slices. Pour the ¼ cup
1elted butter or margarine into a square baking pan and sprinkle in
1e brown or maple sugar. Place rolls, cut side down, in pan. Bake in a
25° F. oven for 25 to 30 minutes, or until browned and done.

CRANBERRY-PEACH BISCUIT CAKE

'his is simply an Americanized *kuchen*. If desired you might use the
ough for the BLACKBERRY KUCHEN (p. 281), but I usually whip this
p as a quick breakfast cake, using the regular dough for MY BISCUITS
p. 266).

1 recipe My Biscuits	1 tablespoon flour
1 #2½ can sliced peaches, drained	1 teaspoon cinnamon
1 cup fresh cranberries	1 cup sour cream
1 cup sugar	½ cup chopped nuts

ress biscuit dough into a buttered 10-inch square pan. Cover with
rained peach slices. Combine cranberries, sugar, flour, cinnamon, and
our cream. Blend. Spoon cranberry mixture over the peaches and
prinkle with chopped nuts. Bake in a 350° F. oven for 40 to 45
1inutes. Cool cake for at least 10 minutes before cutting.

MARVELOUS BUTTER DIPS

'hese tasty and very simple biscuits were developed within the last
ecade. For a "Sweet Butter Dip," increase sugar to ½ cup and work
2 cup each of raisins and chopped walnuts into the dough. If the
·cipe appears too large for your family, cut it by half and make the
ips in a 9 by 13-inch pan.

1 cup butter or margarine	5 teaspoons baking powder
4 cups sifted flour	4 large eggs
1 teaspoon salt	1 cup milk
2 tablespoons sugar	an additional ½ cup flour

Put the butter or margarine into a jelly roll pan and place in a 450° F. oven until melted. Combine dry ingredients and sift into a large bowl. Combine eggs and milk and stir, all at once, into the dry ingredients. Turn out onto a breadboard with the additional ½ cup flour and knead no more than 10 times. As with any biscuit, the less kneading the better. Pat out with the hands to a thickness of ½ inch. Cut into fingers, rounds, or diamonds. Coat each side of each biscuit with the melted butter in the jelly roll pan. Then lay the biscuits in any remaining melted butter, and bake in a 450° F. oven for 15 minutes, or until browned and done.

COTTAGE CHEESE BISCUITS

It is impossible to give the exact amount of cottage cheese needed in this recipe. Depending on the moisture content of the cheese, I have used from 1½ cups to 2¼ cups to make a dough that will hold together. Start with the smaller amount and then add as much as might be necessary to bind the ingredients together. I often add a teaspoon of mixed dried herbs to the dough. Use equal parts of oregano and thyme if the biscuits are to be served with beef, and equal parts of sage and thyme if the biscuits are to be served with pork.

3 cups sifted flour	¼ cup butter or margarine
1 teaspoon salt	2 large eggs
1 tablespoon sugar	1½ to 2¼ cups cottage
5 teaspoons baking powder	cheese

Sift into a large bowl the flour, salt, sugar, and baking powder. Cut in the butter or margarine with a pastry blender or fork. Make a well in the center by pushing flour mixture against the sides of the bowl

ito the well place the eggs and 1½ cups cottage cheese. Work the
ingredients together just enough to bind them, using more cottage
cheese if necessary. Turn out onto a very lightly floured breadboard
and knead very, very lightly. The dough should be just barely smooth
enough to pat out. Pat or roll to a thickness of close to an inch. Cut
with a cutter and place on buttered cooky sheets. Bake in a 450° F.
oven for 12 to 15 minutes or until browned and done.

CORN BREAD OR STICKS

Mary Stuart Smith, in her *Virginia Cookery Book,* published in 1885,
tells us that the simple corn dodger, a flat, oval-shaped bread made
with cornmeal, water, and salt, was the favorite bread of George
Washington. Ash cakes, another popular cornbread of the day, differed
in that they were baked directly on the hearth in front of an open fire.
When the tops of the cakes were firm, the ashes were drawn over
them, to remain until the cakes were cooked through. Particular people,
it was said, laid collard leaves over the cakes before drawing the ashes
over them. And some cooks used cabbage leaves both under and over
the cakes.

Today's cornmeal, unless you buy directly from a miller or from a
health food store, has had the germ and flour removed, so that the
addition of a small amount of flour is necessary to keep the cornbread
from crumbling.

To vary any cornbread, you might add any one of the following:
1 teaspoon chili powder, 1 teaspoon poultry seasoning, some chopped
green chili peppers, some minced and cooked onion, some chopped
pimiento, ½ cup diced cooked ham, ½ cup crumbled cooked bacon.

Remember that the very best cornbreads are baked in heavy, cast-
iron pans, skillets, or corn-stick pans. And for a desirably crisp crust,
preheat the pan with a tablespoon or 2 of butter. Turn the batter into
the pan when the butter is sizzling.

1 tablespoon vinegar
cream, evaporated milk, or
   half and half
1 large egg
1¼ cups coarse ground
   cornmeal
½ cup sifted flour
½ teaspoon salt

1 teaspoon baking powder
½ teaspoon baking soda
1 tablespoon sugar (optional,
   a Southerner will always
   leave it out)
3 tablespoons butter,
   margarine or bacon fat

Put the vinegar into a cup and fill the cup with cream, evaporated mill or half and half. Set aside for 10 to 15 minutes. Then add the egg an beat to blend. Combine this mixture with the cornmeal and stir t blend. Sift the flour, salt, baking powder, soda, and sugar, if used. Sti into the cornmeal mixture and beat all together for a minute. I desired you may add the melted butter, margarine, or bacon fat directl to the batter, and use extra fat in the pans. Some good cooks, howeve prefer to add no fat to the batter, but to depend entirely on that in th pan. Turn into preheated, buttered corn-stick pans and bake in 425° F. oven for 15 minutes, or until done. Makes 12. Or the batte may be turned into a 10-inch cast-iron skillet, preheated and buttered and baked for 25 minutes. Or you may use a 9-inch square pan, pre heated and buttered.

SESAME CORNBREAD

A far cry from the old-time cornbread, we think you will enjoy thi very tasty modern version. It makes a healthful, as well as delicious snack for children. I buy my sesame seeds by the pound at health foo stores and keep them refrigerated.

½ cups sifted flour
⅓ cup sugar
1 teaspoon salt
1¼ teaspoons baking soda
2 cups cornmeal
1 cup wheat germ

½ cup sesame seeds
2 cups buttermilk
½ cup + 2 tablespoons salad
   oil
3 large eggs

Sift together the flour, sugar, salt, and soda. Add the cornmeal, whea germ and sesame seeds. Blend. Combine liquid ingredients and blen

e eggs. Add liquid ingredients, all at once, to the dry ingredients
stir just until the dry ingredients are thoroughly moistened. Too
 beating of any quick bread will make it "tighten," and possibly
Turn batter into a buttered loaf pan and bake in a 375° F. oven
5 minutes, or until browned and done.

GINGERBREAD

 spicy, sweet bread is a generations-old favorite with children and
s alike. Serve it plain as a between-meal or after-school snack.
dessert (or for company) dress up the squares with sweet, heavy
n, whipped cream, ice cream, or WHIPPED CREAM CHEESE TOPPING.
ll the gingerbreads we've tried, this recipe is still the favorite in
family.

cup boiling water, coffee, or	2½ cups sifted flour
orange juice	1 teaspoon salt
cup butter	1½ teaspoons baking soda
cup light brown sugar	1 teaspoon ginger
cup light or dark molasses,	1 teaspoon cinnamon
maple syrup, or honey	1 teaspoon nutmeg
large eggs	

 the boiling liquid over the combined butter, sugar, and molasses.
until the butter is melted, and set aside to cool. When mixture is
d, beat in the eggs. Sift the flour with the salt, soda, and spices and
nto the liquid mixture. Beat just until smooth. Turn batter into a
red 9 by 13-inch baking pan and bake in a 325° F. oven for 1 hour,
ntil done. Serve as suggested above.

WHIPPED CREAM CHEESE TOPPING

ounce package cream cheese	½ teaspoon grated lemon
cup half-and-half	rind, or 1 tablespoon grated
tablespoon sugar	orange rind

bine ingredients and beat, with an electric mixer or in a blender,
 smooth and fluffy. Spoon over squares of GINGERBREAD.

RUTH'S APPLE CAKE

This recipe makes one perfectly marvelous coffeecake.

1 cup finely chopped nuts
½ cup sugar
2 teaspoons cinnamon
1½ cups very thin apple slices
1 teaspoon lemon juice
1 cup butter or margarine
1 cup sugar

3 large eggs
2½ cups sifted flour
1 tablespoon baking powder
1 teaspoon baking soda
1 cup commercial sour cream
1 teaspoon milk

In a small bowl combine the finely chopped nuts, ½ cup sugar, cinnamon, apple slices, and lemon juice. Stir to blend, and set this mixtu aside. Now, cream the butter or margarine and sugar. Beat in the egg one at a time. Sift together the flour, baking powder, and soda. Combine the sour cream and the teaspoon of milk. Add the sifted flou mixture to the creamed mixture alternately with the sour cream, beginning and ending with the dry ingredients. Butter a 10-inch square pa Pour half the batter into the pan and spread with entire apple-nut mixture. Spoon the rest of the batter over the filling. Bake in a 350° oven for 45 to 55 minutes, or until browned and done.

PUMPKIN GINGERBREAD

Although it originated in England, American children have made th homely delights of gingerbread their very own. And country cook again using the ingredients at hand, have added pumpkin to make moist, pleasingly spicy cake.

½ cup butter or margarine
½ cup sugar (brown or
   granulated)
2 large eggs
¾ cup buttermilk or sour
   milk
½ cup mashed pumpkin
½ cup light molasses

2½ cups sifted flour
1 teaspoon baking soda
½ teaspoon salt
1 teaspoon cinnamon
1 teaspoon ginger
1 tablespoon grated orange
   rind

eam butter or margarine with sugar until light and fluffy. Add the
gs, one at a time, and beat in until well blended. Combine the butter-
lk or sour milk, pumpkin (if pumpkin is freshly cooked, whirl it in
blender until smooth), and molasses and stir to blend. Sift the flour
th the soda, salt, and spices. Stir the grated orange rind into the
ur mixture. Now add liquid mixture and flour mixture to the creamed
tter, sugar, and eggs, alternately. Begin and end with dry ingredients.
r to make certain that everything is well blended and the batter is
ooth. Turn into a well-buttered 9-inch square pan. Bake in a 325° F.
en for 45 to 50 minutes or until cake shrinks away from the sides
the pan and tests done with a toothpick or cake tester.

BRANDIED RAISIN COFFEECAKE

e brandy *could* be omitted and another large egg substituted, but the
andy does add an elusive flavor that makes this cake more than just
everyday raisin cake. If desired, you may substitute maple syrup
 the sugar. Simply boil the syrup along with the raisins, butter, and
ter. This cake keeps well.

1 cup raisins	1 teaspoon cinnamon
½ cup butter or margarine	½ teaspoon nutmeg
1 cup water	1 large egg
1½ cups sifted flour	¼ cup cold water
1 cup sugar	¼ cup brandy
1 teaspoon baking soda	½ cup chopped nuts
½ teaspoon salt	

mbine raisins, butter or margarine, and 1 cup water in a saucepan.
ng to a boil and simmer for 5 minutes. Cool to room temperature.
t the dry ingredients together and set aside. Break the egg into a
wl, add the ¼ cup cold water and the brandy, and stir to blend.
w add the cooled raisin mixture. Blend in the sifted dry ingredients
dually and stir just until the flour is thoroughly dampened. Batter
l not be smooth. Fold in the chopped nuts, and pour into a but-
ed 8-inch square pan. Bake in a 350° F. oven for 35 to 40 minutes.
ol on rack for 5 to 10 minutes before turning out of pan. Dust
h powdered sugar while cake is warm.

COCOA-NUT COFFEECAKE

1 cup butter or margarine
1½ cups sugar
4 large eggs
2 teaspoons grated lemon rind
½ teaspoon salt
1 tablespoon baking powder

3½ cups sifted flour
1 large can evaporated milk

TOPPING

½ cup sugar
2 teaspoons cinnamon
2 tablespoons cocoa

Cream butter or margarine and sugar until fluffy. Beat in the eggs one at a time. Stir in the grated lemon rind. Sift together the salt, baking powder, and flour. Add to the creamed mixture alternately with the evaporated milk. Blend ingredients thoroughly. Pour ingredients into a well-buttered Bundt pan, or a 10-inch tube pan. Combine ingredients for topping and stir to blend. Spoon topping over the batter and, using a knife, swirl the topping mixture through the batter. Bake in a 350° F oven 60 to 70 minutes. Cool on rack for 10 minutes before turning out of pan. Dust with powdered sugar while cake is still warm.

RICH CREAM COFFEECAKE

This is just one of the many variations of the sour cream coffeecake that made its entrance some ten years ago. All variations are super.

4 large eggs
1 cup sugar
1 teaspoon vanilla extract
1 tablespoon grated lemon rind
1 cup butter or margarine, melted
2 cups commercial sour cream
2¼ cups sifted flour
2 teaspoons baking powder

1½ teaspoons baking soda
1 teaspoon salt

TOPPING

½ to ¾ cup sugar, granulated or brown
1 cup chopped pecans or walnuts
1 teaspoon cinnamon, or 2 teaspoons cocoa.

ombine eggs, sugar, vanilla, and lemon rind in a large bowl. Using an
lectric mixer, beat at medium speed until light and fluffy. Add melted
utter or margarine and sour cream and mix easily, just until blended.
ift together the dry ingredients and, using a wooden spoon, carefully
old into the butter-sugar mixture, again blending just until smooth.
pread half the batter in a well-buttered 9 by 13-inch pan. Combine
gredients for topping and sprinkle half of topping mixture over the
atter. Cover with remaining batter and top with the rest of the topping.
ake in a 375° F. oven 35 to 40 minutes or until browned and done.
he cake will shrink away from the sides of the pan just a little.

CHRISTMAS COFFEECAKE

his is a must at Christmas time. We love it and we think you will also.

¾ cup sifted flour
½ cup sugar
⅓ cup butter or margarine
1 cup candied fruits
½ cup chopped nuts
2¾ cups + 2 tablespoons
  sifted flour
1 tablespoon baking powder
1 teaspoon salt

¾ cup butter or margarine
1 cup sugar
1 tablespoon grated orange
  rind
1 teaspoon vanilla extract or
  rum flavoring
3 large eggs
⅓ cup milk

ombine the ¾ cup flour, ½ cup sugar and ⅓ cup butter or mar-
rine. Work until mixture is crumbly. Add candied fruits and nuts
d set aside. Sift the remaining flour with the baking powder and
t and set aside. Cream remaining butter and sugar. Add flavorings
d eggs and beat until thoroughly blended. Add sifted flour mixture
 creamed mixture alternately with the milk, beginning and ending
h dry ingredients. Batter should be smooth, but do not overbeat.
oon alternate layers of batter and the reserved candied fruit mix-
e into a well-buttered 10-inch tube pan or Bundt pan. Bake in a
0° F. oven for 50 minutes or until done.

QUICK AND EASY SOUR CREAM COFFEECAKE

Made as easily as muffins, this tender cake is almost as variable. Listed below are some of the things I do with it. I'm sure that you will think of more.

3 cups sifted flour	½ teaspoon salt
1½ to 2 cups sugar	2 cups commercial sour cream
4 teaspoons baking powder	4 large eggs
1 teaspoon baking soda	

Sift dry ingredients together into a bowl. Combine sour cream and eggs and beat well. Stir in dry ingredients and mix to blend. Spread in a lightly buttered 9 by 13-inch pan. Bake in a 350° F. oven for approximately 45 minutes, or until cake tests done.

VARIATIONS

1. Spread a can of apple pie filling (or any desired pie filling) on bottom of buttered pan. Cover with batter and bake as above.

2. Use to make Pineapple Upside-down Cake.

3. Turn a well-drained can of sweet or sour cherries into the batter. Turn into pan and cover with streussel, if desired.

4. Add a cup or two of blueberries to batter. Turn into pan and cover with streussel, or sprinkle with cinnamon and sugar and dot with butter.

5. Spread batter in pan and cover with neat rows of sliced fruit, top with a streussel, or sprinkle with cinnamon and sugar and dot with butter.

Add a cup of chopped nuts and a cup of raisins or dates to batter.

Add a cup of cranberries and a tablespoon of grated orange rind
batter.

BLACKBERRY KUCHEN

his is an Americanized version of Germany's *Kuchen* that our German
iends find quite delicious. As always, the proportion of streussel is sub-
ct to argument. One German friend uses more butter, and rubs it
well with her hands, to make luscious lumps of topping.

EASY KUCHEN DOUGH
2 cups sifted flour
⅓ cup sugar
1 teaspoon baking powder
⅓ cup butter, quite soft
3 large eggs
BERRY FILLING
20-ounce package of frozen,
    unsweetened blackberries,
    blueberries, or raspberries

⅓ cup sugar
¼ cup flour
STREUSSEL
⅓ cup sugar
½ teaspoon cinnamon
⅔ cup sifted flour
⅓ to ½ cup butter or
    margarine

ft together the 2 cups flour, ⅓ cup sugar, and 1 teaspoon baking
wder in a bowl. Stir to blend. Add the soft butter and the eggs.
ork mixture together (I use clean hands) until it forms a dough.
ess the dough against the bottom and sides of a lightly buttered 9
 13-inch pan. Combine ingredients for the filling and stir to blend.
ur filling over the dough. To make the streussel, sift the sugar,
namon and flour into a bowl. Cut in the butter until the flour is
ll-coated and particles are the size of small peas. I have taken the
vice of my German friends, and now work the mixture together
th my hands. The difference is amazing. Spoon the streussel over the
rries and bake in a 350° F. oven for 30 to 45 minutes, or until
e *Kuchen* dough is browned and done. I always make this in a glass
n, as it is much easier to check the dough.

FRUITED COFFEECAKE

We really like this coffeecake, and people are always surprised to find the moist pieces of fruit inside.

2 cups sugar
¼ cup syrup from canned fruit
1 cup salad oil (*not* olive oil)
2 teaspoons vanilla extract
4 large eggs
3 cups sifted flour
1 tablespoon baking powder

½ teaspoon salt
1 cup slivered almonds, or chopped walnuts or pecans
FRUIT FILLING
1-pound can of fruit cocktail; or fruits for salad; or peaches; or pears, drained

In a large bowl combine the sugar, syrup from canned fruit used in the filling, salad oil, vanilla extract, and eggs. Beat with an electric mixer, at medium speed, until thoroughly mixed, 4 to 5 minutes. Now sift the dry ingredients together and, using a wooden spoon, stir into the liquid ingredients, a little at a time, until well blended. Fold in the nuts last. Put half of the batter into a well-buttered Bundt pan or a 10-inch tube pan. Arrange the well-drained fruit over the batter (if fruit is in large pieces, dice it first). Cover with the remaining batter and bake in a 350° F. oven for 1 hour and 20 minutes to 1 hour and 30 minutes. Cool on a rack for 10 minutes and then turn out of pan. Brush lightly with melted butter and sprinkle with powdered sugar.

LEMON COFFEECAKE

¾ cup butter or margarine
2 cups sugar
4 large eggs
1 cup milk
1 tablespoon grated lemon rind
3 cups sifted flour

2 teaspoons baking powder
½ teaspoon salt
1 cup chopped walnuts or slivered almonds
TOPPING
½ cup sugar
⅓ cup lemon juice

ream the butter or margarine and 2 cups of sugar until light and
uffy. Beat in the eggs, one at a time. Stir in the milk and the grated
mon rind just to blend. Sift flour, baking powder, and salt together
id stir into the creamed mixture just until blended. Stir in the nuts
st. Turn batter into a well-buttered Bundt pan or a 10-inch tube pan.
ake in a 350° F. oven for 1 hour, or until cake is browned and
sts done. Cool on a rack for 10 minutes before spooning the top-
ng over the cake. Cool cake completely before turning out of pan.
o make the Topping, combine the sugar and lemon juice and stir
• dissolve the sugar.

OTE. If desired, rum may replace part of the lemon juice. I very
ten use 3 tablespoons of each.

CREAM CHEESE COFFEECAKE

ntil recently we used cream cheese only in fillings for baked products.
ut now we've discovered the smooth richness it adds to pound cakes
d coffeecakes. This one is just great.

½ cup butter or margarine
8-ounce package cream cheese
1¼ cups sugar
2 large eggs
1 teaspoon vanilla extract
2 tablespoons blackberry or
   raspberry jam or preserves
1¾ cups sifted flour
1 teaspoon baking powder

½ teaspoon baking soda
¼ teaspoon salt
¼ cup milk
STREUSSEL
⅓ cup brown sugar
⅓ cup flour
½ teaspoon cinnamon
⅓ cup butter or margarine

ream butter or margarine, cream cheese, and sugar and beat until
ht and fluffy. Beat in the eggs, one at a time, and blend well. Stir
the vanilla and the jam or preserves, just until blended. Sift to-
ther the flour, baking powder, baking soda, and salt, and add to
e creamed mixture alternately with the milk, beginning and ending
th the flour mixture. Turn batter into a well-buttered 9 by 13-inch
n. To make the streussel, combine the brown sugar, flour, and cinna-
on. Now work in the butter until the particles are about the size of
iall peas. Spread this over the batter. Bake in a 350° F. oven for
 to 40 minutes, or until cake tests done.

RICE FLOUR COFFEECAKE

I have a friend who can't eat wheat products. She makes this coffeecake, as delicious as any made with a regular white flour.

¾ cup butter or margarine,
  melted
1½ cups brown sugar
4 large eggs
2½ cups unsweetened rice
  flour (not the sweet rice
  flour that comes packaged in
  small boxes)
2 teaspoons baking powder

1½ cups milk
¾ cup coconut
1 teaspoon vanilla extract
1 teaspoon grated lemon rind
½ cup brown sugar
1 teaspoon cinnamon
⅓ cup rice flour
⅓ cup butter or margarine

Combine the melted butter or margarine and the 1½ cups brown sugar. Cream until light. Add eggs, one at a time, and beat in thoroughly. Combine the 2½ cups rice flour and baking powder. Stir to blend. Add this to the creamed mixture alternately with the milk. Stir in the coconut, vanilla, and grated lemon rind. Pour into a buttered 9 by 13-inch pan. Combine the remaining ingredients in a bowl. Work in the butter until mixture is crumbly. Sprinkle over the batter. Bake in a 375° F. oven for 35 to 40 minutes or until a cake tester comes out clean.

POPPY SEED COFFEECAKE

Reminiscent of the famous European coffeecakes.

⅓ cup poppy seeds
1 cup buttermilk or sour milk
1 cup butter or margarine
1½ cups sugar
4 large eggs
2½ cups sifted flour
2 teaspoons baking powder

1 teaspoon baking soda
½ teaspoon salt
1 teaspoon vanilla extract
  SUGAR MIXTURE
⅓ cup sugar
1 teaspoon cinnamon

ombine poppy seeds and buttermilk or sour milk and let soak over-
ight. Cream butter or margarine and sugar until light and fluffy. Add
ie eggs, one at a time, and blend thoroughly. Sift together the flour,
aking powder, baking soda, and salt. Add the vanilla extract to the
oppy seed-buttermilk mixture. Add the sifted dry ingredients to the
reamed mixture alternately with buttermilk mixture, beginning and
nding with dry ingredients. Turn half the batter into a well-buttered
undt pan or a 10-inch tube pan. Combine sugar and cinnamon and
prinkle this over the batter. Top with remaining batter and bake in a
50° F. oven for 1 hour, or until browned and done. Cool in the pan,
n a rack, for 10 minutes. Then turn out of pan and dust with pow-
ered sugar.

SPICY COFFEECAKE

marvelous, spicy cake that can be whipped up in a moment's time
or the unexpected guest.

2 tablespoons soft butter	½ teaspoon cinnamon
2 tablespoons molasses	1 large egg
½ cup chopped walnuts or pecans	2 cups sifted flour
	2 teaspoons baking powder
½ cup butter or margarine	½ teaspoon salt
½ cup sugar	¼ teaspoon baking soda
3 tablespoons molasses	1 cup commercial sour cream
½ teaspoon ginger	

lend the 2 tablespoons soft butter and 2 tablespoons molasses into
paste. Spread in the bottom of a buttered 9-inch ring mold. Sprinkle
ith the chopped nuts. Set aside. Now cream the ½ cup butter or
argarine, sugar, and 3 tablespoons molasses. Stir in the spices and
ie egg and beat until the mixture is very light. Sift together the
our, baking powder, salt, and baking soda. Stir the sifted dry in-
redients into the creamed mixture alternately with the sour cream,
eginning and ending with the dry ingredients. Spoon batter into the
repared ring mold. Bake in a 350° F. oven for 45 minutes. Cool
n a rack for 5 minutes before turning out of pan. When the cake
turned out of the pan onto the rack, brush it lightly with melted
utter and sprinkle with powdered sugar.

COFFEECAKES MADE WITH STREUSSEL

The *Streussel,* those large lumps of sugary, buttery topping on various cakes, breads, and buns, is the gift of the German immigrant. American cooks like to put a streussel on almost anything, including nut breads and apple pies as well as coffeecakes and buns. I had always made my streussel as directed by the average cookbook, that is, cutting the ingredients together until the consistency of a coarse meal—and I had always been disappointed with the results. I used the pastry blender or two knives or a fork, and while it was clean and neat, it just didn't work. It was a German friend who let me in on the secret of a truly good, lumpy, streussel: it must be mixed with the hands. This impeccable housewife sternly informed me that there are some things that you *must* mix with the hands, and a good streussel is one of them.

PINEAPPLE COFFEE CAKE

½ cup butter or margarine
½ cup sugar
1¾ cups flour, unsifted
1 teaspoon vanilla extract
1 teaspoon grated lemon rind
2 large eggs

1½ teaspoons baking powder
½ teaspoon baking soda
½ teaspoon salt
9-ounce can crushed pineapple, undrained

Cream butter or margarine and sugar. Add ¾ cup of the flour and work it into the creamed mixture with the hands to form a crumb mixture. Remove ½ cup and set aside. To the remaining crumb mixture add the vanilla, lemon rind, and eggs. Beat until smooth. Combine remaining cup of flour with the baking powder, soda, and salt

Stir to mix. Then stir dry ingredients into the egg mixture alternately with the undrained crushed pineapple, beginning and ending with the dry ingredients. Blend well and turn into a buttered 10-inch pie pan. Take the crumb mixture that has been set aside and rub between the hands to make nice large lumps. Sprinkle these over the batter and bake in a 375° F. oven for 35 to 40 minutes or until cake tests done.

BANANA STREUSSEL CAKE

½ cup butter or margarine	½ teaspoon baking soda
¾ cup sugar	½ teaspoon salt
1¾ cups flour, unsifted	½ teaspoon cinnamon
1 teaspoon vanilla extract	⅔ cup mashed bananas
2 large eggs	⅓ cup buttermilk or sour
1½ teaspoons baking powder	milk

Cream butter or margarine and ½ cup of the sugar. Add ¾ cup of the flour and work it into the creamed mixture with the hands to form a crumb mixture. Remove ½ cup and set aside. To the remaining crumb mixture add the remaining ¼ cup sugar, vanilla extract, and eggs. Beat until smooth. Combine remaining 1 cup flour with the baking powder, soda, salt, and cinnamon. Stir to blend. Combine bananas with the buttermilk or sour milk. Add these two mixtures to the egg mixture alternately, beginning and ending with the dry ingredients. Blend well and turn into a buttered 10-inch pie pan. Take the crumb mixture that has been set aside and rub between the hands to make large lumps. Sprinkle over batter and bake in a 375° F. oven for 35 to 40 minutes or until cake tests done.

CITRUS STREUSSEL CAKE

In this delicious cake you can use orange rind and juice, lemon rind and juice, or tangerine rind and juice. We favor slivered almonds in the topping, but chopped walnuts or pecans are good also.

⅔ cup butter or margarine
1 cup sugar
2 cups flour, unsifted
2 teaspoons baking powder
½ teaspoon baking soda
½ teaspoon salt
1 tablespoon grated orange or tangerine rind, or 1 teaspoon grated lemon rind

2 tablespoons orange or tangerine juice, or 1 tablespoon lemon juice
2 large eggs
⅔ cup buttermilk or sour milk
½ cup chopped nuts

Cream butter or margarine and sugar until fluffy. Add 1 cup of the flour and work in well to form a crumb mixture. Remove ½ cup and set aside. Combine remaining cup of flour with baking powder, soda salt, and the grated rind. Stir to blend. Combine juice, eggs, and buttermilk or sour milk, and stir vigorously to blend thoroughly. Add these two mixtures to the remaining crumb mixture alternately, beginning and ending with dry ingredients. Turn batter into a deep 10-inch pie pan. Take the reserved ½ cup crumb mixture and rub it between the hands to make large lumps. Sprinkle over batter. Bake in a 375° F oven for 35 to 40 minutes or until cake tests done.

NUT BREADS

BASIC FRUIT-NUT BREAD

I continued experimenting with the Basic Date-Nut Bread from my earlier book, *A World of Breads,* and however I made it—with dried figs, apricots, and even dried apples—it still proved to be superior to any other recipe. I often double the recipe and bake the loaves in pans rather than 4. The baking time is lengthened but the larger loaves make very nice gifts.

2 or 3 cups raisins, or
chopped, pitted dates
1 teaspoon salt
½ cup butter or margarine
2 cups boiling water (part
may be orange juice)
2 to 4 large eggs
1½ cups white or brown
sugar

1 or 2 teaspoons vanilla
extract, or grated lemon
rind, or 1 tablespoon grated
orange or tangerine rind
(optional)
3 cups sifted flour
(approximate)
1 teaspoon baking powder
1 teaspoon baking soda
1 to 1½ cups chopped nuts

Combine the fruit, salt, butter or margarine, and boiling liquid in a bowl. Stir to melt the butter and set aside. Beat the eggs until light and beat until thoroughly blended with the sugar, and the flavoring, if used. Sift together the flour, baking powder, and soda. Stir the egg-sugar mixture into the well-cooled fruit mixture. Then add the sifted flour mixture and blend in carefully but thoroughly. Do not beat. Overbeating will make a tight, compact loaf. Stir in the chopped nuts. Pour into 2 buttered loaf pans and set aside for 15 minutes. Bake in a 350° F. oven for 1 hour, or in buttered cupcake tins for 30 minutes. Always test carefully.

VARIATIONS

DRIED APPLE.   Use an 8-ounce bag of dried apples. Cut into small pieces with kitchen scissors. Apple juice may replace part of the water. All of the liquid *must* be boiling when poured over the dried apple pieces. Cool, and follow recipe.

DRIED APRICOT OR PEACH.   Use 1 pound of dried fruit. Snip with kitchen scissors dipped in hot water. The peaches should be snipped into smaller pieces than the apricots. Add ½ of a 6-ounce can of frozen concentrated orange juice to boiling water. Use the vanilla extract or the grated orange rind. Because these fruits absorb less of the liquid, you will need more flour, requiring approximately 4 cups in all. It is impossible to tell *exactly* how much flour any particular recipe will take. It may require slightly different amounts at different times, depending on weather and type of flour used. So always start

with a lesser amount and then add as needed. You can *add* flour, bu
you cannot remove it if you've used too much.

DRIED FIG. This is my favorite! Use 3 cups of dried figs and cu
them into pieces with kitchen scissors dipped in hot water.

HOLIDAY. Decrease sugar in basic recipe to 1 cup and add 1 cu
of any desired candied fruits.

APPLE BUTTER NUT BREAD

A delicious tea bread. If desired, you can use any other fruit butte
of like consistency.

1½ cups + 2 tablespoons sifted flour	¼ cup butter or margarine, melted
2 teaspoons baking powder	½ cup apple butter
½ cup sugar	¼ cup milk
1 teaspoon cinnamon	¼ cup apple cider
¼ teaspoon salt	½ cup chopped nuts
1 large egg	

Sift 1½ cups of the flour with the baking powder, sugar, cinnamo
and salt into a bowl. Make a well in the center. In the well place th
egg, melted butter or margarine, apple butter, milk, and cider. Usin
a kitchen fork or a mixing spoon, combine mixtures until dry i
gredients are thoroughly moistened, but be careful not to overmi
Combine remaining 2 tablespoons flour with the chopped nuts an
fold into the batter. Turn into a well-buttered 9 by 5 by 3-inch lo
pan. Let stand for 15 minutes. Bake in a 350° F. oven for 45 minute
Turn out of the pan onto a rack and cool completely before storin
Wrap and keep refrigerated.

CHRISTMAS NUT BREAD

This recipe uses ready-made, or homemade cranberry-orange relis
Make this bread at least 24 hours before serving.

3 cups sifted flour
1 tablespoon baking powder
½ teaspoon baking soda
1 teaspoon salt
⅔ cup sugar

½ cup butter or margarine
1 large egg
¾ cup milk
1 cup cranberry-orange relish
1 cup chopped nuts

Sift dry ingredients into a bowl. Add the butter or margarine and cut it in until the mixture is like coarse meal. Combine the egg and milk and stir into the flour-butter mixture, stirring just until blended. Stir in the relish and the nuts. Turn the batter into a well-buttered 9-inch tube pan, or a mini-Bundt pan. (These are new on the market, and hold no more than a 9-inch tube pan. The regular Bundt pan holds the same amount of batter as a 10-inch tube pan.) Bake in a 350° F. oven for 55 to 60 minutes or until done. Cool on rack for 10 to 15 minutes before turning out of pan. Cool thoroughly before wrapping and storing. If desired, the bread may be drizzled with a thin icing or sprinkled, while warm, with sifted powdered sugar.

QUICK GRAHAM BREAD

This is a coarse-textured, homely, sweet bread, easily made and delicious. Remember that graham flour and whole-wheat flour are always interchangeable.

2½ cups graham flour
¼ teaspoon salt
1 teaspoon baking soda
2 large eggs
⅓ cup mild molasses
⅓ cup brown sugar

¼ cup oil, or melted butter
  or margarine
1 teaspoon vanilla extract
1 teaspoon grated lemon rind
⅔ cup yogurt or sour cream
½ cup chopped nuts
  (optional)

Combine flour with salt and baking soda. Stir to blend. Combine remaining ingredients and stir, all at once, into the dry mixture. Stir just until dry ingredients are thoroughly moistened. Turn into a buttered loaf pan and bake in a 375° F. oven for 50 to 60 minutes, or until bread tests done.

HAWAIIAN NUT BREAD

In our fiftieth state they use macadamia nuts in this tasty bread. Indeed, the crunchy macadamia nuts can replace any type of nut used in any recipe. One can even use them in fruitcakes.

2 cups sifted flour
1 teaspoon baking soda
2 teaspoons baking powder
½ teaspoon salt
½ cup butter
1 cup sugar

2 large eggs
1 cup mashed bananas
9-ounce can crushed pineapple, undrained
⅓ cup orange juice
2 cups chopped nuts

Sift dry ingredients together and set aside. Cream the butter and sugar until light and fluffy. Add the eggs and beat to blend. Combine bananas, crushed pineapple, and orange juice. Stir into creamed mixture alternately with the sifted dry ingredients, beginning and ending with the dry ingredients. Stir in the nuts last. Turn into a well-buttered loaf pan and set aside for 15 to 20 minutes. Then bake in a 350° F. oven for 1 hour to 1 hour and 15 minutes.

LEMON NUT BREAD

½ cup butter or margarine
1 cup sugar
2 large eggs
1¼ cups sifted flour
1 teaspoon baking powder
½ teaspoon salt

½ cup milk
½ cup chopped nuts
1 teaspoon grated lemon rind
⅓ cup sugar
¼ cup lemon juice

Cream butter or margarine and the 1 cup sugar until fluffy. Add eggs and beat until thoroughly blended. Sift flour with baking powder and salt. Add the flour mixture to the creamed mixture alternately with the milk, beginning and ending with the dry ingredients. Fold in the chopped nuts and the grated rind. Turn into a buttered 9 by 5 by 3-inch loaf pan and let stand for 15 minutes. Bake in a 350° F. oven for 50 minutes to an hour, or until loaf is browned and done. Dissolve the remaining ⅓ cup sugar in the lemon juice and spoon this over the hot loaf. Cool in the pan on a rack for 20 to 30 minutes before turning out of pan.

BLUEBERRY NUT BREAD

I've used other types of berries in this bread, and they all work well as long as they are not too soft.

1½ cups white or brown sugar	1 teaspoon salt
½ cup melted or very soft butter or margarine	5 cups sifted flour
	2 tablespoons baking powder
1¾ cups milk	2 cups berries, canned or fresh
2 large eggs	½ cup chopped nuts

Combine sugar, butter or margarine, milk, and eggs. Beat, with the electric mixer at medium speed, just until well blended. Sift together the salt, flour, and baking powder. Add the berries and the nuts and carefully stir them through the dry ingredients. Now stir this mixture into the liquid ingredients just until the dry ingredients are thoroughly moistened. Pour into 2 well-buttered loaf pans and let stand for 15 to 20 minutes. Bake in a 350° F. oven for 1 hour, or until browned and done. Test loaves before removing from oven.

CITRUS TEA BREAD

I use a plain tea in this bread. However, one friend uses a more exotic tea, such as Jasmine, or one of the various teas that are blended with spices and fruit rinds.

¼ cup butter or margarine
¾ cup white or brown sugar
1 large egg
1 teaspoon grated lemon rind
1 teaspoon grated lime rind
1 tablespoon grated orange or tangerine rind
3 cups sifted flour

½ teaspoon salt
¼ teaspoon cinnamon
1 teaspoon baking powder
1 teaspoon baking soda
¾ cup orange or tangerine juice
½ cup tea
½ cup chopped nuts

Cream butter or margarine and sugar until light and fluffy. Add the egg and grated rinds and blend in thoroughly. Sift the dry ingredients together. Combine juice and tea. Add the sifted dry ingredients and the liquid mixture to the creamed mixture alternately, beginning and ending with dry ingredients. Fold in nuts last. Turn into a well-buttered loaf pan and let stand for 15 or 20 minutes. Bake in a 350° F. oven for 50 minutes or until loaf is browned and done.

MAPLE NUT BREAD

Anywhere we might use brown sugar, we may also use maple sugar for its superb flavor. In New England it is used in pies, cakes, breads, and even in baked beans.

2 cups buttermilk
½ teaspoon baking soda
1 cup maple syrup
1 teaspoon salt
1 cup sifted white flour

2 teaspoons baking powder
3 cups graham flour
1 cup raisins
½ cup chopped nuts

Combine buttermilk, baking soda, and maple syrup. Set aside. Sift the salt, white flour, and baking powder together. Add the graham flour to the sifted ingredients and stir through. Now add the dry ingredients to the liquid ingredients all at once, stirring just until dry ingredients are thoroughly moistened. Do not beat. Fold in the raisins and nuts. Turn into a well-buttered loaf pan and set aside for 15 to 20 minutes. Then bake in a 325° F. oven for 1¼ to 1½ hours. Turn out and cool on a rack.

HONEY NUT BREAD

This is a simple, very good bread. If desired, you could use maple syrup for another "Maple Nut Bread."

1 cup mild-flavored honey or maple syrup	2 egg yolks
1 cup milk	2¼ cups sifted flour
½ cup sugar	1 teaspoon baking soda
¼ cup butter	½ teaspoon salt
	½ to 1 cup chopped nuts

Combine honey or maple syrup, milk, sugar, and butter in a saucepan. Heat slowly until sugar is dissolved and butter melted and the mixture is well blended. Cool. Pour into a large bowl. Sift the dry ingredients together and carefully fold them into the honey mixture. Fold in the nuts. Butter a large loaf pan, line it with waxed paper and butter the paper. Pour in the batter and let stand for 15 to 20 minutes. Bake in a 350° F. oven until done, about 1¼ to 1½ hours. Cool on a rack.

QUICK MINCEMEAT BREAD

This easily made quick bread is best made with homemade mincemeat. If in doubt, use a bottled mincemeat. If you are making the bread for company, or to give away, stir 1 or 2 tablespoons brandy or rum into the mincemeat 15 or 20 minutes before using. This is to allow the raisins in the mincemeat to soak in the liquor.

2 cups sifted flour	½ cup butter or margarine, softened
1 cup sugar	
¼ teaspoon salt	2 medium eggs
¾ teaspoon baking powder	2 cups prepared mincemeat
½ teaspoon baking soda	chopped walnuts, or a combination of nuts

Combine the dry ingredients and sift into a large bowl. Add the butter or margarine, eggs, and mincemeat. Using an electric mixer at low

speed, beat for several minutes, or until batter is well blended. Turn
into a well-buttered 5 by 10-inch loaf pan. Let stand for 15 minutes.
Sprinkle thickly with chopped nuts and bake in a 350° F. oven for
1 hour or until bread is done. Test carefully. Sprinkle with powdered
sugar while bread is hot.

PINEAPPLE NUT BREAD

If desired, ½ cup coconut or scalded, drained raisins may be added
to the batter.

¾ cup white or brown sugar
⅓ cup butter or margarine
2 large eggs
9-ounce can crushed pineapple,
    undrained
½ to 1 teaspoon vanilla
    extract
1 cup chopped nuts
2¼ cups sifted flour

2 teaspoons baking powder
¼ teaspoon baking soda
¼ teaspoon salt

TOPPING
1 tablespoon sugar
¼ teaspoon cinnamon
(optional)
¼ cup chopped nuts

Cream sugar and butter or margarine until light and fluffy. Add the
eggs and beat just enough to blend. Stir in the undrained pineapple,
vanilla extract, and 1 cup chopped nuts. Sift together the flour, baking
powder, soda, and salt. Stir sifted dry ingredients into the pineapple-
butter mixture just until blended and there are no more dry lumps of
flour. Do not beat. Turn into a well-buttered loaf pan and set aside for
15 to 20 minutes. Combine the ingredients for the topping and sprinkle
over the batter. Then bake in a 350° F. oven for 1 hour or until the
bread tests done.

PUMPKIN NUT BREAD

This makes a delicious nut bread. If you wish to cook fresh pumpkin
simply cut it in half from top to bottom, clean out the seeds and strings,
and lay it, cut side down, on a cooky sheet. Bake in a 325° F. oven

until a cake tester goes through it easily. Cool and then scoop out the pulp. Old-time cooks pushed the pulp through a ricer, but I whirl it in the blender, adding a little liquid if necessary. It keeps, refrigerated, for quite a while, and makes a startling difference when used instead of canned pumpkin for pies and breads. In this bread, and in any pumpkin pie, you can use cooked, mashed, Hubbard of banana squash. No one will know the difference. The recipe makes 3 large loaves which freeze well.

4 cups sugar	1 teaspoon baking powder
1 cup butter	1 tablespoon baking soda
6 large eggs	½ teaspoon cloves
3 cups cooked, mashed	1 teaspoon cinnamon
pumpkin	1 teaspoon salt
1 cup water	1 cup chopped nuts
5 cups sifted flour	1 cup chopped dates or raisins

Cream sugar and butter until light. Add eggs and beat thoroughly. Stir in pumpkin and water and blend. Sift dry ingredients together and carefully fold them into the liquid ingredients, mixing just until dry ingredients are thoroughly moistened. Add nuts and fruit. Pour into 3 well-buttered loaf pans and set aside for 15 minutes. Bake in a 350° F. oven for 1 hour or until cake tester comes out clean. Cool on racks.

SOY BREADS

FRUITED SOY BREAD

In this fine bread you might use a combination of dried fruit and nuts or the nuts alone. Our favorite combination is 1 cup each of chopped, pitted dates and pecans. But dried figs and walnuts are excellent also. Plump dried apricots are good, and at holiday time you might use a cup of candied fruit mix in place of a cup of the nuts.

¼ cup butter, margarine, or oil

2 cups honey

2 large eggs

¼ cup grated orange rind

4 cups sifted flour

½ cup soy flour

5 teaspoons double-acting baking powder

1 teaspoon salt

1 teaspoon baking soda

1½ cups orange juice

1½ cups chopped nuts or dried or candied fruits

Cream the shortening used with the honey and eggs, blending until mixture is smooth and thoroughly blended. Add the grated orange rind. Sift flours, baking powder, salt, and baking soda. Stir into the creamed mixture alternately with the orange juice, beginning and ending with the dry ingredients. Stir in the nuts or fruits last. (Flour these lightly and then shake out any excess flour.) Pour into 2 well-buttered and waxed-paper-lined loaf pans. Push the batter up a little with spoon, so that the center is lower than the sides. Set aside for 15 minutes and then bake in a 325° F. oven for 1 to 1¼ hours. Cool on a rack for 10 minutes before turning out of pan. Do not cut for 24 hours.

SOY GINGERBREAD

Children generally love gingerbread. This recipe produces a fine, sweet bread that tastes delicious and is, as with all the recipes in this section, nutritious enough for them to grow strong on.

1¾ cups sifted flour

¼ cup soy flour

¾ teaspoon baking soda

1 teaspoon double-acting baking powder

½ teaspoon cinnamon

¼ teaspoon cloves

1 teaspoon ginger

½ teaspoon salt

¼ cup light or dark brown sugar

¾ cup mild molasses

1 large egg

1 cup apple cider

¼ cup butter, margarine, or oil

Sift together the flour, soy flour, baking soda, baking powder, spices, and salt. Set aside. Blend the brown sugar, molasses, and egg, beating until thoroughly blended. Heat the cider to boiling and add the butter, margarine, or oil, stirring until the butter or margarine is melted.

Pour this over the brown sugar mixture. Now add the sifted dry ingredients gradually, stirring just until blended, as you would if making muffins. Do *not* beat the batter. Turn into a well-buttered 9-inch square pan. Bake in a 300° F. oven for 40 to 45 minutes, or until browned and done. If using for a dessert serve the gingerbread topped with the following topping.

WHIPPED-CREAM TOPPING.   Blend whipped cream with an equal amount of applesauce, jelly, marmalade, or other fruit pulp, such as apricot pulp.

SOY CREAM BISCUITS

These biscuits are easily varied. The heavy cream eliminates any need for fat.

3½ cups sifted flour	2 teaspoons salt
⅓ cup soy flour	2 cups heavy cream, whipped
2 tablespoons double-acting	until stiff
baking powder	

Sift all the dry ingredients together into a bowl. Make a well in the center and add, all at once, the whipped cream. Stir the mixture and work it lightly until dry ingredients are thoroughly moistened. Turn out onto a lightly floured breadboard and pat or roll to ½-inch thickness. Cut and bake on an unbuttered cooky sheet in a 400° F. oven for 15 minutes or until done.

VARIATIONS

1. The tops of the biscuits may be sprinkled with brown sugar or shaved maple sugar before baking.

2. 2 teaspoons grated lemon, orange, or tangerine rind may be stirred into the dry ingredients.

3. If a sweet biscuit is desired, stir in ½ cup each chopped nuts and figs, or pitted chopped dates.

COFFEE TWISTS

These fine twists are easily made and the recipe may be doubled or halved. Any marmalade or stiff preserve may be used.

3½ cups sifted flour
⅔ cup soy flour
2 tablespoons sugar
1½ teaspoons salt
2 tablespoons double-acting
baking powder

1 cup butter or margarine
1⅓ cups milk
marmalade or thick preserve
chopped nuts

Combine the flours, sugar, salt, and baking powder. Sift into a bowl. Add the butter or margarine and cut it in until mixture is like coarse meal. Stir in enough of the milk to make a soft dough. Turn dough out onto a floured breadboard and knead as you would biscuits, very lightly. Roll dough into an oblong. Spread with soft or melted butter. Combine equal parts of marmalade or a thick preserve and chopped nuts. Spread on the dough. Roll dough up as for a jelly roll. Cut strips about ½ inch wide. Twist these strips into S-shaped rolls. Place on buttered cooky sheets and bake in a 400° F. oven for 12 to 15 minutes or until done.

SOY PANCAKES

½ cup soy flour
1½ cups white, whole-wheat,
or graham flour
1 tablespoon brown sugar
½ teaspoon salt

2 large eggs, separated
1¾ cups milk
2 tablespoons oil or melted
butter

Combine dry ingredients and sift. (Graham flour cannot be sifted. Spoon it carefully into a cup measure, and level the top with a knife.) Combine egg yolks, milk, and oil or melted butter. Add, all at once, to the sifted ingredients. Beat the egg whites until they stand in stiff peaks. Fold into the batter. Bake as for regular pancakes. Best made into small pancakes.

7. Yeast Breads and Coffeecakes, Sour Dough Breads

Although I love to cook, period, no other culinary project is as personally rewarding to me as baking with yeast. Bread is the oldest and simplest of "made" foods, and Man, I believe, is born with a basic, inborn hunger for *good* bread. Not the refined, cottony loaves that sell so many for the dollar but rather the crusty, full-of-flavor, stick-to-the-ribs loaves that earned—and merited—the title, "staff of life." Fortunately for women—although more men than you might realize enjoy reputations as champion breadmaker—making bread is fun. Part of the fun is in the varied forms and shapes that a single loaf of bread can take. You might bake some breads in Bundt pans or in tube pans, first rolling the dough into small balls, then coating each ball of dough with melted butter or melted butter with garlic, and finally rolling the balls in sesame seeds. Baked together in the pan, the fragrant balls of dough are easily pulled apart for delightful eating. Following are some of the shaped breads that I most frequently make.

TWIST.   Divide dough for each loaf into 2 parts. Roll each part into a thick rope about half again as long as the pan. Take the 2 ropes and twist them together. Place in buttered pan, tuck ends under, let rise, and bake as directed in recipe.

BRAIDED LOAF.   Divide dough for each loaf into 3 parts. Roll each part into a long rope, again about half again as long as the pan. Braid these 3 ropes together. Tuck ends under and place in buttered pan. Let rise and bake as directed in recipe.

TWO-TONE BREAD.   If you bake a lot, you can manage this very simply by making several batches of bread at one time and freezing the extra loaves. Or you can cut the recipes so that you only end up with enough dough to make 1 or 2 loaves. Make 2 recipes, one for any white or yellow bread, and one for any whole-grain type of bread. Make a twist, using a strand of each type of bread. Or make a 4- or 6-strand braid, using 2 types of dough. Or make a checkerboard loaf by rolling out strands of dough that just fit into the loaf pan. Alternate white and whole-grain strands in the loaf pan, filling the pan no more than ⅔ full. Or wrap one sheet of one type of dough around a loaf of another type of dough. In all cases, then let loaves rise until double and bake as directed in recipes.

FRENCH FLUTE.   Unless you are using a typical hard-crusted bread (any type that is baked on a cooky sheet rather than in a loaf pan), you will need to add a little more flour to the recipe. Otherwise the dough will be too soft to hold its shape well. Shape the dough into long rolls—the longer the better—about half as big around as your wrist. In France these rolls are often several feet long, a feat not accomplished in any domestic oven. Brush with SALT WATER GLAZE (page 307) and at the very last moment, just before popping into the oven, make several slashes in the loaf with a razor blade or a *very* sharp knife.

Do this quickly and neatly. If the knife is not sharp enough, you run the risk of making the bread fall; then you must let it rise again.

ITALIAN LOAF.   As with the "French Flute," unless you are using a hard-crusted bread recipe, you will need to add a little more flour to the dough. The dough should be shaped into a long oval (or a nice circle for a round loaf). At the last minute, brush with SALT WATER GLAZE (page 307) and slash the loaf decoratively.

SESAME RING.   As with the "French Flute" or the "Italian Loaf," make a recipe for a hard-crusted bread, or add more flour to the dough. Shape dough into a large ring. Brush with EGG WHITE GLAZE (page 348) and sprinkle heavily with sesame seeds just before popping into the oven.

HOMEMADE HAMBURGER BUNS.   Use any favorite bread or roll dough, or a hot roll mix. Butter as many 4-inch-diameter aluminum-foil tart pans as you wish buns. After the dough has risen once, punch it down and form the dough into smooth balls, about 2 inches in diameter. Place in the pans and press slightly to flatten. Brush with EGG WHITE GLAZE (page 348), and sprinkle with sesame seed or poppy seed, or with sautéed minced onion. Cover and let rise until doubled. Bake in a 400° F. oven for about 15 minutes, or until browned and done. Cool a few minutes before turning out of pans. These slice easily and can be frozen if desired.

CHRISTMAS TREE BREAD.   Make small balls of dough. Place close together, on a cooky sheet, in the shape of a Christmas tree. Let rise and bake. Decorate with a heavy powdered-sugar frosting and green and red candied cherries. The balls pull apart for easy eating. A "New Year's Eve Bread" may be made in the same way by arranging the balls of dough in the shape of a bell complete with clapper. The finished bread can be frosted and then sprinkled with silver shot.

BRAID ON BRAID.   Beautiful breads are made by doubling a recipe, or by using a recipe that calls for about 7 cups of flour, and then making several layers of braids. Put the largest braid on the bottom and a long, very narrow braid on the top. In making all braided breads, be careful to allow the bread to rise until completely doubled before baking. This will prevent the cracking of the braids.

BREAD SCULPTURE.   The bread sculptor uses a baker's clay, or a very heavy bread dough, made by using only the basic bread ingredients: water, yeast, flour, and salt. Do not use any shortenings or eggs, as these will limit the life of sculpted breads, which are not edible. The dough should be made very heavy. It can then be worked into any number of very intricate shapes. I make lovely "Easter Birds." by forming this dough into a long, thick rope, and then knotting it loosely so that the thickest part makes the body. The tail, coming out from under the body, is easily snipped with scissors into "feathers," and the head can be shaped with the fingers, pinching part to form a beak. The heavier the dough, the better it will hold a particular shape. The dough will not rise much, but do let it rise, and then bake in a 350° F. oven until very well done. The best "frosting" for these breads is a thick coating—or several thick coatings—of Elmer's Glue. If sprayed with a lacquer the breads will keep for years.

GENERAL INFORMATION

1. Use the best ingredients. Your finished product will only be as good as what went into it. I prefer unbleached flour. This is a cream-colored white flour that has no preservative added. I buy the unbleached bread flour, which is a hard wheat flour that makes excellent bread. An all-purpose flour may be used, but all-purpose flours are made with the hard winter wheats *and* the soft spring wheats. This is done so that you can make breads *or* cakes, both of which require different types of flour. To achieve this all-purpose flour, something must be sacrificed and it usually is: all-purpose flour will make both, but neither will be quite as good as it should be. As no recipe can specify exactly how much flour will be required, it is best to start out with a lesser amount of flour. You can add as needed, but you cannot remove if too much has been used.

2. For the liquid you may use water, potato water, fresh milk that has been scalded and cooled, evaporated milk blended with an equal amount

of water, or whey if you sometimes make cottage cheese. I have experimented with using a flavored broth, such as a mild chicken broth, when making dinner breads and/or rolls, and I find that it adds a delightful flavor, especially if combined with a pinch of dried herb.

3. Dry yeast and compressed yeast are interchangeable. Refrigerated, dry yeast will keep for at least a year. Compressed yeast must be kept refrigerated and should be used within 30 days. The yeast should always be dissolved in a small amount (usually ¼ to ½ cup) water before adding to the dough. The water should be lukewarm. Too hot or too cold a temperature will kill the yeast, which is delicate and must be coddled a bit.

4. Unless otherwise specified, kneading is essential to a good loaf of bread. Indeed, it is almost impossible to work a bread dough overly much. The more kneading, the finer the texture of the finished bread.

5. The kneaded dough should be placed in a buttered bowl and the top of the dough brushed with more butter to prevent a crust from forming. Cover the bowl with a clean towel and set aside to rise until doubled.

6. When the dough has risen enough, punch it down and turn out onto a lightly floured breadboard. Knead it lightly, enough to work out any air holes, and then cut it into as many pieces as you wish loaves. Cover and let the dough rest for 10 minutes. This allows the dough time to "loosen," and the shaping is then much easier.

7. I do not roll the dough out and fold as directed in most books. I consider this a laborious and time-consuming method that often results in large air pockets in the finished loaf. I simply pat the dough into shape with my hands and then place it in a buttered loaf pan, unless otherwise directed in a specific recipe.

8. All breads freeze successfully.

9. A friend once called me and, with great chagrin, told me that she had made up the dough for several loaves of bread and then discovered that she had absent-mindedly left out the yeast! Here is the remedy. Take the required amount of yeast and soften it in about ½ cup of

lukewarm water. Then, very carefully and *very* thoroughly, work it into the dough. It will take a bit of kneading—quite a bit—and possibly a little more flour. Then continue as directed in the recipe. It works.

SOUR DOUGH RYE BREAD

This makes an absolutely marvelous bread, the equal of any quality bakery bread. It's a complicated recipe, which may explain why the best *rye* breads come from good bakeries. Start the dough the day before you want the finished bread. I use part white flour, but some good cooks use all rye flour, or part whole-wheat or graham flour. Each produces a hard-crusted, extremely flavorful bread, and if you've grown up on processed store bread, a taste of this will be proof enough of why bread used to be termed "the staff of life." The first day make the sour dough as follows:

½ cup rye flour   ½ cake compressed yeast
¼ cup warm water   (do not use dry yeast)

Combine and work together. Cover tightly and keep in warm place for 24 hours. Then add to the sponge and work in:

¾ cup warm water   1 cup rye flour

Let the combined mixtures ferment, covered, for another 4 hours. Then add and work in to make a smooth but firm dough:

1¾ cups rye flour   ½ cake compressed yeast,
                                    dissolved in 1 or 2
                                    tablespoons lukewarm water

Cover the dough and set it aside to ferment until it rises, and then falls back on itself. This will take longer in the winter than it will in spring or summer. But it should take no longer than approximately 2 hours. When it has risen, and then fallen, add and work in:

1¾ cups rye flour   1 cup water
1¾ cups white flour, or rye,
    whole-wheat, or graham
    flour

Cover the dough, and set it aside to rise and fall back on itself again. Then add:

1 cup warm water
1 tablespoon salt

1¾ cups flour (rye, white,
  whole-wheat, or graham)
1 tablespoon caraway seed

Work this into the dough thoroughly. Then cover the dough and let it rest for 15 to 20 minutes, to loosen. Then turn the dough out onto a floured breadboard and knead it with:

1½ to 2 cups white, rye, whole-wheat, or graham flour

Knead in just enough of the flour to make a stiff dough that will not spread and lose its shape. Cut the dough into 2 parts and shape into 2 round or oval loaves. Place on a greased cooky sheet that has been sprinkled with cornmeal or flour. Cover and let the loaves rise until not quite double. If the loaves rise too much they will fall while baking. I start baking the loaves when they are just half-risen. Bake in a 350° F. oven 1 to 1½ hours. A pan of very hot water should be placed on the oven floor. For a professional crust, brush loaves with SALT WATER GLAZE (see below) just before putting the loaves in the oven, once during the baking, and then immediately upon removing the loaves from the oven. Cool loaves on a rack, away from drafts.

SALT WATER GLAZE.   Combine 1 teaspoon salt and ½ cup water, and stir to dissolve the salt.

CINNAMON TOAST BREAD

This bread reaches its peak of flavor when toasted, and also makes a marvelous French toast. It must be refrigerated for at least several hours before baking, and is easily made the day before baking.

2 cakes yeast
½ cup warm water
1½ cups milk, scalded and
  cooled
1 large egg
¼ cup sugar

2 teaspoons salt
¼ cup butter or margarine,
  melted
1 tablespoon cinnamon
5½ to 6 cups sifted flour

Dissolve the yeast in the warm water. Stir in the milk and egg and stir vigorously to blend. Stir in the sugar, salt, melted butter or margarine, and cinnamon. Add 2 cups of the flour and beat until batter is smooth. Now stir in enough of the remaining flour to make a smooth, soft dough. Turn out onto a lightly floured breadboard and knead until smooth and elastic, about 7 or 8 minutes. Cover the dough with a towel and let stand for 15 to 20 minutes. Then cut the dough in half and pat and shape each half into a loaf. Place in buttered glass loaf pans (these generally measure smaller than the aluminum pans), brush the dough with melted butter and cover loosely with waxed paper or plastic wrap. Place pans in refrigerator for at least 2 hours, or up to 30 hours. When ready to bake, remove pans from refrigerator and let stand, uncovered, for 15 minutes. Bake in a 400° F. oven for 30 to 40 minutes, or until loaves test done. Remove from pans and cool on racks.

CALIFORNIA MISSION OVERNIGHT BREAD

Up and down the state of California, usually within a very few miles of *El Camino Real* (The King's Highway, now route 101), are the Missions. There are twenty-one of them, from San Diego to San Francisco. They were founded by the Spanish missionaries. Many of them have been restored, and religious services are still held in some. In others you can still walk through and see the huge old kitchens with their sometimes numerous ovens, and mammoth barbecues that could hold an entire steer or several lambs. And in San Miguel Arcangel, a few miles north of Paso Robles, they still grind their own wheat, and make this bread in the old oven. The recipe calls for a minimum amount of yeast and an overnight rising period. If desired, the yeast may be increased to 1 or even 2 cakes and the entire batch, from start to finish, made in just a few hours. Follow directions for any regular bread if more yeast is used.

2 tablespoons lard
1 tablespoon sugar
2 teaspoons salt
2 cups hot water

¼ cake yeast
¼ cup lukewarm water
6 to 7 cups sifted flour

Combine lard, sugar, and salt in a bowl. Add hot water and stir to melt the lard. Cool to lukewarm. Dissolve yeast in the lukewarm water. Add to the cooled lard-water mixture. Stir in 3 cups of the flour and eat thoroughly, until the batter is smooth. Now add enough of the remaining flour, a little at a time, to make a stiff dough. Use a sharp knife and cut through the dough several times. Now turn the dough out onto a lightly floured board and knead thoroughly, about 7 or 8 minutes. When kneaded enough, the dough will be smooth and elastic. Place in a buttered bowl and spread the top of the dough with oil, or with melted butter or lard. Cover with a towel and let stand overnight. In the morning, punch the dough down and turn out onto a floured board again. Knead for 7 or 8 minutes, then cut dough in half, cover and let rest for 10 minutes. At the end of the 10 minutes, pat and shape the dough into loaf shapes. Put each into a buttered loaf pan. Cover and let rise again until double, several hours, and then bake in a 400° F. oven for 50 minutes to an hour, or until browned and done.

SOUR DOUGH BREAD

This isn't a true sour dough bread, but simply requires ½ cup leftover dough from a previous batch of bread. Any batch will do. Just keep out ½ cup and store it in a container in the refrigerator until you make the next batch of bread, hopefully no longer than a week, by which time you just might have a really sour dough bread. Anyway, it makes a good sturdy, no-nonsense loaf of bread, the kind (lacking the wheat germ) that your grandmother probably made and your grandfather grew strong on.

½ cup dough from previous batch of bread
4½ cups warm water
1½ cakes yeast

4 cups whole-wheat or graham flour
8 or 9 cups sifted white flour
2 tablespoons salt
1 cup wheat germ

Combine the starter and 3 cups of the warm water in a bowl. Let stand for several hours, stirring it whenever you happen to think of it. Then add the yeast, dissolved in the remaining 1½ cups warm water, the whole-wheat or graham flour, and 2 cups of the white flour. Stir until batter is smooth. Cover and let stand until light and bubbly, about 1½ hours. When sponge is bubbly, stir it down and add remaining ingredients, working them in until you have a smooth, firm dough. Turn

out onto a well-oiled breadboard and knead for at least 5 minutes.
Return to the bowl, spread with oil or melted butter, cover and let
stand until doubled, about 1½ hours. Then punch the dough down
and divide into 3 parts. Cover and let rest for 10 minutes, then pat and
shape the pieces into loaf shapes. Place in buttered loaf pans, cover
and let rise again until doubled, about an hour. Bake in a 400° F. oven
for 45 to 50 minutes, or until loaves are browned and done.

COTTAGE BREAD

Combination breads always have a rich, nutty flavor from the mixture
of flours. They come in handy also to use up any small amounts of
leftover flour. Just remember that the finished bread will only be as
good as the flour that went into it. Flour with an off-odor should be
discarded. It won't freshen in the baking. This recipe makes a particularly fragrant, nutty-flavored loaf.

⅓ cup butter, margarine, or lard	1 cake yeast
	¼ cup warm water
2 tablespoons molasses or brown sugar	1¾ cups coarsely ground cornmeal
1½ teaspoons salt	1¾ cups whole-wheat or graham flour
1 cup scalded milk	
1 cup hot water	1¾ cups rye flour

Combine butter, molasses or brown sugar, and salt in a bowl. Pour
scalded milk and hot water over them and stir to melt the butter. Cool.
Dissolve yeast in the warm water and stir into the cooled mixture. Add
the cornmeal and flours and beat in. The bread is not firm enough to
knead, but is more of the batter type. Beat mixture with a wooden
spoon for 2 minutes. Cover bowl and let the dough rise until doubled.
When it has doubled, punch it down and let it rise until doubled again.
Do this twice more, making four times in all. Turn the dough into a
buttered 1-quart casserole. Brush top with melted butter, cover, and
let rise until doubled. Bake in a 425° F. oven for 15 minutes. Then
reduce heat to 350° F. and bake another 30 minutes.

NOTE.   White flour may replace the whole-wheat flour in this recipe.

CRACKED WHEAT BREAD

A delicious bread. Cut the hot bread into wedges and serve with plenty of butter.

2 cups boiling water
1¼ cups cracked wheat
½ cup brown sugar
1 teaspoon salt
¼ cup butter or margarine

2 cakes yeast
⅔ cup warm water
2¼ cups sifted flour
¼ cup wheat germ

Pour boiling water over the cracked wheat. Add the brown sugar, salt, and butter or margarine. Stir to melt the butter, and let stand until mixture is cooled. Dissolve yeast in the warm water and stir into the cooled cracked-wheat mixture. Stir in the flour to make a soft dough. Stir in the wheat germ last. Turn dough out onto a floured breadboard and knead for at least 5 to 7 minutes, or until dough is smooth and elastic. You will have to keep your hands well floured as the dough remains fairly sticky. Place in a buttered bowl and brush top of dough with melted butter or oil. Cover and let rise until doubled, about 1 hour. Punch the dough down and let rise for another 30 minutes. At the end of 30 minutes, punch the dough down again and turn out onto a floured breadboard. Cut the dough in half and press each half into a well buttered 9-inch pie pan. Cover and let rise until dough is rounded above the pans. Brush with melted butter and bake in a 350° F. oven for 1 hour or until loaves are done.

BEER BREAD

The men in the family will especially like this flavorful bread. We like it with ham.

1 cup dark beer (bock beer is
    preferable)
1 cake yeast
3 to 3½ cups sifted flour
2 tablespoons light or dark
    brown sugar

1 teaspoon salt
1 large egg
¼ cup butter or margarine
½ cup wheat germ

Warm the beer just to lukewarm. Pour into a mixing bowl. Stir in the
yeast and let stand until bubbly, about 5 minutes. Add 2 cups of the
flour along with the sugar, salt, and egg. Beat until smooth. Melt the
butter or margarine and stir it into the batter along with another cup
of flour and the wheat germ. Mix thoroughly, adding the rest of the
flour as needed to make a smooth dough that cleans the bowl. Turn
out onto a lightly floured breadboard and knead for 5 to 7 minutes,
or until smooth and elastic. Place in a buttered bowl, brush the top
of the dough with melted butter or oil and cover the bowl. Let rise
until doubled. When dough is doubled, punch it down and turn out
onto a lightly floured breadboard again. Let the dough rest for 10
minutes. Then, using the hands, gently smooth and shape the dough
into the shape of a loaf. Place in a buttered 9 by 5 by 3-inch loaf pan.
Cover and let rise again until doubled in bulk. Bake in a 375° F. oven
for 35 to 40 minutes. Turn out of pan and tap the bottom of the loaf
with the knuckles to see if it is done. Cool on a rack.

MILWAUKEE'S BEER RYE BREAD

Milwaukee's German residents love to use beer in their cooking, and
serve this good bread with a sharp cheese spread.

1 cake yeast
1 tablespoon sugar
¼ cup warm water
2 cups sifted white flour
4½ cups rye flour
1 cup whole-wheat or graham
    flour

1 cup buttermilk or sour milk
¾ cup beer
2 teaspoons salt
2 or 3 tablespoons caraway
    seeds

Combine yeast, sugar, and warm water. Stir to dissolve the yeast. Let
stand until the yeast bubbles, about 3 to 5 minutes. Stir in ½ cup of

the white flour and let mixture stand until bubbles form, approximately 30 to 45 minutes. Add the remaining white flour, the rye flour, whole-wheat or graham flour, buttermilk or sour milk, beer, salt, and caraway seeds. Blend mixture, with a wooden spoon, until it forms a nice dough. Turn out onto a lightly floured breadboard and knead until smooth and elastic, about 5 to 7 minutes. Place dough into a buttered bowl. Brush top of dough with soft butter or with oil, cover with a towel and let rise until dough is doubled, about 1½ hours. When dough is doubled, punch it down and form into 2 loaves, or a pan of rolls. Place in buttered loaf pans, or onto a buttered cooky sheet, preferably one with low sides. Cover and let rise again until doubled. Bake the loaves in a 400° F. oven for 10 minutes, reduce heat to 350° F., and continue baking until loaves are browned and done, about 1 to 1¼ hours longer. The rolls should be baked at 400° F. for 10 minutes, the heat then reduced to 350° F. and the rolls baked for another 25 to 35 minutes, or until they are lightly browned and done.

HERB CHEESE BREAD

The tantalizing aroma of this flavorful bread is bound to bring your family running. Remember though, that aroma and flavor depend on the quality of cheese that is used. For best results buy ungrated, imported Romano or Parmesan cheese and grate it yourself. The blender does an excellent job of this if you first cut the cheese into small squares.

1 cup milk	½ cup grated Parmesan or
⅓ cup butter or margarine	Romano cheese
2 tablespoons sugar	½ teaspoon oregano
1½ teaspoons salt	¼ teaspoon marjoram or
1 large egg	sweet basii
1 cake yeast	4½ cups sifted flour
½ cup lukewarm water	

Scald the milk. Add the butter or margarine, sugar, and salt. Stir to melt the butter and dissolve the sugar and salt. Cool to lukewarm. When mixture has cooled add the egg and beat to blend ingredients. Dissolve the yeast in the lukewarm water. Now add yeast mixture to milk mixture and stir to blend. Stir in the cheese, herbs, and 2 cups of the flour. Beat until smooth. Add the remaining flour and work it in with your clean hands. Turn dough out onto lightly floured breadboard and knead until dough is smooth and elastic, about 5 to 7 minutes. Place dough in buttered bowl, brush top of dough with melted butter or oil, cover with a clean towel, and let rise until doubled, about 1 hour. Turn dough out again onto a lightly floured breadboard. Knead for several minutes longer and then let the dough rest, covered, for 10 minutes. Now, using your hands, mold and shape it into a loaf. Place in a buttered loaf pan and let rise again until doubled, about 45 minutes. Bake in a 400° F. oven for 45 to 50 minutes, or until nicely browned and done. Cool on a rack.

OUR FAVORITE GRAHAM BREAD

This makes what must be the world's finest graham bread. It has never received anything but raves. Remember that whole-wheat flour and graham flour are interchangeable.

2 cakes yeast	1 cup hot water
¼ cup warm water	½ cup softened butter
¼ cup brown sugar	⅓ cup brown sugar
2¾ cups lukewarm water	8 cups graham flour
4 cups sifted flour	(approximately)
1 tablespoon salt	

First you must make a sponge as follows: Dissolve the 2 cakes of yeast in the ¼ cup warm water. Add the ¼ cup brown sugar and stir until dissolved. Now stir in the 2¾ cups lukewarm water, white flour, and salt. Beat with a wooden spoon until smooth. Cover and let the sponge rise until light, about 1 to 1½ hours. When sponge is light stir it down with a wooden spoon. Pour the 1 cup hot water over the softened butter and stir to melt the butter. Add the ⅓ cup brown sugar and stir to dissolve it. Now turn this butter-brown sugar mixture into the sponge. Add 4 cups of the graham flour and blend the ingredients together thoroughly. Add the rest of the graham flour gradually, using only enough to make a medium-firm dough. I have found that this bread generally requires the full amount of flour suggested in the recipe.

Turn out onto a lightly floured breadboard and knead for 5 to 7 minutes, or until smooth and elastic. The dough should not be sticky. Place in a buttered bowl. Brush the top of the dough with melted butter or with oil. Cover with a clean towel and let rise until doubled, approximately 1½ to 2 hours. When dough is doubled, punch it down and turn out onto a lightly floured breadboard again. Divide dough into 3 parts. Shape each into a ball, cover with a towel and let rest for 10 minutes. At the end of this time use your hands to mold and shape the dough into loaves. Place in 3 buttered loaf pans. Cover and let rise until doubled again, about 1 to 1½ hours. Bake in a 375° F. oven for 45 to 50 minutes. Brush hot loaves with soft or melted butter and cool on racks.

POTATO LOAF

This makes a moist, beautifully textured bread with good keeping qualities due to the potatoes.

1½ cups cooked potatoes, unseasoned
¼ to ½ cup butter or margarine
1 or 2 tablespoons sugar
1 teaspoon salt
1 cup milk, scalded
1 or 2 cakes yeast
⅓ cup lukewarm water
6 cups sifted flour

Mash the hot, unseasoned potatoes and add the butter or margarine, sugar, and salt. Pour in the scalded milk, and stir to blend ingredients and melt the butter. Cool to lukewarm. Now dissolve the yeast in the lukewarm water and stir into the potato-milk mixture. Stir in 3 cups of the flour and beat until smooth. Gradually blend in the rest of the flour to make a medium dough. Turn dough out onto a lightly floured breadboard. Knead for 5 to 7 minutes, or until dough is smooth and elastic. Place in a buttered bowl, brush top of dough with melted butter or oil, cover the bowl and let rise until doubled. When dough has doubled, punch it down and turn out onto a floured breadboard again. Divide dough into 2 parts. Cover with the towel again and let rest for 10 minutes. Then mold and shape the dough, with the hands, into 2 loaves. Place in 2 buttered loaf pans. Cover and let rise until double again. Brush with beaten EGG WHITE GLAZE (page 348) and sprinkle with poppy seeds. Bake in a 400° F. oven for 10 minutes and then reduce heat to 350° F. and bake for another 40 to 45 minutes.

BRAIDED POTATO LOAF. To make the loaf into braids, as suggested in the title, cut the dough, after the first rising period, into 2 parts. Cut one part into 3 equal pieces and roll out into strips about 18 inches long. Braid these 3 strips together, tucking the ends under. Place on a lightly buttered cooky sheet. Now divide ⅔ of the remaining part into 3 equal pieces, roll out, and braid as above. Place this braid on top of the first braid. Now, take the remaining piece of dough and roll it out, twist it, like a curlicue, and place this twisted strip of dough on top of the uppermost braid. If you think it necessary, seal the ends with a very little water. Carefully cover the braided loaf, being careful not to disarrange the braids, and let rise until *completely* doubled. You must not cheat by even 5 or 10 minutes, for if you do the braids will split while baking. When ready to bake, brush with EGG WHITE GLAZE (page 348), and sprinkle with sesame or poppy seeds. Bake in a 400° F. oven for 10 minutes. Reduce heat to 350° F. and bake until bread is well browned and done, approximately 45 to 50 minutes longer.

NOTE. This bread also makes delicious, and very attractive, rolls. Cut or shape into whatever shapes you desire, brush with Egg White Glaze and sprinkle with poppy or sesame seeds. When rolls are doubled, bake them at 400° F. for about 20 minutes.

COUNTRY BRAIDS

The good cook—and the good cook generally finds baking with yeast a rewarding and creative pastime—likes to take a smooth, elastic bread dough and shape it. She makes long, narrow loaves like the French Flute, or she makes round, fat loaves, or she makes intricate braids like this exceptionally pretty and delicious loaf.

1 cup milk, scalded	2 cakes yeast
½ cup butter or margarine	¼ cup lukewarm water
¼ to ⅓ cup sugar	3 large eggs
1 teaspoon salt	6 to 7 cups sifted flour

Pour the scalded milk over the butter or margarine, sugar, and salt. Stir to blend and melt the butter, and to dissolve the sugar. Cool to lukewarm. Now dissolve the yeast in the lukewarm water. When dissolved, stir yeast into cooled milk mixture. Add the eggs and beat mixture to blend ingredients. Stir in 3 cups of the flour and beat with a wooden spoon until smooth. Now blend in 3 cups of the remaining flour. Add enough of the remaining cup of flour as is needed to make a medium-stiff dough. A looser dough will not hold its shape while baking. Turn dough out onto a lightly floured breadboard and knead until smooth and elastic, about 5 to 7 minutes. Place dough in a buttered bowl, brush top of dough with melted butter or with oil, cover the bowl, and let the dough rise until doubled, about 1 to 1½ hours. When dough has doubled, punch it down and turn out onto a floured breadboard again. Divide dough into 2 parts. Cut one part into 3 equal pieces and roll each piece out into a long strip about 18 inches long. Braid, tucking the ends under. Place on lightly buttered cooky sheet. Now, divide ⅔ of the remaining part into 3 equal pieces and braid as above. Place this braid on top of the first braid. Take the remaining piece of dough and roll it out into a long strip of dough. Twist it, like a curlicue, and place this twisted strip of dough on top of the uppermost braid. If desired, seal the ends with a very little water. Cover with a towel, being very careful not to disarrange the braids, and let rise until completely doubled. It not *completely* doubled before placing in the oven, the braids will crack and slide during the baking time. When ready to bake, brush the braids with EGG WHITE GLAZE (page 348), and sprinkle with sesame seeds if desired. Bake in a 375° F. oven for 40 to 45 minutes, or until loaf is well-browned and tests done when tapped on the bottom with the knuckles.

TAOS BREAD

This bread, the bread of the Pueblo Indians of New Mexico, is a simple, basic, white bread recipe, but shaped and baked into enchanting, lopeared loaves. The pragmatist might ask why they are shaped this way, and even complain because the loaves can't be cut into the nice even slices so loved by practical people. But the romantic—and all good cooks must be romantics—tells her family that this bread comes from the outdoor ovens of the Pueblo Indian villages, high in the mountains of New Mexico. They make the loaves for the festival held each September, where the young Indians run dawn races, and dance their traditional dances in the autumn sunset, and eat these charming, oddly shaped, crusty loaves.

3 tablespoons butter, margarine, lard, or oil	1 tablespoon sugar
1½ cups very hot water	2 cakes yeast
1 tablespoon salt	½ cup lukewarm water
	7 to 7½ cups sifted flour

Combine butter, hot water, salt, and sugar. Stir to melt the butter. Cool to lukewarm. Dissolve the yeast in the lukewarm water. Stir yeast mixture into the butter-water mixture, stirring to blend. Now add 4 cups of the flour and blend into a smooth batter. Blend in 2 cups of the remaining flour, working it into the dough with a wooden spoon or nice clean hands. Turn the dough out onto the heavily floured board and knead the dough quite vigorously, working in as much as the flour as the dough will hold. Knead for 5 to 7 minutes, although more— should you want to work off your hostilities—certainly won't hurt the bread. When kneaded enough the dough will be smooth and elastic. Place dough in a buttered bowl and spread the top of the dough with more butter or oil. Cover and let rise until doubled, about 1 to 1½ hours. When dough is doubled, turn it out onto that floured board again. Cut dough into 3 pieces and punch it around a little to work out any air holes. Now divide the dough into 3 equal parts. Roll each part into a ball, cover with a towel and let rest for 10 minutes. At the end of 10 minutes the balls of dough will be loose enough to work easily. Now, pat each ball into a flat circle about 8 or 9 inches in diameter. Take each circle and fold almost, but not quite, in half. The top circular edge should be about 1 inch from the bottom circular edge. With kitchen scissors or a very sharp knife make 3 or 4 gashes in the dough, cutting from the circular edge to about ⅔ of the way to the straight, folded edge. Place each cut circle of dough into a buttered 9 or 10-inch pie pan, spreading the gashes a little so that they do not seal together in the baking. Cover with a towel and let rise until doubled. When doubled, bake loaves in a 350° F. oven for 50 minutes to an hour. If desired you may place a pan of hot water on the oven floor to make a crustier bread. However, the bread is nicely crusty anyway. Tear loaves apart to serve.

EARLY CALIFORNIA EGG BREAD

This is a recipe apparently going back to the early Spanish settlers in the American West.

1 cake yeast	½ cup butter
2 cups lukewarm water	1 to 1½ cups sugar
2 tablespoons sugar	1 teaspoon salt
6 cups sifted flour	2 large eggs

Dissolve yeast in ¼ cup of the lukewarm water. When dissolved, add to the remaining water along with the 2 tablespoons sugar. Stir in 3 cups of the flour and beat until smooth. Cover and let rise until doubled, about 1½ hours. Cream the butter, the remaining sugar, salt, and eggs. Beat until creamed and thoroughly blended. When the sponge is doubled, punch it down and combine the two mixtures. Stir in the remaining 3 cups flour, a little at a time, until you have a medium dough. It will be a little sticky. Turn dough out onto a lightly floured breadboard and knead thoroughly, until dough is smooth and elastic. Place in a buttered bowl, spread top with oil or melted butter, cover with a towel and let rise until doubled, about 1½ hours longer. When dough has doubled, punch it down and cut in half. Cover dough and let it rest for 10 minutes. Then pat and shape into loaves. Place in buttered pans, let rise until doubled, and then bake in a 350° F. oven for 40 to 45 minutes, or until done.

BASIC DINNER ROLLS

These easy-to-make, delicious rolls may be shaped or filled, as desired. I give a few ideas; you will think of many more.

2 cakes yeast	1 teaspoon salt
½ cup lukewarm water	2 large eggs
½ cup scalded, cooled, milk	4½ cups flour, sifted
⅓ cup sugar	½ cup butter, softened

Combine yeast and lukewarm water in a bowl. Stir to blend, and allow yeast to dissolve. This will take approximately 3 minutes. Then stir in the cooled milk, sugar, salt and eggs. Beat, using a wooden spoon preferably, until blended. Then stir in 3 cups of the flour and the softened butter and blend thoroughly. Work in the fourth cup of flour and turn the dough out onto a breadboard on which you have spread the remaining ½ cup of flour. Knead for approximately 5 to 7 minutes, or until dough is smooth and elastic. Place dough in a buttered bowl, cover with a clean towel and let rise until doubled in bulk. When the dough has doubled, punch it down again and turn out onto a lightly floured breadboard. (At this point the dough may be refrigerated, if desired, and it will keep for 3 or 4 days. As it rises, punch the dough down to keep it from souring.) Shape and bake the rolls as suggested below.

VARIATIONS

CLOVERLEAF ROLLS. Form dough into small round balls no larger than a walnut. Place 3 balls in each buttered muffin cup. They may be sprinkled, or not, with sesame seed or poppy seed. Let rise until doubled in bulk. Bake in a 425° F. oven for approximately 15 to 18 minutes.

DINNER ROLLS. Form dough into small oblong cushions with tapered ends. Place on lightly buttered cooky sheets. Cover and let rise until doubled. Bake in a 425° F. oven for 15 to 18 minutes, or until browned and done.

FAN-TANS. Roll the dough into a thin rectangle, approximately ¼-inch thick. Brush the dough all over with melted butter, and sprinkle with sesame seed or poppy seed if desired. Now cut the dough into strips about 1 inch wide. Stack the strips one on the other, about 6 deep. Cut into pieces about 1 inch by 1½ or 2 inches. Place the pieces, cut side down, in buttered muffin pans. Cover with a towel, and let rise until doubled in bulk. Bake in a 425° F. oven for 15 to 18 minutes, or until done.

PAN ROLLS. Form dough into balls about the size of a small or medium lemon. Place, with sides almost touching, in a buttered, square or oblong baking pan with sides. Brush with melted butter and sprinkle with sesame seed or poppy seed if desired. Cover with a clean towel and let rise until doubled in bulk. Bake in a 425° F. oven for 15 to 18 minutes, or until browned and done.

PARKER HOUSE ROLLS.   Roll the dough into a rectangle a little less than ½ inch thick. Spread with very soft, but not melted, butter, and cut into 3-inch rounds. In each round of dough make a crease, slightly off center, with the back of a knife. Fold the circles so that the smaller half of each round slightly overlaps the larger half. Press the ends of the crease together to prevent the rolls from opening. Place close together on buttered cooky sheets or baking pans with sides. Cover with a clean towel and let rise until doubled in bulk. Bake in a 425° F. oven for 15 to 18 minutes, or until done.

TWISTS.   Roll dough into an oblong shape about ¼ inch thick. Spread with melted butter and fold, lengthwise, so that you have 2 layers of dough with the buttered halves together. Now cut the dough into strips about ½ inch wide and 6 inches long. Now twist the strips of dough and form into figure 8's, snails, or simple twists. Place on lightly buttered cooky sheets, cover with a clean towel and let rise until doubled in bulk. Then bake in a 425° F. oven for 15 to 18 minutes, or until done.

FILLED ROLLS

For these, use the dough for BASIC DINNER ROLLS (p. 319). The dough may be rolled and cut into rounds and then wrapped around a frankfurter or a cooked sausage. Place the rolls, seam side down, on a lightly buttered cooky sheet, cover, and let rise until double. Bake in a 425° F. oven for 15 to 18 minutes, or until browned and done. Or you may use any of the following suggestions.

CHEESE-FILLED ROLLS.   Combine 1 cup of grated Cheddar cheese with 2 tablespoons sesame seed or poppy seed and 1 tablespoon soft butter. Roll the dough to a thickness of no more than ⅛ inch and cut into circles. Place some of the filling in the center of each circle (how much depends on how large your circles are). Fold over and seal the edges. Place on lightly buttered cooky sheets, cover, and let rise until doubled in bulk. Brush with melted butter and sprinkle with more seed. Bake in a 400° F. oven for 20 minutes, or until browned and done.

GREEN ONION–FILLED ROLLS.   Take 2 cups of finely chopped green onions and sauté in ⅓ cup butter until wilted and cooked, but not browned. Season with salt and pepper and allow to cool. Roll the dough to a thickness of no more than ⅛ inch and cut into circles as large or as small as you wish. Place some of the filling in the center of each circle of dough and fold over, sealing the edges with water. Place on lightly buttered cooky sheets, cover, and let rise until doubled in bulk. Brush with melted butter and sprinkle with sesame seed if desired. Bake in a 400° F. oven for 20 minutes, or until browned and done.

CRACKED-WHEAT LONG ROLLS

This recipe makes two very tasty, very long rolls. Cut in half, and filled with sliced meats, cheeses, tomato slices, purple onion slices and romaine lettuce, you have a lunch or supper to satisfy a longshoreman, or possibly even a teen-age boy.

½ cup milk, scalded	1½ cups lukewarm water
3 tablespoons sugar	1 cup cracked wheat
1 tablespoon salt	5½ cups sifted flour
¼ cup butter or margarine	coarse salt (optional)
1 cake yeast	

Pour the scalded milk over the sugar, salt, and butter or margarine. Stir to melt the butter. Cool to lukewarm. Dissolve the yeast in the 1½ cups lukewarm water. When dissolved turn into the cooled milk mixture. Add the cracked wheat and 3 cups of the flour. Beat until as smooth as a dough with cracked wheat can get, which admittedly isn't any too smooth. Now stir in enough of the remaining flour to make a dough that is not sticky, but a little on the soft side. Turn dough out onto a lightly floured breadboard and knead until smooth and elastic, about 5 to 7 minutes. Place in a buttered bowl, brush dough with melted butter or with oil, cover with a towel and let rise until doubled, about 1 hour. When dough has doubled, punch it down and turn out on that floured breadboard again. Divide dough into 2 parts. Cover with a towel and let rest for 10 minutes. When ready, roll each piece of dough into a long, thin roll and place on a lightly buttered cooky sheet. Cover and let rise until doubled, about 30 minutes. Brush rolls with melted butter and sprinkle with coarse salt if desired. Bake in a 400° F. oven for 30 minutes, or until rolls are done when tapped on the bottoms with the knuckles.

WHOLE GRAIN ROLLS

These delicious rolls can be used for Parker House rolls, or baked in muffin tins, or shaped as desired. I sometimes add chopped nuts and candied fruits to make a fine sweet roll. They may be frosted or not, as desired. The rolls make up very quickly, requiring no more than 2 to 2½ hours from start to finish.

2 cups sour milk or buttermilk	⅓ cup light or dark brown sugar
1 cake yeast	
6 to 7 cups sifted flour	1 teaspoon salt
2 large eggs	¼ cup oil or melted butter

All ingredients should be at room temperature. Combine the sour milk or buttermilk with the yeast and stir to dissolve the yeast. Now add 3 cups of the flour and the rest of the ingredients. Beat thoroughly. Then add enough of the remaining flour to make a smooth elastic dough. Turn out onto a lightly floured breadboard and knead for 5 minutes. Place dough in a buttered bowl, brush the top with oil, cover the bowl with a clean towel and set aside for 20 to 25 minutes. Punch the dough down and turn out again onto a lightly floured breadboard. Pat or roll the dough to a thickness of about ⅓ inch. Cut with a biscuit cutter or shape as desired. Place on a buttered cooky sheet and brush the rolls with oil or with melted butter. Cover and let rise until doubled, about 45 minutes. Bake in a 350° F. oven until done, about 25 minutes.

SOUTHERN BUTTER ROLLS

These great rolls have a crispy, buttery crust and always bring raves.

1 cake yeast
¼ cup lukewarm water
1 cup hot water
¼ cup softened butter
¼ cup sugar

1 teaspoon salt
1 large egg
4 cups sifted flour
melted butter

Dissolve the yeast in the lukewarm water. Pour the hot water over the softened butter, sugar, and salt. Cool to lukewarm. Add the dissolved yeast and the egg and stir to blend. Now stir in the flour and blend thoroughly. Brush the top of the dough with melted butter to prevent a crust from forming and chill the dough in the refrigerator, overnight preferably, but at least for 5 or 6 hours. Remove dough from refrigerator and let stand at room temperature for 1 hour. Now turn the dough out onto a floured breadboard and roll out to a rectangle ⅛ inch thick. Brush top of dough with melted butter, fold the dough over and brush the top again with melted butter. Fold the dough in half again (it should by now be no more than ½ inch thick) and once again brush the top with melted butter. Cut into circles with a biscuit cutter and place the rolls in buttered muffin pans. Cover with a clean cloth and let rise in warm place until doubled, about 1 hour. Bake in a 400° F. oven for 20 minutes, or until browned and done. Makes 24 rolls.

Some gave them white bread,
And some gave them brown;
Some gave them plum cake,
And drummed them out of town.
WILLIAM KING: *Useful*
Transactions in Philosophy (1708)

FLAKY ROLLS

2 cakes yeast
1¼ cups lukewarm water
⅔ cup butter or margarine,
   melted (half may be lard)
2 cups freshly mashed,
   unseasoned potatoes

1 teaspoon salt
2 tablespoons sugar
2 large eggs
6 to 7 cups sifted flour

Dissolve yeast in ¼ cup of the lukewarm water. Pour melted butter or margarine over the mashed potatoes, salt, and sugar. Stir to blend. Now add the dissolved yeast, the remaining cup of water, and the eggs. Stir to blend thoroughly. Add 3 cups of the flour and beat with a wooden spoon. Batter should be fairly smooth. Now add 3 more cups flour, making 6 cups total. Use the last cup of flour only if needed to make a smooth, non-sticky dough. Knead lightly in the bowl. Brush with melted butter or oil, cover, and let rise until doubled, about 1 hour. When dough has doubled, punch it down and divide in half. This division is simply to make the dough easier to handle on the breadboard. Turn half onto a lightly floured breadboard and roll to a thickness of no more than ¼ inch. Cut into 2-inch circles and place on buttered cooky sheets. Brush tops with butter. Roll out remaining dough and cut into circles. Place these circles on top of the others, making two-layer rolls. Cover and let rise until light, about 45 minutes. Bake in a 400° F. oven for 20 minutes, or until browned and done. Makes 36 rolls.

Mama, why mayn't I, when I dine,
Eat ham, and goose, and drink port wine?
And why mayn't I, as well as you,
Eat pudding, soup, and mutton, too?
Because, my child, it is not right,
To spoil the youthful appetite.

MRS. TURNER: *Cautionary Stories*
(LATE 19TH CENTURY)

BUTTER-FILLED SOUTHERN ROLLS

These rolls are a specialty of one well-known Southern cook. Any roll recipe could be shaped and filled this way for added flavor and interest.

¾ cup milk or half-and-half
2 tablespoons sugar
1 teaspoon salt
¼ cup butter (no substitute)

1 cake yeast
about 3 cups sifted flour
1 egg
more butter (no substitute)

Scald milk or half-and-half and pour it over the sugar, salt, and butter. Stir to melt the butter and cool to lukewarm. When mixture has cooled, stir in the yeast and blend. Add 1 cup of the flour and beat until smooth. Cover with a clean towel and let rise until bubbly, about 30 minutes. Add the egg and enough of the remaining 2 cups flour to make a smooth dough. Blend well. Turn out onto a lightly floured breadboard and knead until the dough is smooth and elastic. Try not to handle this dough too much as it should be a delicate dough. Place in a buttered bowl, brush top with melted butter, cover with a clean towel, and let rise until doubled. Turn out of the bowl onto a very lightly floured breadboard again. Pat or roll the dough to a thickness of no more than ⅛ inch. Cut into small rounds, preferably no more than 1 or 1½ inches across. In the center of each round place ¼ teaspoon of butter. Top with another round and pinch the edges together to seal. Butter a shallow pan and place the rounds, pinched edges down, close together in the pan. Let rise, covered, until doubled. Bake in a 400° F. oven 15 to 20 minutes or until lightly browned and done.

WATER-RAISED BUTTER ROLLS

3 cups sifted flour
1 teaspoon salt
½ cup butter
2 cakes yeast
2 tablespoons sugar

½ cup milk, scalded and cooled
3 large eggs
1 teaspoon vanilla extract
1 cup chopped nuts mixed with ½ cup sugar

Place 1½ cups of the flour in a bowl. Add salt and butter, cutting the butter into the flour as for pie crust. Stir the yeast and sugar into the cooled milk. Stir into the flour mixture, beating until batter is smooth. Cover and let this sponge rise 20 to 30 minutes. Now, stir in the eggs and beat vigorously. Add the vanilla and the remaining 1½ cups flour. Work this in with a wooden spoon or clean hands. Dough will be firm but sticky. Take a clean, white tea towel or several thicknesses of cheesecloth and tie the dough loosely, to give it room to rise in, into the cloth. Now drop the whole works into a large bowl filled with lukewarm water. The dough will sink to the bottom at first, but will gradually rise to the top of the water. When it does this, in approximately 45 minutes to an hour, the dough is risen enough. Untie the dough and cut off pieces about the size of an egg. Roll each piece of dough in the chopped nut-sugar mixture. Twist the coated dough into a figure eight and place on a well-buttered cooky sheet. Let rise for 10 to 15 minutes and then bake in a 425° F. oven for 10 to 15 minutes, or until well browned and done. Makes 20 rolls.

PINWHEELS

If you wish these delicious rolls for breakfast, simply bake them the day before, leave in the pan and cover. When you wish to serve them, reheat in a 350° F. oven for 20 minutes. Invert onto a hot plate to serve.

1 cup milk, scalded	½ cup raisins or chopped dates or figs
⅓ cup sugar	
⅓ cup butter	½ cup chopped nuts
½ teaspoon salt	1 teaspoon grated lemon rind
1 cake yeast	1 tablespoon grated orange rind
¼ cup lukewarm water	
2 large eggs	1½ cups brown sugar
4½ cups sifted flour	2 tablespoons butter
	⅓ cup orange juice

Pour the scalded milk over the ⅓ cup sugar, ⅓ cup butter, and salt. Stir to melt the butter. Cool to lukewarm. Dissolve yeast in ¼ cup lukewarm water. Add the yeast mixture and the eggs to the cooled milk mixture. Stir to blend. Add 4 cups of the flour and blend in well. Spread the remaining ½ cup flour on a breadboard and turn the dough out onto the floured board. Knead for about 5 minutes. Place dough in a buttered bowl, brush with oil or melted butter, cover, and let rise until doubled, about 1 hour. When dough is doubled, punch it down and turn out onto the floured board again. Roll out to a rectangle about 24 by 12 inches. Combine fruit, nuts, and fruit rinds with ½ cup of the brown sugar. Blend and then spread on the rolled-out dough. Beginning with the wide side of the dough, roll up tightly, as for a jelly roll. Cut the dough with a very sharp knife into pieces about 1½ inches wide. In a saucepan combine the remaining cup of brown sugar with the 2 tablespoons butter and the orange juice. Cook, stirring, until mixture comes to a boil. Divide brown sugar syrup into 2 well-buttered 8 or 9-inch square pans or pour into 1 large pan with sides. Arrange pinwheels in pans. Brush lightly with butter. Cover and let rise until doubled, about 45 to 50 minutes. Bake in a 350° F. oven for 35 to 40 minutes, or until lightly browned and done. Invert to serve.

HOLIDAY RUM ROLLS

These are a must for New Year's morning breakfast. I make plenty for the drop-in company, but the recipe is easily halved.

1 cup milk, scalded	3 tablespoons rum
1 cup sugar	½ teaspoon cinnamon or
2 teaspoons salt	nutmeg
¼ cup butter or margarine	ICING
2 cakes yeast	1½ cups powdered sugar
½ cup lukewarm water	2½ tablespoons rum
5 to 6 cups sifted flour	2 teaspoons water
2 large eggs	chopped nuts

Pour the scalded milk over ½ cup of the sugar, salt, and butter or margarine. Stir to dissolve the sugar and melt the butter. Cool. Dissolve yeast in lukewarm water. Add to cooled milk mixture along with 2 cups of the flour, the eggs, and rum. Beat until batter is smooth. Now add 2½ cups more flour and work in. Turn dough out onto a floured bread board and knead in enough of the remaining flour to make a smooth satiny dough. Turn into a buttered bowl and brush top of dough with oil or melted butter. Cover and let rise until doubled, about 1½ to 2 hours. When dough has doubled, punch it down and turn out onto a floured surface again. Cut dough into 2 pieces and roll each piece into a rectangle about 8 by 16 inches. Brush with melted butter. Combine the remaining ½ cup of sugar with the cinnamon or nutmeg and sprinkle on the dough. Starting at the wide side, roll up as for a jelly roll. Cut each roll into pieces 1½ inches wide. Place close, but not too close, in 2 buttered 9 by 13-inch pans or in buttered muffin pans. Brush tops with melted butter, cover, and let rise until doubled. Bake in a 375° F. oven for 25 to 30 minutes, or until browned and done. Turn out of pans and frost with the Icing while slightly warm. Sprinkle heavily with chipped nuts. To make icing, combine the powdered sugar with the water, rum, and chopped nuts.

SALLY LUNN

According to tradition, this sweet bread is named after the young girl who devised the recipe, and sold the bread on the streets of Dickensian England. It has, however, been served with afternoon tea in homes of prominent Southern families for at least 8 generations. Spread thin slices of this bread-cake with whipped butter or cream cheese.

4 cups sifted flour	1 cup rich milk, scalded and
¼ to ⅓ cup sugar	cooled
1½ teaspoons salt	4 large eggs, separated
1 cup butter, melted	1 cake yeast, dissolved in 2
	tablespoons lukewarm water

Sift the flour with the sugar and salt. Set aside. Combine the melted butter and milk and beat into the egg yolks. Add the dissolved yeast and then the sifted flour mixture. Beat until batter is smooth. Beat the egg whites until stiff and fold into the batter. As the batter is thick, the egg whites are best folded in using the hands. Brush with melted butter, cover with a clean towel, and set aside to rise until doubled, about 2 to 3 hours. When the dough has doubled, punch it down and beat it, using a heavy spoon or a dough-whip attachment on a heavy-duty mixer, for 3 to 5 minutes. Then turn the dough into a well-buttered 9-inch tube pan, or mini-Bundt pan. Cover and let rise again until doubled, about 1½ hours. Bake in a 350° F. oven about 40 to 50 minutes, or until the loaf is golden brown and done.

WHEAT-NUT COFFEECAKE

This divinely fragrant bread is nutritious and tasty.

1½ cups very hot water
⅓ cup butter or margarine
½ cup mild-flavored honey
2 teaspoons salt
2 cakes yeast
½ cup lukewarm water
2 large eggs

½ cup wheat germ
2¾ cups sifted flour
1¾ cups graham or
   wholewheat flour
1⅓ cups chopped nuts
¼ cup water
⅓ cup sugar

Combine very hot water, butter or margarine, honey, and salt. Stir to melt the butter. Cool. Dissolve yeast in lukewarm water and then stir into honey mixture. Add eggs, wheat germ, and 1½ cups of the white flour. Beat until batter is smooth. Stir in the remaining white flour, the graham flour, and 1 cup of the chopped nuts. Mixture will be sticky so do not attempt to knead. Divide the heavy batter-type dough into 2 well-buttered loaf pans. Brush tops with melted butter, cover with towel, and let rise until loaves are about 1 inch from tops of pans. Bake in a 375° F. oven for 40 to 50 minutes. While loaves are baking combine the ¼ cup water and the sugar in a small saucepan and boil until syrupy, about 2 minutes. Brush the baked, hot loaves with the hot syrup and sprinkle with remaining ⅓ cup chopped nuts, or more if desired.

CHOCOLATE CHIP COFFEECAKE

¾ cup milk, scalded
½ cup butter or margarine
⅓ cup sugar
1 teaspoon salt
2 cakes yeast
¼ cup lukewarm water
3 large eggs
3½ cups sifted flour
½ cup chocolate chips

COFFEE TOPPING
½ cup sifted flour
½ cup sugar
½ cup butter or margarine
½ cup chopped walnuts
⅓ cup chocolate chips
1 teaspoon instant coffee
1 teaspoon vanilla extract

'our hot milk over butter or margarine, sugar, and salt. Stir to melt
he butter. Dissolve yeast in lukewarm water. Stir into the cooled milk
mixture. Add the eggs and 2 cups of the flour. Beat until smooth.
Blend in the remaining 1½ cups flour and the chocolate chips. Turn
dough into a well-buttered 10-inch tube pan. Sprinkle with COFFEE
TOPPING. Cover the pan and let dough rise in a warm place until
doubled, approximately 1 hour. Bake in a 400° F. oven for 35 to 40
minutes or until done. Turn out of pan immediately.

To make coffee topping, combine flour, sugar, and butter or margarine. Rub together with the fingers, to make coarse crumbs. Add
and blend in the nuts, chocolate chips, instant coffee and vanilla extract.

SALT-RISING BREADS

Salt-rising bread, a truly American invention, was very popular in our
grandmother's time, when all yeasts were homemade, often unreliable,
and always difficult to keep. Its leavening agent is the natural fermentation which occurs when the cornmeal or potato starter mixture is kept
in a warm place. (Its curious, sweetish flavor has many avid devotees.)
A modern way to hasten fermentation is to set the container with the
starter mixture in water in a deep electric frying pan, or an electric
saucepan, and set the control at 120° F. The starter will ferment a little
faster, generally requiring 12 to 15 hours rather than the 24 hours
required the old-fashioned way.

2 medium potatoes
¼ cup coarse, water-ground
   cornmeal
2 tablespoons sugar or honey
1 tablespoon salt
4 cups boiling water (part
   may be milk)

2 cups milk, scalded and
   cooled to lukewarm
¼ teaspoon baking soda
14 cups sifted flour,
   . approximately
4 or 5 tablespoons lard or
   other shortening

Peel the potatoes and slice thinly. Turn into a bowl or pitcher which
can be placed in a larger container. Add the cornmeal (it must be
water-ground, and must *not* be the degerminated kind found in boxes,
which won't work), sugar or honey, and salt. Add the boiling water.
Cover the bowl with cheesecloth and place it in a container of water

(see above) that is about 120° F. It should not be too hot to put your hand in. Keep in a warm place so that the water will stay lukewarm If you do not use an electric appliance, the starter will take about 24 hours to ferment. It should have a "yeasty" odor. If it doesn't smell "yeasty," and look foamy, do not proceed. You will have to begin anew. When the starter has fermented and is yeasty, strain it into a bowl, discarding the potatoes. Add the milk, baking soda, and enough of the flour (about 6 cups) to make a sponge. Beat this until smooth cover with a clean towel, set in a warm place, and let the mixture rise until it is light and bubbly, about 1½ hours. Sift the remaining flour with the salt and add to the sponge, working in the shortening as you go along. Use as much flour as is necessary to make a workable dough that is not sticky. Turn dough out onto a lightly floured bread-board and knead until smooth and elastic, about 10 minutes. Divide the dough into 3 pieces and shape each piece (do not allow this dough to rest as recommended with other bread recipes) into a loaf. Place in but-tered bread pans. Cover and let rise until not quite doubled in bulk Bake in a 350° F. oven for 1 hour or until browned and done.

WHOLE WHEAT SALT-RISING BREAD

An unusual recipe that makes a delicious, flavorful bread.

4 cups very hot water	7 to 8 cups whole-wheat or
3 tablespoons coarse, water-	graham flour
ground cornmeal	1 tablespoon salt
2 teaspoons sugar or honey	3 tablespoons lard or oil

In the morning combine in a bowl or pitcher 2 cups of the hot water and the cornmeal. Cover the bowl with cheesecloth and set it in a pan of warm water, about 120° F. Let stand until it ferments. When properly fermented the mixture will be light and will be filled with gas bubbles which have a distinct odor. When the starter has fer-mented, stir in the sugar or honey and 2 cups of the flour. Beat until smooth, cover with a clean towel, and let rise again until doubled about 1½ to 2 hours. At the same time that you have set this sponge aside to rise, combine, in another bowl, the remaining 2 cups hot water the salt, lard or oil, and 3 cups of the remaining flour. Beat well, cover, and set aside. When the sponge containing the starter has doubled, combine the 2 mixtures, adding enough of the remaining flour to make an easily workable dough. Turn out onto a lightly floured breadboard and knead thoroughly, using enough flour so that the dough is not sticky. Turn the dough into a buttered bowl, brush with oil, cover and let rise again until doubled. Then punch the dough down and turn out onto a very lightly floured breadboard. Cut the dough into 2 pieces and shape into loaves. Place in buttered loaf pans, cover, and let rise until doubled, about 1½ hours. Bake in a 375° F. oven until done, about 50 minutes to an hour.

SOY BREADS

Experiments at the Cornell University School of Nutrition have proved that the soybean is an excellent protein food. Here, because this is a book devoted to baking, we will concern ourselves with the flour. In spite of its name, soy flour is a highly concentrated protein food rather than a true flour. It is also 15 times as rich in calcium and 10 times as rich in iron as regular wheat flour. For these reasons, soy flour makes an important nutritional addition to the daily diet, especially for low-income families, but in my opinion it should be used wherever there are children.

Because soy flour lacks the gluten needed to develop yeast doughs, it cannot be used alone. The usual addition is 2 tablespoons of soy flour in each cup of regular flour, although some good cooks use up to 20% or even 30% of the soy flour in their bread recipes. The Cornell Triple-Rich Formula, which will make any bread the staff of life that it should be, is as follows:

CORNELL TRIPLE-RICH FORMULA

1 tablespoon soy flour   1 teaspoon wheat germ
1 tablespoon skim-milk
   powder

Add the above ingredients to the bottom of each cup of flour befor
sifting in the flour. This is done so that the ingredients are not inad
vertently *added* to the flour measurement. If you use the formula reg
ularly, make a notation at the side of each recipe as to the total table
spoons used and then write the required flour adjustment. The formul
may be used with breads, cakes, pancakes, muffins, cookies, and eve
in pie crusts.

SOY BREAD

This makes a delicious, soul-satisfying bread.

¼ cup butter, margarine, or   1 cake yeast
   soya oil   ½ cup lukewarm water
½ cup brown sugar or honey   5¾ cups sifted flour
1½ teaspoons salt   1¼ cups soy flour
2 cups homogenized milk or
   soy milk

Place butter, sugar or honey, and salt in a bowl. Scald the milk an
pour over. Stir to dissolve the butter and sugar. Cool to lukewarm
Dissolve the yeast in the lukewarm water and stir into the milk mixtur
Combine the two flours. Work in enough of the flours to make a mediun
stiff dough. Turn dough out onto a floured breadboard and knead tho
oughly. Place dough in a buttered bowl, cover, and let rise until double
When dough has doubled, punch it down and turn out onto a floure
breadboard again. Cut dough into two parts, cover, and let set for 1
minutes. This allows the dough to loosen enough to make it easier

hape. Then pat and shape the dough into 2 loaves. Place in buttered
oaf pans, cover, and let rise until doubled. Bake in a 350° F. oven for
0 to 45 minutes, or until browned and done.

WHOLE WHEAT SOY BREAD

his fine-flavored bread can be made from start to finish in less than
 hours. The bread cuts without crumbling, something that can't be
aid about most homemade whole-wheat breads no matter how delicious
nd healthful they may be. The dough may also be used to make yeast
iscuits, buns, rolls, or cinnamon rolls. It may also be shaped into
arker House rolls, twists, or any other desired shapes.

1½ cups hot water	½ cup lukewarm water
2 teaspoons salt	4 cups graham or whole-wheat
⅓ cup honey or brown sugar	flour
2 tablespoons soya oil	1 cup soy flour
1 cake yeast	

'ombine the hot water, salt, honey or sugar, and oil in a bowl. Stir
) melt the honey or dissolve the sugar. Cool to lukewarm. Dissolve
ie yeast in the lukewarm water and stir into the honey mixture. Beat
 2 cups of the flour, cover the bowl and set it aside for 20 minutes.
Iow add the soy flour and enough of the remaining graham flour to
ake a dough that is not sticky. Knead the dough on a floured bread-
oard. Shape as desired. If making loaves, it is best to make 2 small
aves in the smaller Teflon loaf pans, rather than 1 large loaf. How-
ver you shape the dough, into loaves or various roll shapes, place
nmediately in an oven set at 250° F. Leave at this temperature for
0 minutes. The bread will finish rising during this time. After 20
inutes, raise oven temperature to 350° F. and continue baking until
one, about 35 to 45 minutes for loaves and a slightly shorter time
)r rolls.

IOTE.   Soy milk, homogenized milk, or potato water may be used
 place of water. All should be scalded first.

REFRIGERATOR SOY ROLLS

This dough may be used as you would use any refrigerator dough. The recipe doubles easily.

½ cup hot water
1 teaspoon salt
¼ cup brown sugar or honey
⅓ cup butter, margarine, or oil
½ cup homogenized milk or soy milk

1 cake yeast
¼ cup lukewarm water
1 large egg
½ cup soy flour
3½ cups sifted flour

Pour the hot water over the salt, sugar or honey, and butter or other shortening. Stir to melt the butter or margarine, if used. Scald and cool the milk. Dissolve the yeast in the lukewarm water. Combine the mixtures. Add the egg, soy flour, and 1½ cups of the flour. Beat well. Add enough of the remaining flour to make a dough that is not sticky but is not stiff either. Turn dough out onto a floured breadboard and knead thoroughly. Place dough in a buttered bowl, cover, and store in the refrigerator. Punch it down several times the first day. After that once each day should be enough. When ready to use, remove the amount of dough desired, shape into rolls, and place on buttered or oiled pans. Cover and let rise until doubled. Bake in a 350° F. oven until browned and done, about 20 minutes.

SOUR DOUGH BREADS

For a while sour dough breads seemed to have gone the way of the horse-drawn buggy but the past few years have seen, if you will excuse the pun, a rising interest in this oldest of raised breads. So much so that some cooks are laboring excessively to find new ways in which to use the sour dough flavor. Or so it seems to me. We love the various sour dough breads, biscuits, and pancakes, and maintain a cool detachment towards all the sour dough fruitcakes, cookies, etc. The true sour dough is leavened by wild yeasts in the air. If you use your kitchen a great deal for cooking and baking, a recipe for a true sour dough should work well for you. If you don't cook and bake much, you had best "fudge" a little and use a sour dough starter that requires yeast.

One very old recipe for an excellent starter is made thus: Combine 2 cups flour, 1 or 2 tablespoons sugar, 1 tablespoon salt, 1½ cups lukewarm water and 1 tablespoon vinegar. Beat until batter is smooth and place in a bowl or glass container (never use metal for sour dough). Cover and let stand for 12 hours. After each usage replenish starter with equal amounts of flour and water and occasionally add a teaspoon of sugar. My favorite starter, repeated from my earlier book, *A World of Breads*, is made as follows.

MY FAVORITE STARTER

1 or 2 cups milk   equal amount of flour

Put the milk in a sterilized glass or pottery container, cover with cheesecloth, and let stand at room temperature for 24 hours. Then stir in an equal amount of flour and stir to blend well. Cover with cheesecloth and set jar outdoors in a protected place for 12 to 24 hours. Now put the jar in a warm place, the back of the stove will be fine, until it starts to bubble and becomes full of bubbles. This will take from 2 to 5 days, depending on the weather and on the wild yeast cells in the air. Put the starter in a covered container, being careful to leave room enough in the container for the starter to rise without spilling over, and store it in the refrigerator. Each time it is used, replenish the starter by stirring in equal amounts of milk and flour. My batch of starter is so good that I have on occasion used all but a few tablespoons of it and, upon stirring in 1 cup each of milk and flour, had it bubbling almost immediately. You have to learn by experience the amount of replenishing that the leftover starter will take. If I have quite a bit of starter left and am planning to use a large amount very soon, I stir in several cups each of milk and flour. But if only a small amount is left, ½ to 1 cup each of milk and flour is best to start with. Stir in more as the starter reaches the bubbling point.

NOTE.   All starters are interchangeable.

HINTS ON USING SOUR DOUGH

1. Never store sour dough starters in metal. Crockery is ideal. However, I use a refrigerator container.

2. Keep starter refrigerated. It will literally keep indefinitely if used regularly. Some good cooks have starters that have been in use for close to a hundred years. Or so they claim.

3. When you replenish the starter, let it stand at room temperature until it bubbles and then refrigerate.

4. If you do not use the starter at least once a week or every 10 days, freshen it by pouring off half the starter and adding an equal amount of warm water and flour, or in the case of the My Favorite Starter, milk and flour.

5. Never cap a jar of starter tightly. The first time I made starter, I didn't allow room for expansion, and ended up with bubbly starter all over a small kitchen floor.

6. If you are concerned about using a bread recipe that is leavened *only* by a starter, it is all right to fudge a bit. Simply add a cake of yeast dissolved in ¼ cup warm water to the sponge. The recipe will require a bit more flour but you can work this out as you go along.

SOUR DOUGH BISCUITS

1½ cups flour
2 teaspoons double-acting
　 baking powder
¼ teaspoon baking soda

½ teaspoon salt
¼ cup melted butter
1 cup starter

ſt the dry ingredients together. Work in the butter and starter. Pat
ℓ dough out on a floured board, adding a little more flour if neces-
ιy. Cut and place on buttered cooky sheets. Cover and let rise un-
light. Bake in a 425°F. oven for 20 minutes or until browned
d done.

SOUR DOUGH SOY BREAD

2 cups warm water
4 to 5 cups sifted flour
2 tablespoons sugar
¾ cup starter
2 tablespoons brown sugar

1½ teaspoons salt
3 tablespoons oil or melted
　 butter or margarine
1½ cups soy flour

the winter make the sponge in the evening and allow it to stand
ernight. In warm weather the sponge may be set in the morning.
ιmbine 1 cup of the warm water, 2 cups of the flour, the 2 table-
ɔons sugar, and starter. Beat thoroughly. Cover and let stand until
ht and foamy. In the morning, or when the sponge is light, add the
maining cup of water, the brown sugar, salt, oil, and soy flour.
:at in. Now add 2 more cups of the remaining flour and work in.
•read remaining cup of flour on breadboard and turn the dough
.t onto it. Knead the dough thoroughly, kneading in as much flour
is needed to make a smooth, non-sticky dough. Place in a buttered
wl, brush dough with oil or melted butter, cover, and let rise until

it has doubled, about 2 to 2½ hours. Punch down and divide doug
into 2 parts. Turn out onto breadboard again and let rest for 1
minutes. Then pat and shape the dough into loaves. Place in 2 bu
tered loaf pans, cover, and let rise again until doubled. Bake in
350° F. oven for 40 to 50 minutes, or until browned and done.

SOUR DOUGH POTATO BREAD

This makes a delicious, light bread. I coil the dough before puttin
into the loaf pans. It comes out very professional-looking.

1 cup starter
1½ cups lukewarm water
2 cups sifted flour
¾ to 1 cup mashed,
   unseasoned potatoes
¾ cup warm water
2 teaspoons salt

⅓ cup oil or melted butter or
   margarine
⅓ cup sugar
6½ to 7 cups of flour (part
   may be wheat germ or
   wheat germ and middlings)

Combine starter, 1½ cups water, 2 cups flour and mashed potatoe
Beat until thoroughly blended, cover, and set aside until light. Th
will take several hours in warm weather, overnight in cool weathe
When sponge is light, stir it down and add the ¾ cup warm water, sal
oil or melted butter or margarine, sugar, and half the flour. Beat wel
Gradually stir in enough of the remaining flour to make a medium-firr
dough. Turn dough out onto a floured breadboard and knead thor
oughly, using as much or as little flour as is necessary to make a nor
sticky dough. Place dough in an oiled bowl and turn the dough aroun
so that it retains a thin film of oil. Cover and allow the dough to ris
until doubled, about 2 hours. When dough has doubled, punch it dow
and turn out again onto a lightly floured board. Cut the dough in hal
cover, and allow it to rest for 10 minutes. Then pat and shape th
dough as desired. I roll each piece into a thick rope, coil each rop
separately, and place each coil in a buttered loaf pan. Cover and let th
dough rise until doubled again. When doubled, bake in a 375° F. ove
until browned and done, about 45 to 50 minutes.

8. *Miscellaneous Recipes*

This brief chapter includes recipes that just didn't seem to fit anywhere else but are too good and too useful to leave out. Knowing how to freeze whipped cream can save us needed time; the use of coconut milk can add much to various cakes and cookies. And other recipes, that may or may not be frequently used, are often interesting to read about.

BASIC POPOVERS

Popovers may be served hot with any meal, and seem to go as well with roast beef as with the more delicate salad luncheons with which they are more usually served. The single most important thing to remember is

that the batter must be beaten until perfectly smooth. You might u
a strong arm or an electric mixer, but a blender does the best job, a
indeed makes the making of the ideal popover batter so ridiculous
simple that even the newest bride can make a perfect popover.

The batter may be baked immediately upon mixing, or it may
made when convenient, poured into the cups, and stored in the refri
erator for several hours or overnight. Bake as directed. For those wl
like their hot breads *hot,* this makes it a simple matter to have fres
hot popovers for even the most rushed meal.

Remember that hot popovers make good containers for scrambl
eggs, creamed chipped beef, and creamed chicken or shellfish. A
with the addition of 1 teaspoon sugar to the batter, the hot popove
can be filled with sugared fresh fruit.

1 cup sifted flour	1 cup milk
½ teaspoon salt	1 tablespoon melted butter,
2 large eggs	bacon drippings, or salad
	oil

Sift the flour and salt into a bowl. Beat the eggs and add to the mi
and melted butter. Pour, all at once, into the dry ingredients and be
until perfectly smooth. Pour into buttered muffin pans, iron popov
pans, custard cups, or tall pottery cups. Fill pans no more than ha
full. Bake large popovers in a 400° F. oven for 35 to 40 minute
smaller popovers will bake through in 25 to 30 minutes. If desire
the popovers may be placed in a *cold* oven, then set the control f
425° F., and bake for 45 to 50 minutes. Regardless of how you bak
your popovers, *do not peek.*

BLENDER POPOVERS.   Follow basic recipe, putting ingredients i
to blender container. Cover and blend on high speed for 15 to 20 se
onds, or until batter is perfectly smooth. Pour into buttered pans an
bake as directed.

CHEESE POPOVERS.   Add 1 cup grated sharp Cheddar cheese, an
use 3 or 4 large eggs. Serve with a main meal or luncheon.

GARLIC POPOVERS.   These are a real treat when served with roa
beef. Add 1 or 2 mashed cloves of garlic to batter.

AWAIIAN POPOVERS. Add 2 teaspoons mild-flavored honey,
nd ½ cup of ground macadamia nuts to the batter. Other nuts could
e used.

ORANGE POPOVERS

hese sweet, orange-flavored popovers are excellent when served with
a. For added flavor add ½ cup ground walnuts, pecans, or almonds.

2 cups sifted flour	¾ cup milk
½ teaspoon salt	1 cup orange juice
3 large eggs	1 tablespoon grated orange
1 tablespoon honey	rind

ft the flour and salt into a bowl. Beat the eggs with the honey, and
ld to the combined milk, orange juice, and rind. Beat with an electric
ixer until perfectly smooth. Or whirl in the blender for approximately
) seconds. Pour into buttered pans, filling to no more than half full.
ake in a 400° F. oven for 35 to 40 minutes for large popovers, or 25
30 minutes for smaller ones. Other baking directions given with the
cipe for BASIC POPOVERS (p. 341) may also be used.

COCONUT MILK

oconut milk is called for in various recipes throughout this book, and
here called for, it gives a far more pleasing flavor than plain milk.
oconut milk should be kept refrigerated if not used immediately. It
eezes very well and can be used to flavor various frostings and glazes;
makes excellent creamed chicken; use it as part of the milk for
JSTARD SAUCE (p. 102), but do not let the coconut milk boil. Bring

it just *to* the boil. To make 2 cups of coconut milk, you will need the following:

4 cups grated coconut (preferably fresh grated coconut, but shredded will do)

2 cups boiling water

Pour the boiling water over the coconut. Let stand for 20 to 25 minutes. Strain through several thicknesses of cheesecloth, pressing and squeezing to remove all of the liquid. Bottle and refrigerate immediately if not to be used right away.

FROZEN WHIPPED CREAM

Whipped cream freezes so easily and so beautifully that there is no need to be caught without this graceful topping for cakes and pies. You can mound it from a spoon, or pipe it through a decorating tube (the large kind) into attractive rosettes, or even shape the whipped cream (using a decorating tube) into hearts and letter shapes. Be fancy when you have the time, and enjoy the results later.

Beat 1 cup of heavy cream until almost stiff and then beat in from 1 to 3 tablespoons of sugar. Flavor with any one or more of the following: ½ teaspoon vanilla extract; ¼ teaspoon almond extract; 2 teaspoons grated lemon rind; 2 teaspoons instant coffee; 1 tablespoon cocoa; 1 tablespoon grated orange or tangerine rind. Beat until stiff, but be very careful not to overbeat or you will end up with sweetened flavored butter! When stiff, drop from a tablespoon, or pipe as directed above, onto waxed paper which has been placed on heavy cardboard, a cooky sheet or a jelly roll pan. Place in the freezer and leave until the cream is solidly frozen. Then place the frozen mounds of whipped cream in freezer bags or freezer containers. Return to freezer. These will keep for 2 to 3 weeks.

ROSE PETAL SYRUP

This syrup, which is easy to make and requires no special equipment, was well-known to Colonial housewives, and has been used for thou sands of years in the Middle East. It may be used in place of rose water in the various cake recipes in this book. A tablespoon or 2, according to taste, may flavor cake or cooky frostings or glazes; it lends delightful flavor and fragrance to whipped cream and custard sauce; it can be used in almost any cake recipe and in many cooky recipes. Its flavor and fragrance can best be appreciated in simple pound cakes, angel food cakes, sponge cakes, and white or yellow layer cakes. Use up to ½ cup, tasting as you go along, in fruitcakes, where more is required to keep its flavor from being lost. And ¼ cup of the syrup, warmed and carefully spooned over any pound cake, angel food cake, or sponge cake, makes an exotic delight.

For best flavor and fragrance, the rose petals should be picked before they are full-blown, as full-blown roses often have a slightly bitter taste. The roses should be picked early in the day, before the sun is at its height. Make certain that the roses are *unsprayed*. Clean the petals gently, but well, and clip off the green or white base of each petal. Use glass or enamel pans to make the syrup. Do not use metal pans. There seem to be as many variations of this basically simple recipe as there are snow crystals, but this one is my favorite. A bottle or two of the delectable syrup will keep indefinitely, and you will find many uses for it beyond my suggestions.

4 cups clean, unsprayed rose petals (see above)	1 or 2 tablespoons fresh lemon juice (optional)
1½ cups cold, distilled water	1 vanilla bean (optional)
4½ cups sugar	

Combine the rose petals and the water in a pan (see above) and bring just to a boil. Gradually stir in the sugar and the lemon juice if used, and simmer for 10 minutes. Turn off the heat and let the syrup stand for another 5 to 10 minutes. Then strain the rose petals out, and pour the syrup into a well-sterilized bottle. Refrigerate for at least 10 days before using.

NOTE. If you use the vanilla bean, place the bean in the bottle with the syrup. The vanilla bean can be removed after 2 weeks and used for other purposes. Or you can simply leave it there.

YOGURT I

Yogurt, called *Leban* in Syria and Lebanon, *Madzoon* in Armenia, and *Dadhi* in India, has in recent years become very popular in diet-conscious America. And with typical ingenuity the American housewife puts it to all kinds of uses. She combines equal parts of yogurt and mayonnaise or an oil dressing to make a delightful salad dressing; she makes a delicious sauce for fruits by adding honey or brown sugar to yogurt and beating until smooth; and she makes a fruit sauce for cake by beating the yogurt with brown sugar until smooth and adding sliced or crushed fresh fruit. The firmer, custard-type yogurt can substitute for sour cream in most recipes, and the thinner yogurt can always be used in place of buttermilk or sour milk.

Some housewives are rebelling against the high cost of commercial yogurt by making it themselves for little more than the cost of the milk it is made with. The single most important factor in making yogurt at home is the temperature. And although I made yogurt for fifteen years without a candy thermometer, and housewives before me have made it for thousands of years without such an aid, I do consider it well-nigh indispensable. The bacterial culture that thickens yogurt grows rapidly between the temperatures of 90° F. and 115° F. Higher temperatures will kill it and lower temperatures will result in simple sour milk. A candy thermometer is the only way of guaranteeing good results by enabling you to keep an eye on the temperature of the milk during the incubation period.

Any milk or combination of milks can be used to make yogurt. have used whole milk, non-fat milk, half-and-half, non-fat milk powder and evaporated milk either whole or non-fat. However, since I feel that if you are going to make yogurt in the first place, you might as well make it even more nutritious, I prefer a combination of milk and skim milk powder, or of milk and evaporated whole or non-fat milk, in proportions that just about double the nutritional value.

If you eat yogurt frequently, a yogurt maker is a good investment. These can be as simple or as complex as you wish. Mine is an 8-quart pot over an electric heating unit. I put warm water in the pot, and put

y containers of milk in the water. This keeps the milk just warm
ough to incubate properly. Other yogurt makers have containers in
hich you make *and* store the yogurt. For thousands of years house-
ives wrapped the milk in heavy towels or blankets to incubate. But
have found that the water bath works best.

This recipe makes 2 quarts of a thinner yogurt that can be spooned
om a bowl or drunk from a cup. It is very good mixed with fruit
ices, especially orange juice, and can be used in any recipe calling
r buttermilk or sour milk.

½ quarts whole or non-fat milk
3½-ounce can whole or non-fat evaporated milk
cup culture (yogurt from a previous batch, or commercial yogurt)

ave all ingredients at room temperature. Blend the yogurt culture
ith the evaporated milk until smooth, and then blend evenly into the
ilk. Pour into a container or containers that are meticulously clean.
et in a water bath where you can maintain a constant temperature of
10° F. Depending on the weather, the mixture will "jell" in from 3
5 or 6 hours. Cool, and keep refrigerated.

YOGURT RECIPE II

his recipe makes a firmer, custard-type yogurt. Please note that *all*
omemade yogurts are sweeter than the commercial yogurt, although
ven homemade yogurt will become more tart after several days.

6 cups lukewarm water
1½ cups skim-milk powder
(the non-instant type)

⅓ to ½ cup culture (yogurt
from a previous batch, or
commercial yogurt)
13½-ounce can evaporated
whole or non-fat milk

ombine in a blender: 2 cups of the water, the milk powder, and the
ogurt culture. Whirl for a few seconds or just until thoroughly blended
nd smooth. Blend with the evaporated milk and the rest of the water.
our into a container or containers that are meticulously clean. Set in a
ater bath where you can maintain a constant temperature of 110° F.
should "jell" in from 3 to 6 hours. Keep refrigerated after thickened.

NOTE. To make the thicker yogurt, housewives used to heat the milk on the stove until it would rise in the pan, about 180° F. Then it would have to be cooled to 110° F. before blending in the culture. The above method is much easier and more reliable, as heating milk over direct heat sometimes results in a scorched taste.

FRUIT-FLAVORED YOGURT. Before incubating, sweeten the milk with ⅓ cup honey and add ⅓ cup of your favorite preserves. Incubate as usual.

EGG GLAZE

For this simple glaze for breads, just beat 1 large egg with a tablespoon of water.

EGG WHITE GLAZE

Beat 1 egg white with 1 tablespoon of water. Beat just to blend and brush on bread once before placing in oven, and several times during the baking.

PREPARATION OF NUTS

Since nuts are used so much in baking, it is a good idea to keep plenty on hand. Most of us buy the nuts we use already shelled and in packages. But the packages will not keep the nuts from turning rancid, and rancid nuts have ruined many an otherwise fine cake or pastry. So unless you are planning to use them immediately, keep all nuts refrigerated or frozen. Frozen, they will keep for several years.

BLANCHED NUTS. Blanched almonds are frequently called for in various cookies and pastries. To blanch almonds or other nuts, pour

oiling water over the shelled nuts and let them stand for several min-
tes. The skins will then slip right off. The nuts should always be al-
)wed to dry thoroughly before being used. Since they do not need
) be used immediately after blanching, they can be allowed to dry and
ten frozen for use when needed, thus saving time.

'OASTED NUTS. Spread blanched or unblanched nuts in an even
tyer on an ungreased cooky sheet or baking pan. Toast, stirring
equently to keep them from burning, in a 300° F. oven for 20 to 30
tinutes.

;RATED OR GROUND NUTS. Many recipes call for grated or
round nuts. Unless otherwise specified (as in Almond Paste), the nuts
tould always be ground or grated in a Mouli-type grater. This grates
te nuts without releasing the oils, thus resulting in a dry, fluffy, grated
ut.

ALMOND PASTE

'his homemade almond paste is far better than most you can buy.
1 European countries almond paste is molded into small fruits and
ipped in chocolate to be eaten as a confection. In most recipes using
rated or ground nuts, it is important that a Mouli-type grater be
sed so that the nuts remain dry. But for almond paste the use of a
rinder or a blender is preferable.

cups blanched almonds, thoroughly dry but not toasted
½ cups sifted powdered sugar
4 cup (about 2) egg whites
teaspoon almond extract or 1 tablespoon Kirsch
or rose water

irind the almonds 3 or 4 times through the finest blade of a meat
rinder or a nut grinder. Using the hands, blend the ground nuts with
te sifted powdered sugar, egg whites, and flavoring. Blend thoroughly.
fold the paste into a ball, wrap in plastic wrap, and place in an air-
ght container. Store in the refrigerator for 5 to 8 days before using.

Table of Equivalents

Butter	2 cups	=	1 pound
	1 cup	=	16 tablespoons
Coconut			
Grated	3½ ounces	=	1 cup
Shredded	3½ ounces	–	1⅓ cups
Flaked	3½ ounces	=	1⅓ cups
Eggs	4–5 large	=	1 cup (about)
	6–7 medium	=	1 cup (about)
Egg whites	8 large	–	1 cup (about)
	10 medium	=	1 cup (about)
Egg yolks	12 large	–	1 cup (about)
	14 medium	–	1 cup (about)
Flour			
Bread	4 cups		1 pound
All-purpose	4 cups, sifted	=	1 pound
Cake	4¾ cups, sifted	=	1 pound
Whole-grain	3¾ cups	=	1 pound

Honey	1⅓ cups	=	1 pound
Sugar			
Granulated	2 cups	=	1 pound
Superfine	2¼ cups	=	1 pound
Brown	2⅓ cups	=	1 pound
Powdered	3½–4 cups	=	1 pound
Lemon (fresh)	1 medium	=	3 tablespoons juice
			2 teaspoons grated rind
Orange (fresh)	1 medium	=	¼ to ⅓ cup juice
			2 to 3 tablespoons grated rind

Table of Substitutions

IF YOU DO NOT HAVE	USE
square unsweetened chocolate	3 tablespoons cocoa + 1 tablespoon butter
ounce semisweet chocolate chips	1 ounce sweet cooking chocolate
teaspoon double-acting baking powder	1½ teaspoons phosphate or tartrate baking powder
cup milk	½ cup evaporated milk + ½ cup water
cup buttermilk	1 cup sour milk, or 1 cup thin yogurt
cup sour milk	1 cup buttermilk, or 1 cup minus 1 tablespoon fresh milk + 1 tablespoon lemon juice or vinegar (let stand 10 minutes)
cup maple sugar	1 cup brown sugar

INDEX